France today

Introductory
studies

Fifth edition

Edited by
J.E. Flower

Methuen
London and New York

First published in 1971 by
Methuen & Co. Ltd
11 New Fetter Lane, London EC4P 4EE
Second edition 1973
Third edition 1977
Fourth edition 1980
Fifth edition 1983
Published in the USA by
Methuen & Co.
in association with Methuen, Inc.
733 Third Avenue, New York,
NY 10017
© 1971, 1973, 1977, 1980 and 1983
Methuen & Co. Ltd
Printed in Great Britain at the
University Press, Cambridge

British Library
Cataloguing in Publication Data

France today. – 5th ed.
1. France – Civilization – 1901–
I. Flower, J.E.
944.083'7   DC402

ISBN 0–416–35010–0

Library of Congress
Cataloguing in Publication Data

France today.
(University paperbacks; 415)
Includes bibliographies and index.
1. France – Civilization – 1945–
I. Flower, J.E. (John Ernest)
II. Series.
DC415.F73   1983   944.08
83–12133

ISBN 0–416–35010–0 (pbk.)

Contents

Foreword to the fifth edition

In May 1981, François Mitterrand was elected to the Presidency of France and a Socialist government controlled the country for the first time during the history of the Fifth Republic. The economic and social problems which Mitterrand inherited were, like those of most western European countries, the results not simply of the policies of previous governments, but of a worldwide recession and an international oil crisis. The new government's attempts to solve these problems and to revitalize the nation met at first with approval. The spirit of constructive reform appealed to many, including some hitherto wary of Socialism and in particular of the possible influence of the Communist Party. Decentralization, reflation of the economy, the promise of new attitudes to foreign policy, the reassessment of the position of immigrants and some educational reforms were all watched with interest. Before long some modification was necessary, however, and reactions have, in some quarters, been strong. Just how much more Mitterrand will be obliged to cut back on his original plans and how resistant he will be to increasing pressure from the Right remains to be seen.

Once again this edition of *France Today* is as up-to-date and as informed as publishing schedules allow. I would like to thank my fellow contributors for their efforts and welcome Richard McAllister who has taken over the chapter on trade unions from Malcolm Anderson. I am grateful to our publishers for their continued support and to Sarah Jones for her copy editing and index.

John Flower
Exeter, 1983

One

Social structures

Andrée Shepherd

Introduction

French society today can no longer be neatly divided into the traditional units of ruling class, middle class, working class and peasantry. During the last hundred years in particular, wars and revolutionary movements, shifts of population and developments in industry, science and technology, have all helped to create a kind of uniformity and standardization which makes any clear-cut divisions of this nature difficult. This trend has also been emphasized by the evolution of the more traditional institutions of society – the Church, the family, the educational system and even military service. French society has changed and is still very much on the move, a fact which has only been recognized fairly recently in a number of important administrative changes – an attempt to break down excessive centralization and encourage the development of regions as more autonomous units, the spreading of social and cultural services and changes in social legislation. Much remains to be done however, and the economic crisis weighs on the future.

Population

Today France has just under 54 million inhabitants including some 4 million foreigners. With low birth and death rates, and with immigration now virtually at a standstill, the population is still increasing but at a much slower rate. By the year 2000 it is expected to reach only 56 to 58 million. During the last forty years French governments have been in favour of larger families – the *Code de la Famille* was first drafted in 1939 though not put into effect until after the Second World War and more recently still there have been large-scale press campaigns to encourage French people to have more children. However, in spite of government incentives (in the form of increased benefits and allowances for families with three or more children), the birth rate has fallen to 1.8 (which is below replacement level), and family-forming habits seem to have settled into a stable pattern: people marry later, divorce more (one in six marriages ends in divorce) and have two rather than three children, or less. Except perhaps in working class and immigrant groups, large families are very much a thing of the past. With increasing numbers of women at work (often in low-paid, insecure and part-time jobs), there seems to be little chance of a reversal of recent trends, and the present balance between the 23 million economically active (out of which, in 1982, over 2 million were unemployed) and the 30 million or so dependent members of the population is unlikely to improve. One in every three people is still under twenty and almost one in five over sixty: with longer education, earlier retirement and steadily increasing unemployment, there is bound to be a mounting burden on health, social and educational services.

A large proportion of the population lives in towns – 36 million in 1975 compared with 17.5 million in 1911 – with the migration from countryside to town continuing at a faster rate than ever before. But what is more significant still is the fact that the population is becoming tripartite: 16 million in towns proper, 20 million in suburbs and *grandes banlieues* (expected to increase to 25 million in the next twenty years), and the remaining one-third spread over a countryside of about 500,000 sq. km. This growing suburbia is creating new challenges and new problems. The architectural horror of Sarcelles north of Paris, for example, brought with it fresh social problems. The very existence of this type of dormitory-suburb, catering for vast numbers of industrial and office workers, has had unexpected consequences, one of which is a growing tendency to introduce the continuous working day, which only ten years ago would have been anathema to French workers used to one-

or two-hour lunch breaks. But the solution may be elsewhere: these distant suburbs may, for example, be developed into viable economic units. From 1956 to 1965, Sarcelles grew from 8400 to 30,000 inhabitants: a *grand ensemble* with no life of its own. Socio-cultural facilities have gradually changed it into a proper town. Sarcelles 1983, with its (now stable) population of some 54,000 inhabitants, regional commercial centre, grammar and secondary schools, town library and cultural centre, industrial development zone and municipal bus service, no longer relies on Paris, although it is only nine miles away. A few miles to the west the new town of Cergy Pontoise is being built around new factories, office blocks and schools in an attempt to avoid previous mistakes, but with only limited results. Together with the other eight New Towns in France – five of them in the Paris area – Cergy Pontoise suffers from a too rapid growth rate and a closeness to the capital. Another problem is the change in the overall plan, especially in the development of the Paris area: originally the five New Towns were supposed to be large autonomous units, close to but not dependent on Paris. They are now seen as an integral part of a re-structured greater Paris, a megalopolis of 14 million inhabitants by the year 2000.

The massive exodus of French people from the land towards the expanding towns has meant a radical change in the distribution of the population between agricultural and other activities: over the last thirty years, the number of people employed in agriculture has decreased from 25 per cent to 9 per cent of the active population today, while the professionals and *cadres* grew from 9 per cent to 20 per cent. This points to a large-scale reorganization of the socio-economic structure. A direct comparison between agriculture and industry (still strong, with 36 per cent of the population in blue-collar jobs in 1980) leaves aside the most important sector of activity known as the tertiary sector – transport, distribution and services. Today, this 'non-productive' sector (which accounts for 55 per cent of the active population) is larger than the other two put together and still growing apace: most of the new jobs are in non-manual occupations and are filled by an increasing proportion of women. Industrial growth is greatly impaired by the effects of the economic crisis with large-scale redundancies resulting from restructuring in all the major industries. A further factor is the regional imbalance between the hard-hit areas in the North and in Lorraine and the still developing Rhône-Alpes area. A continuation of these trends because of further technological change, mechanization and rationalization may be expected to lead to a society in which only a minority will be directly involved in production, with the majority occupied in administrative and servicing activities. In such a situation there may be a number of consequences. On the one hand the division between manual and non-manual workers could become more marked, leading to a greater proletarianization of a smaller manual working class, and to an intensification of the class struggle. On the other hand, with a large number of workers facing redundancy, unless extensive retraining facilities are developed quickly, the wealth created by automation will heighten the problem of inequality and a new class of 'unemployables' will emerge.

Country v. town

Where have all the peasants gone?

France used to be described as a nation of small farmers; as F.C. Roe once put it, a 'garden in which millions of peasants dig, plough, hoe and weed from sunrise to sunset'. This is undoubtedly no longer true, as the widely-used phrase 'the death of the peasantry' indicates. But this does not mean that the countryside has become a desert: moving away from agriculture has not necessarily meant moving out of the countryside. Many former farmers have only moved a short distance away to the nearest market town in search of a job, or even continue to live in their village and commute to work. Many families are now earning part of their income from the land. The husband may, for example, remain a farmer but a supplementary (and regular) income is provided by his wife who has become a nurse or a teacher, or by his sons and daughters who work as secretaries, shop-assistants or factory-workers. This may not be by choice, but rather out of necessity since small family farms are no longer viable economic units. Many small farmers and agricultural labourers are among the poorest in the

French community, while the regrouping of land, modernization of farming methods and judicious reconversion to intensive fruit, cereal or meat production have enabled the few (who
may also draw high profits from the Common Market) to
become very wealthy indeed. Whether or not they are still
deriving their income from the land, villagers can no longer be
sharply distinguished from the rest of the population in their
way of life. In the 1960s they became bitterly aware of the fact
that, far from being protected by the Welfare State, they had
not joined the consumer society and were not receiving their
fair share of the national income in spite of the fact that they
were doing more than their fair share of work: harder work,
longer hours, lack of cultural facilities and modern con-
veniences were their lot. This is no longer the case and
increasingly, village, suburb and town dwellers alike watch
television, own a car and do their Saturday shopping in a
neighbouring hypermarket. They may not all have a bathroom
and indoor toilet, but they have a deep-freeze (well-stocked
with home-produced as well as pre-packed food) and a washing-
machine. In the last fifteen years, country life has in fact
become an attraction for former town-dwellers who now
return to the land at weekends, or even turn what was
originally a weekend cottage into their permanent home. The
farming community has become a minority on its home
ground and village life has often been transformed out of
recognition by these 'neo-villagers' who have sometimes
captured key positions on local councils.

Generalizations are of course dangerous: historians and sociologists have repeatedly demonstrated through case studies that
the contrast between town and countryside within a given area
is less striking than the often extreme regional differences. The
great plains of the Paris basin with their rich crops of wheat
and intensive farming, the mixed-crop farming of Brittany or
the Rhône valley, the vine-growing areas and the mountain
deserts of central France present widely differing problems and
prospects. The healthy areas seem to be of two kinds: the
capitalist type of intensive farming; and the more traditional
type of mixed farming, which, by increasingly involving co-
operative enterprise, fulfils the need for skilful crop rotation
and division of labour. Future prospects are certainly favour-

able given certain conditions: namely concentration on products in high demand (fruit, vegetables, high quality wine); sufficient organization (co-operatives); and well-planned marketing. In some favoured areas like the Côte d'Or, the agricultural labour force (vineyard labour) earns salaries comparable to those of the Dijon factories nearby. In less prosperous areas, like Brittany, however, some poultry farmers are worse off than industrial labourers. A large firm may deliver them day-old chicks and chicken food and impose precise planning. After nine weeks they collect the chickens for slaughtering. The farmer is a home-labourer paid to work according to conditions laid down by the firm. He may own his poultry farm, but this is probably a liability as he is usually tied down by debts and is entirely dependent on the firm employing him. Some poultry farmers have managed to organize themselves into co-operatives, but these are exceptions. For the majority, proletarianization has reached the countryside in a brutal form, and even in the richer Rhône valley there are increasing tendencies for the farmers to contract with freezing and canning firms like the American firm Libby's. All too often the farmers' share in the profits is a minor one, and agricultural incomes vary even more than industrial ones.

In the last thirty years or so, a certain amount of government planning has been introduced to improve the lot of rural communities very often in answer to growing unrest and insistent demands by younger farmers who first began to organize themselves in the early 1950s around a Catholic youth organization, the JAC (*Jeunesse agricole chrétienne*). From Bible meetings and socials to study groups on accountancy and farming techniques, they developed a growing awareness of their lack of formal schooling and absence of cultural facilities. They soon openly entered the trade union arena, led by Michel Debatisse who had coined the phrase 'the silent revolution of the peasants' to describe their aim. The main farmers' union, the FNSEA (*Fédération nationale des syndicats d'exploitants agricoles*), was controlled by the older, richer, conservative farmers. But its moribund youth section, the CNJA (*Centre national des jeunes agriculteurs*) could be revived. They took it over and gradually captured key posts in the trade union movement, while using their position as a platform to advocate new policies. They claim that peasant unity is a myth, that there are rich and poor farmers whose interests are different. They admit that the rural exodus is normal – most of the small family farms are not economically viable – but they want it to be 'humanized' by the provision of proper training facilities. They do not deny the importance of maintaining prices (the French farmers' lobby is a powerful one in the EEC), but wish to give greater importance to structural reforms (land and marketing). Finally they question the sacred principles of property ownership and individualism: 'The fishermen do not own the sea. Why do we need to own the land?' They have started implementing their own proposals by renting rather than owning their farms, by establishing group enterprises for marketing and shared production, by supporting the government agency set up for buying land and letting it in order to prevent speculation and by encouraging the regrouping of land (parcelled as a result of equal inheritance laws dating back to Napoleon). The movement has not always been peaceful, however, and there were famous riots in Brittany in 1961, for example, when ballot boxes were burned. Michel Debatisse himself has now become an establishment figure, while the *jeunes agriculteurs* have found younger, more militant leadership. Constant campaigning of the government has been effective; greater concentration and specialization has also had some benefit; agricultural schools and training have been developed, new regional investments are co-ordinated through the EPR (*Etablissements publics régionaux*) created in 1972, government grants are given to young farmers willing to settle in depopulated areas, loans for equipment are now easier to obtain, and the old-style co-operatives have federated into vast units and modernized their methods. There are also industries contracting out work over large areas of countryside. This *saupoudrage industriel* as it is called provides regular work for women at home or winter occupation for the whole family. This is the case with watch-making in the Jura, textiles in the Loire, footwear around Cholet (near Nantes) and cutlery in the Lozère, though it can and does lead frequently to the exploitation of cheap labour.

Finally, the extension of tourism may also help bring a new lease of life to areas which are often beautiful but deserted (mountainous areas in particular). But the development of the tourist potential must provide new jobs (as ski instructors or in hotels in the mountains) if the local youth are to stay in the village and earn a proper and regular wage, while in the coastal areas, those responsible for development must beware of ecological – and architectural – disasters. The growth of the tourist industry, if properly controlled by local communities rather than by capitalist sharks, may help provide extra income and facilities for country folk while answering the need of town-dwellers for open–air leisure activities and rest – thus further bridging the gap between the 'two nations'.

Paris and 'the French desert'

And yet, it remains traditional to underline both the contrast between town and country and the divorce between Paris and the provinces – a metropolis in 'the French desert'. Taine put it in a nutshell in 1863:

> There are two peoples in France, the provinces and Paris, the former dines, sleeps, yawns, listens; the latter thinks, dares, wakes and talks; the one dragged by the other like a snail by a butterfly, now amused now worried by the capriciousness and audacity of its leader.

As the focus of national life in France, Paris is unrivalled and the Parisian has a somewhat haughty attitude towards anybody who does not belong there. This is somehow surprising to outside observers who happen to know that while one in every five Frenchmen lives in Paris or the Paris region, relatively few have been established in the capital for more than a generation, and one in five Parisians is a foreigner. In spite of the pressure of life in the capital, the constant rush and noise (1 million commuters spend two or more hours travelling to and from work every day), the desperate housing situation, and the very high cost of living, the prestige and desirability of life there were unaltered until recently. Stifled by cars which encroach even on the pavements, much of the old Paris is being demolished and replaced by tall tower blocks, or tastefully renovated at high cost, thus driving the original slum inhabitants into the distant suburbs. In general there is a definite move towards the outskirts of the city – a pheno-menon which is true of all the large towns – and since 1968 the number of provincials moving into the capital has consistently been smaller than the number of Parisians moving away.

Just as it is a social centre, so, too, is Paris an intellectual one: with its thirteen university campuses and its flood of students it contrasts sharply with quieter provincial university towns. But is prestige necessarily matched by excellence? Certainly it appears to be so. In a centralized and fiercely competitive system, a Paris appointment is often seen as promotion for teachers, as indeed for most civil servants; and students compete for places in the *grandes écoles* which are still more often to be found in the Paris conurbation than outside. Paris used also to be considered the world's cultural capital. It is still a very lively but expensive centre. Many of the new films can now be seen in provincial towns for one-third of the price of an *exclusivité* on the Champs-Elysées or the Boulevards, but while the decentralization policy for the arts and the increasing number of summer festivals have made culture available to more provincials than ever before, it is often at such a high price that many lower paid people are effectively debarred from enjoying it.

With industry the situation is similar and in spite of efforts to decentralize the city is bursting at the seams. Tax rebates are awarded to industries moving outside the Paris area. Thus, between 1968 and 1975, half a million new jobs were created in provincial cities. But the general underdevelopment of the provinces (communications in particular are poor though improving) counteracts government incentives. While Paris itself, with its 2.3 million inhabitants, lost 11 per cent of its population between 1968 and 1975, the greatest increases in population were in the other areas of the *Ile de France* (the Paris conurbation) which grew from 9.2 to 9.9 million, and includes five New Towns. Recent years have also seen the fostering of provincial conurbations to serve as poles of attraction, such as the Rhône-Alpes region, with the already enormous Lyon complex (well over 1 million inhabitants) and much publicized expansion of the Winter Olympics town of

Grenoble. Only five towns have 500,000 (Lyon, Marseille, Lille, Bordeaux, Toulouse); another nine have over 300,000. Compared with the size of the Paris conurbation, this shows a lack of balance greater than in Britain.

Efforts to fight the growing suffocation of Paris have been extended by a policy of regionalism, which is still causing a great deal of controversy. Regionalism is a positive effort to adapt to the requirements of contemporary life and needs. It involves the formation of viable and autonomous economic units, rather than a negative rejection of the arbitrary division into *d'epartements* and a resulting return to historical provinces. The ninety-five departments have thus been grouped into twenty-two economic regions, and the eight largest towns have been singled out as *métropoles d'équilibre*. But real administrative and industrial decentralization is proving difficult. Too many Paris-based firms are setting up one or even several factories in the provinces while retaining their *siège social* in Paris. As a result, decisions are taken in Paris without enough direct knowledge of local conditions. Recently the system of regional development has been diversified, to include both the *métropoles d'équilibre* and the *villes moyennes* (50,000 to 80,000 inhabitants), helped by better road and rail communications between towns (like the Paris-Lyon-Marseille *turbotrain*), and by greater specialization of each industrial centre to avoid costly competition within one region. However, the *question régionale* still remains, with its political, economic and cultural undertones, and is especially used in political and electoral manoeuvring. Regional cultures and languages, which the introduction of compulsory schooling and the imposition of the French language had helped to destroy, are being revived in the South and in Brittany. Nationalist, political or religious minorities act as pressure groups, attempting to restructure local communities. This quest for local, regional roots may be part of a search for identity in a mass society in which so many local and traditional features have been ironed out.

Young and old, men and women

In the early 1960s, the cult of youth invaded advertising, fashion and the entertainment and holiday industries. And *les jeunes* were the basis of France's faith in its political and economic future. This faith was shaken by the explosion of May 1968 when young workers and students were suddenly seen as a threat to the establishment. Until then rebellious minorities had largely been ignored by the wider public. Even pop culture was tame. It was the reign of *'les copains* walking hand in hand' and listening to Françoise Hardy and Johnny Halliday on their transistor radios – nothing resembling the wild English or American crowds. They were on the whole conforming to accepted patterns of behaviour. The more culturally aware formed the audience for Georges Brassens, Juliette Gréco and other upholders of the poetical or political tradition of the *chansons*; the more politically minded were militant in innocuous-looking *groupuscules* torn by in-fighting.

Rebellious youth was brought to the fore in May 1968 – untamed university and secondary school students, unorganized union militants all defying the establishment. They questioned authority in all its manifestations and won some concessions. Although student unrest now seems to have receded, protest will continue to simmer under the surface as long as educational reforms are not properly implemented, and this will take years, thousands of new teachers and millions of francs. As the youth of the early 1960s now reaches adulthood and enters a labour market dominated by unemployment, older generations often react with hostility and fear; statistics indicate that a crisis may not be far away.

Today, in spite of the successive youth employment schemes (*Pacte national pour l'emploi*), over 40 per cent of the unemployed, among whom two-thirds are women, are under twenty-five. Worse still, according to the *Agence nationale pour l'emploi* (ANPE), 35 per cent are still unemployed after six months, the jobs they find are often temporary (*emplois intérimaires*), and unqualified school-leavers only represent a small proportion of those who gain admission to one of the government schemes – a situation which the Mauroy government is trying to remedy with special measures for the sixteen-to-eighteen age group. A hard core of unqualified young unemployed is slowly emerging and it is hardly surprising that suicide and criminal rates are increasing. But accusations of apathy, rejection of adult values or downright laziness are misguided for a number of reasons. These accusations both ignore educational and social disparities (a university graduate has three times more chance than an unqualified school-leaver of finding a first job), and do not acknowledge the fact that most young people share the same values as their elders. Recent opinion polls and government reports alike paint a more positive picture: most young people do not reject their own family and wish to have one of their own; they want to work and are worried about their prospects in a society which only offers them insecure and uninteresting jobs with no prospects of obtaining further qualifications. Work, therefore, is no longer the central value in their life since it will bring them neither satisfaction nor social recognition: their questioning of traditional hierarchical models, of repetitive fragmented tasks, their demand for greater autonomy and a sense of purpose are aspirations they share with many adult workers. They did not invent the consumer society, they were born with it and want to join it – though it may be true to say that they prefer spending their money on going out dancing and buying stereo equipment rather than a colour television or a new settee. And their life styles often imply different values, rather than a rejection of all values: cohabitation before marriage may be read as the sign of a search for marital harmony and true respect for marriage itself.

One reason for the tension between young and old may be that adults fear the approach of old age. While earlier retirement is welcomed by those for whom work has been synonymous with physical strain, repetitive tasks, noise and long hours, those who find fulfilment in their job are often loath to retire. Nevertheless, there are already signs that retirement no longer means relinquishing an active social life: pensioners have their own clubs (*clubs du troisième âge*), travel, take up university courses and enjoy leisure activities – all the more so when they receive a decent pension and have not been worn out by a life of toil. Moreover, the pensioners of today are the last pre-war generation of workers; the grandparents of tomorrow will have spent their active life in the prosperous 1950s and will probably not have the same value systems. Society must adapt to the new distinction between the 'younger pensioners' whose needs are psychological as well as economic, and the 'very old' (*le quatrième âge*) for whom isolation and health will remain the main problems.

Women, both young and old, are claiming their place in French society. Fairly recently, legislation granted them formal equality with men: joint choice of the matrimonial home (1965), freedom to work, open a bank account and own property without the need for the husband's consent (1965), equal pay (1972), protection from sex discrimination (1975), birth control (contraception and abortion Acts of 1974 and 1975), divorce reform (1975). Yet French women, who represent 40 per cent of the work force, constitute a majority in unskilled industrial jobs, while in white-collar occupations they rarely rise to a position commanding responsibility and initiative. As a result, they remain lower-paid (in the proportion of 2 to 1 for the lowest wages, of 1 to 7 for the highest), and are twice as likely to become unemployed. Such inequalities were officially recognized in 1981 with the appointment of a Minister for Women's Rights who is busy introducing new protective legislation.

Some observers are quick to point out that, paradoxically, women may have lost more than they gained by leaving their home for the world of work: the subordinates of men at work, they have also lost 'control' over the home since the domestic tasks are shared – though often unequally – and they may well have the worst of both worlds. Yet most women, except perhaps the unskilled labourers, claim that having a job has meant an overall improvement in their lives, and many young mothers choose to continue working after the birth of their first child. Thereafter, however, economic and practical difficulties may force a choice between outside employment and the birth of a second or third baby. But for over 3 of the 9 million women at work, there is little freedom of choice: they are single wage-earners, many of them with dependent children. Though still a minority in militant trade union, political or cultural organizations, they are beginning to assert themselves. Opinion is divided as to the social consequences of these continuing trends.

Social classes

The general improvement in the standard of living, the development of hire-purchase and changing patterns of consumption in the (relatively) affluent society have caused a blurring of former class distinctions. The family car and the television set have entered working-class homes, holidays are no longer the privilege of the rich and even home ownership is spreading, though it is still less common than in England. Could this mean a destruction of class barriers and the end of the struggle for control and power which were the hallmark of pre-war French society, with its powerful working class and strong Communist Party? The language of the class struggle may have changed; but it does not necessarily mean that a classless society is emerging.

Wealth and income

Between 1950 and 1980, the purchasing power of the average annual wage has more than trebled and the introduction, in 1968, of the index-linked minimum wage – the SMIC (*Salaire minimum interprofessionnel de croissance*) – has helped to reduce the gap between high salaries and low wages: a gap which is still greater in France than in any other European country apart from Italy. In 1981, a comparison between the top and bottom 10 per cent of the salaried workers showed a ratio of 1 to 15: over 34,000 francs (about £3000) a month for *cadres supérieurs*, less than 2200 francs (about £200) for unskilled manual workers. Even more serious perhaps is the fact that, since 1976, the growth of wages has not kept pace with the cost of living. Low-paid workers are among the new poor, and below them and excluded from the consumer society, we find the 'submerged' – the unemployed, the old, the immigrants, and the handicapped who barely survive on social security. For these people a new expression has been coined – le 'quart-monde' (the Fourth World).

At the other end of the social scale, the wealthy *grande bourgeoisie* still possesses considerable power and influence, particularly in the *Chambre des députés* (the legislative assembly) and in the Civil Service, especially, for example, in the Foreign Office. The economic rule of this class remains undisputed, though the frequency of mergers and take-overs by foreign firms causes signs of strain to appear. In the educational, social and cultural spheres, its influence is less marked.

State education, which is anti-clerical and fairly democratic (but perhaps more a formal than a real democracy), has almost completely escaped its grasp; but it still controls élite recruitment through private education and the prestigious *grandes écoles*. There is an ever-widening gap between the very rich and very poor, but if we exclude the two extremes, we may agree with Peter Wiles's comment in his survey of the distribution of disposable income per household carried out for the OECD: 'France is more equal than she thinks.'

The working class

The traditional condition of the working class has changed considerably in the last fifty years. The growth of unionization, the system of social security and the increased mechanization of industry leading to an overall higher level of training and skill, have certainly improved the lot of the workers. However, some problems remain; others are heightened. There is in particular a sense of insecurity at a time when many industries are under threat: mining, as in Britain, is declining; the car industry is shaken by regular crises; bankruptcies have caused regional disasters; even in more advanced sectors like the aircraft industry, rationalization has led to redundancies on a large scale.

Class consciousness seems to have remained sharper than in Britain. It may be due in part to the 20 per cent of Communist voters who, while not being a 'revolutionary' force, still keep alive a certain language or jargon and an analysis based on the class struggle; it may also be due to a labour movement which, until the electoral victory of the Left in May 1981, had not been torn apart to the same extent as in England by the compromises of participation in government. Union action welds workers together in the class struggle, but the best unionists form a minority of the workers, and the commitment of workers to their unions seems to be changing: the very militant are probably becoming more politically conscious and active, while those on the fringe of union activity only snatch a limited amount of time and energy from their main commitment to a better standard of living. The search for security is a key word for working class people, who now favour the monthly-paid status to the hourly-paid insecurity of the past. Secure employment can guarantee them the maintenance of a newly-acquired standard of living now under threat. Only then, as the shorter working week spreads, will they be able to satisfy their new cultural and leisure requirements, though time thus gained is too often wasted commuting to distant suburbs.

The new middle classes

The new extended middle classes are not a purely French phenomenon. But there are some specific French characteristics: the number of minor Civil Servants (*petits fonctionnaires*), who often earn less than manual workers, do a repetitive and often tiring type of office work, and yet consider their position as a promotion, mainly on account of the 'image' (white-collar worker) and the security (no fear of redundancy and a guaranteed retirement pension) which such posts offer.

It must be remembered that the French Civil Service includes, besides administrative workers, other sections of the working population like teachers and post-office workers. The social status of teachers is certainly higher than in Britain, though large numbers of supply teachers (a quarter of the total number) have low pay and no security of employment. Teachers are generally held to belong to the very French category of *cadres*, which forms a new middle class largely corresponding to the growth of the service sector. The *cadres* are distinguished from managers because they are salaried workers, not employers. They may be responsible for a large section of a factory or administration (*cadres supérieurs*) or only a smaller group of workers (*cadres moyens*). In some industries, they represent 3 per cent of the salaried workers only (mining), in others 12 per cent (mechanical and chemical industries), and even 18 per cent (power) or 19 per cent (oil). They enjoy a high standard of living, due to the relative security of their jobs; but they too are increasingly suffering from unemployment and inflation. Their number has been estimated at around 1.5 million and it is still rising. They mainly enjoy a better education, are more numerous in large towns and differ from the traditional bourgeoisie by their more reckless way of life with a tendency not to save but rather to consume.

Social mobility: a myth or a reality?

It is generally acknowledged that it takes three generations for the gradual change from the worker/peasant class to post-graduate or professional status to be achieved. But formal education, which plays such an important role in this, is not always attainable: scholarships and grants are scarce and in most cases insufficient to ensure reasonable chances of success. Of course, the unification of syllabuses, the *tronc commun* for all the children between eleven and fifteen, and centrally-organized examinations, though criticized for being overdone, are to some extent helping to standardize things. But inequalities remain, between those who are deemed capable of following the three-year *lycée* courses leading to the *baccalauréat* (*cycle long*) and the others, who join technical schools for shorter courses of study, enter apprenticeship, or drift out of school with no qualification at all. Although all the *lycées*, in theory, cater for anybody according to ability, they do in fact have different clienteles. The best *lycées classiques* are still largely a preserve of the bourgeoisie while the others, because of geographical distribution and lack of prestige, get more working class and fewer brighter children. Access to the very top of the social structure remains the privilege of the very few: recruitment to the administrative élite (executive class of the French Civil Service) may be considered to be predominantly incestuous. However, there is considerable mobility around the middle of the occupational scale: investigation into the family background of the *cadres moyens* shows their extremely varied social origins, but this is also the case for the manual workers and the unemployed: mobility is not always upwards.

Institutions: stability and change

In May 1968, after ten years of stable Gaullist rule, France woke up in turmoil. The country came to a standstill, the regime itself was threatened. Everything seemed to be called into question: parliament and political parties, trade union bureaucracies, the educational system, the mass media, bourgeois culture. With the breakdown of normal communications – press, radio, television – came what has been called an 'explosion of the word'. Everybody talked to everybody else, in university lecture theatres and cafés and on the streets (this was of course, more true of large towns than villages, of Paris rather than the provinces, of young people than of old). For a short while, there was an impression of liberation from the constraints of normal life, an awakening, for people normally held down by routine. Theatre companies, journalists, writers, television personalities who visited the occupied factories and universities, were struck by the overwhelming response of their audiences. People became aware of the censorship of the government-controlled radio and television, of the cultural desert in which they were kept. But romanticizing is of no avail: the wave of excitement was followed by a Gaullist landslide victory. The staying power of institutions had proved stronger than the wind of change.

The stability of the basic institutions of the State is not at stake; and the electoral victory of the Socialists in 1981 has not meant a radical departure from the past. The government is not attempting to change the 'Gaullist' Constitution of the Fifth Republic and will be content to introduce reforms within the existing framework. Nor will it lead a frontal attack against the Church in the form of a straightforward nationalization of private schools which are often 'Catholic' schools, nor an attack against the Army by abolishing conscription or altering defence policy. The institutions closer to economic and social life are of course being modified, but not out of recognition. Nationalization itself is not new – cars (Renault), banks (Crédit Lyonnais), railways and cigarettes were already nationalized. The reform of the judiciary and the symbolic transfer of the guillotine to a Paris museum have not meant a radical transformation of the system: the Home Secretary, faced with the continuing problem of terrorist bomb attacks and insecurity, has repeatedly asserted confidence and pride in his police force. Social and education policy may be trying to reduce inequalities, but the school and university system are so far unaltered, and the survival of the family as a basic element in the social fabric is still encouraged by government incentives.

And yet, consumer groups and lobbies of all kinds are sprouting everywhere, organizing protest, putting pressure on civil service and local authorities, on trade union and political bureaucracies. Over the last fifteen years, a new consciousness seems to have developed, however diffuse. It is revealed through many initiatives and practices which are growing at local level, close to the grass roots; just as if the French, realizing the rigidity of their institutions, were constantly trying to find ways of by-passing bureaucracies in a constant battle against an abstract enemy – the 'administration'. Thus, unofficial strikes and claims for workers' control over production and organization of work (*autogestion*) are often given equal weight with more traditional wage claims, all the more so in a trade union like the CFDT (*Confédération française et démocratique du travail*) which is less centralized than the vertically-structured CGT (*Confédération générale du travail*). Grass-roots militancy has also developed within political parties: the Socialists are often faced with minor revolts from their rank and file, whilst the right-wing parties hold regular 'summer schools' hoping to develop a new image among the young by extending the activities of their local branches outside election periods. Christian associations openly debate problems of doctrine, young magistrates and judges criticize the judicial system, conscripts demand new rights of association, and discipline has been transformed beyond the wishes of many teachers and administrators in the *lycées*. More say in decision-making is the order of the day, even though 'participation' tends to be quickly formalized, and therefore anaesthetized in the process.

This may be painting too bland (or too fragmented?) a picture: militants will remain a minority in a population which is above all trying to survive economically and snatch as many crumbs as possible from the cake of affluence. The fabric of society is being changed, but this does not necessarily mean a lack of continuity.

The best example is perhaps the family: its death has been prophesied; some deplore the loss of many of its former functions while others attack it for curbing the development of its individual members. And yet the French family is going strong. When asked about ideal family size many people say they would like to have three or more children, and yet they only have one or two. This contradiction may be partly explained by factors like poor housing and economic difficulties which bring them down to earth. Young parents are not willing to have larger families at the expense of a standard of living which has been painfully attained through the added source of income of the increasingly numerous working wives and mothers. Indeed, as a result of the number of working mothers, there are twice as many places in *crèches* for young children in France than in England. Young people seem to favour 'juvenile cohabitation' rather than marriage and a large-scale survey carried out by the INED (*Institut national d'études démographiques*) shows that 44 per cent of the couples who married in 1976–7 had lived together before marriage as against 17 per cent in 1968–9. At the same time their decision to have children is usually linked with the decision to legalize the union and illegitimate births are only 10 per cent of all births.

Close ties still exist everywhere between the small family unit (parents and children), and the extended family (grandparents, uncles, cousins, and so on) – ties which have survived the move of the children to the city. Parental authority, respect and politeness are on the whole more sternly enforced than in England, though all this is being eroded in urban communities. In this respect, French society seems nearer to Irish than to English society, though just how far this is due to a common Roman Catholic tradition is difficult to ascertain. Kinship links remain important in all social groups: they are useful when you look for a job, or a home; grandparents look after children after school and at holiday time; and with the widespread search for cultural roots, they recover a role they had lost in most western societies – transmitting to the younger generations the traditions and language of their own family past, thus helping to bridge the gap between young and old, between peasant origins and urban living.

Another unifying element between social groups, conscription, is still enforced, and young men face twelve months of military service. Until the Second World War, this period *sous les drapeaux* used to create a real melting pot, some kind of initiation rite in which young men from varying backgrounds shared. It still remains a meeting ground, but offers less social mixing. Great numbers of students used to obtain several years' delay, but the law is trying to enforce early military service for all young men of eighteen, and attempting to reduce the number of exemptions from military service. However, students still tend to serve their time as teachers in ex-colonial countries or, if they serve in the armed forces, very often do so as NCOs, and in any case do not mix well because of their age and different interests. So the rift between the educated and uneducated is no longer bridged as it once was by this common experience of army life. Conscription itself provokes bitter controversy, and the Socialist election promise to reduce the length of military service to six months is yet to be fulfilled.

Some new or forthcoming changes, however, must not be minimized. The most momentous will probably be 'decentralization' (the Act came into force in March 1982), hailed by the Socialists as 'a quiet revolution' (*une révolution tranquille*), an attempt to bring decision-making closer to the people affected by these decisions – hence greater democracy. Inevitably it has been denounced by their opponents as a divisive measure and a wasteful manipulation of committees and personnel, since the local and regional assemblies will need brains trusts and advisers to help them perform their new functions. The *préfet* was the eye of the Home Secretary in each *départment*; he now becomes a *commissaire de la république*, the local representative of the executive. Will he be a mere delegate, or the new referee over problems which will no longer need to be referred to Paris? Time, and decisions over financing, will decide. Decentralization may help defuse the Corsican time-bomb; may bring a new lease of life to regions like Brittany, the Jura, or the Dordogne, for which distance from the Paris Ministries meant files sometimes 'getting lost' on their way through the red-tape of administration, and in any case resulted in long delays. If fully implemented despite Civil Service resistance and powerful lobbies, the Act will certainly mean diversification – a departure from the long tradition of Jacobin centralization.

Leisure and culture

There are now in France two Ministries in charge of leisure and cultural activities. First is the *Ministère de la Culture* which is responsible for the development of libraries and museums, music, theatre and the cinema. Second is the *Ministère du Temps libre* which deals with problems connected with leisure: the timing of holidays to avoid the August mass migration and its consequences for both the tourist industry and the economy; the development of the tourist potential of the country areas to counterbalance the dominant choices of seaside or mountain holidays; the diversification of State subsidies to enable the less affluent members of the community to enjoy a holiday away from their urban or village homes; the balancing of work and leisure (*aménagement du temps de travail*). This concern with holidays and leisure is not new, but it has recently become a leading issue. The pressure of urban living, longer life expectancy and earlier retirement, rising unemployment (hence the slogan *travailler moins pour travailler tous* – 'shorter hours mean jobs for all') have combined with the return of a Socialist government committed to fulfilling the task started by the Popular Front in 1936 which was for a shorter working week (forty hours, now reduced to thirty-nine with the aim being a thirty-five hour week) and an annual paid holiday for all (recently increased from two to five weeks).

Holidays

The French seem to live obsessively for *les vacances* – eleven months of noise, work and stress, of scrimping and saving for an annual spending spree. Two-thirds of the population regularly migrate south and west in the summer while farmers account for nearly half of those who remain behind. Half the holidaymakers rush to the seaside and the sun. The spectacular success of such institutions as the *Club Méditerranée*, with its thatched-hut villages built around the Mediterranean as well as in more exotic places like Tahiti, is a witness to this trend. But the majority of holidaymakers either stay with friends or relatives (35 per cent), go camping (23 per cent), or rent a flat or a cottage (*gîtes ruraux*). Among the less affluent, school-children often go away without their parents, staying with grandparents or in *colonies de vacances* (holiday camps) – the social security system partly footing the bill. Disadvantaged children from the towns frequently have only the streets and some adventure playgrounds for their holidays, and confrontation with the police for their excitement – a problem which, after the hot summer of 1981 (with the news-catching 'rodeos' involving stolen cars in a Lyon suburb), the government at last seems to be tackling with more humanity and less repression.

When they can afford it, families go away together with organizations like *Villages-Vacances-Familles*, *Les Maisons Familiales*, *Vacances-Loisirs-Familles* and so on which offer family accommodation, communal catering and leisure activities for all ages. A more recent trend is the distribution of holidays over a (longer) summer and a (shorter) winter period. Even skiing holidays, still a preserve of the upper-middle class (only 8 per cent of the population can afford them), are in a minor way open to the underprivileged. This is through the system of *classes de neige* whereby primary schools from town areas can in turn send one or more classes to the mountains for a month, complete with teacher and skiing equipment, to combine normal teaching in the morning with outdoor activity in the afternoon. This is still far too sporadic for it to be effective in any general way, and too expensive for all children concerned to be able to go, but it does point to a future when what used to be the privilege of the better-off may be available to many more.

Pastimes and leisure

Besides holidays proper, leisure activities of all kinds develop in all social groups – the advent of a 'civilization of leisure' has even been prophesied. People often say they would prefer a longer weekend to a bigger pay packet: time is too often 'wasted' in the mad rush to earn a living ('on perd sa vie à la gagner') and increasingly, the French insist on 'choosing' how to divide their life between work-orientated and leisure activities (*le temps choisi*), or increasing the amount of time to be devoted to non-work (*le temps libéré*).

Pastimes vary greatly depending on social class and

education but gardening has become a national pastime for rich and poor alike; one Frenchman in three now mows his lawn, grows vegetables or flowers, and may even decorate his garden with plastic gnomes or reproduction nymphs. Radio, television and newspapers are part of most people's daily lives, though they were only mentioned by a tiny minority as being among their 'favourite pastimes' in a recent IFOP survey, while reading and sports vied for the lead followed by music, needlework, do-it-yourself (*bricolage*) and gardening. 'Sports' of course means different things for teenagers and adults, for workers and professionals. Football and cycling are the popular sports and are more often watched than actively practised, with the ritual *Tour de France* taking over from cup matches in July on television. Elite sports like tennis, horse-riding, sailing and wind-surfing are becoming accessible to increasing numbers of young people through the multiplication of municipal clubs and investments. However, cultural activities outside the home remain largely the preserve of the middle and upper classes: few people frequently attend concerts (7 per cent) or go to the theatre (12 per cent), though one person in five still goes out to the cinema at least once a week – the highest percentages being amongst the *cadres* and Parisians. More films are watched on the family television than on the screen, however, and video clubs are sprouting.

There is certainly greater demand for cultural activities now than ten or twenty years ago, as the success of classes for classical or modern ballet dancing, learning languages, pottery, playing the guitar and other instruments has demonstrated. However, the dream of a popular culture bridging class differences remains, at present, a pious dream. The gap between the cultured and the deprived (rural communities, the working class) seems likely to remain for quite a long time. Formal education at present is insufficient, and adult education sadly underdeveloped. Industrial workers may be alienated for a number of reasons: work on a machine; closed community living; lack of time and facilities or the poor quality of the mass media, for example. This alienation causes a reversion to what one such worker calls 'illiteracy' when he compares the reading and writing abilities of adult factory workers to that of their children still in junior schools. But the role of associations of all kinds in developing an awareness of cultural needs has led to initiatives – both private and public – for extending cultural activities to an ever-growing audience, and the dominance of Paris is beginning to be challenged.

Decentralization of culture

There are 1200 *Maisons des jeunes et de la culture* (youth and arts centres) in France, with some 600,000 members (half workers, half students and schoolchildren). They are subsidized partly by the State, partly by local councils, and each centre is administered by a permanent head (who nearly always has experience outside the educational profession) and by a house council elected by the young members themselves. Very often the centre is the only meeting-place for young people in a small town, apart from the local café, and is used for amateur dramatics, film shows, lectures, concerts, dances, and other indoor leisure activities; it also serves as a base from which to organize outings, holidays and so on. A high proportion of the worker members of the MJC are active trade unionists, and their members in general are among the most literate young people apart from students. Recently they have been under attack for being hotbeds of politicization of youth, and for wasting public money through bad administration. Both charges have been denied, but action has been taken against them. Under the pretext of decentralization, State subsidies have been reduced by 13 per cent, and more financial responsibility has been placed on local councils who thus became direct employers of the staff. The consequences of this are tighter control over cultural policy by the local councils (generally Right of Centre) and a tendency to demand that what is supposed to be a public service should also be economically viable.

The MJC were born of the post-war spirit, out of a desire to provide young people with places to meet – youth clubs rather than purely arts centres. For the *Maisons de la culture*, however, the purpose was clear and voiced by André Malraux who wanted to give a single 'home' to all the arts, where culture would be represented with its many facets, and where various types of audience could meet under one roof. The fifteen *Maisons de la culture* created since 1961 in provincial cities (except for Créteil and Nanterre near Paris) have helped the development of a variety of cultural projects and practices. They have three principal missions. The first is creativity (*création*), the presentation of new high-quality productions often undertaken by permanent theatre or ballet companies (Grenoble and La Rochelle), by teams of film-makers (Le Havre) or musicians (Amiens), and sometimes with the collaboration of specially invited and well-known artists. The second is cultural dissemination (*diffusion*) and outside companies, itinerant exhibitions and orchestras are welcomed. The third is cultural *animation*, an encouragement for all forms of cultural activity, especially those which favour confrontations and exchanges between actors, designers, musicians and their public, thereby encouraging cross-fertilization and experiment. Though the *Maisons de la culture* have developed into lively arts centres transforming life in their city, they are plagued by a shortage of funds and often have to curtail their own most adventurous projects and instead invite well-known companies on tour in order to boost the bookings. Unfortunately the development of a real cultural policy is bound to be inhibited by the need to make a profit.

The *Maisons de la culture* regularly welcome the regional theatre companies, themselves formed as a result of the decentralization policy for the arts and also fighting for survival. When Jean Vilar's *Théâtre National Populaire* in Paris (founded in 1951) was forced to close down through lack of government subsidy in 1972, Roger Planchon (who had gathered together his company in Lyon during the early 1950s) inherited the title of *national* theatre for his *Théâtre de Villeurbanne*. This may have been a victory for decentralization but it also meant the disappearance of the stronghold of popular theatre in élitist Paris. In the provinces, nineteen *Centres dramatiques* sprang up, with financial support from both government and local councils: the *Comédie de l'Est* (Strasbourg), . . . *de l'Ouest* (Rennes), . . . *du Centre* (Bourges), and so on. Their policy is to serve both the town where they are based and the surrounding rural community by regular tours, and their 'consecration' comes when they are invited to Paris for a season. Their aim is obviously to reach out to a working-class audience, and they partly succeed: some 30 per cent of the audience of Planchon's *Théâtre de Villeurbanne* is *populaire*. But the public reached is mainly skilled workers, foremen and the like – perhaps because the ordinary workers have fewer contacts with the trade union bureaucracy that handles the bookings. There is now an increasing realization that the theatre must go out to people in their normal surroundings; the general difficulties then are how to combine artistic quality with mobility, and to ascertain what degree of effort can be demanded of the audience. Much more specific is the financial problem.

In 1981, only 0.5 per cent of the national budget went to support the arts. In 1977, State help to the *Centres dramatiques* increased by only 7 per cent, even though a 25 per cent increase had been written into the contracts. The same year, the prestigious *Centre Georges Pompidou* opened, absorbing in running costs almost half the total state budget allotted to the arts. Mitterand's choice of a well-known personality of the arts, Jack Lang, as his Minister of Culture, and a government commitment to a larger share of the national budget may help make culture available to all. Whether this is a democratic phenomenon or a new form of twentieth-century bourgeois patronage remains to be seen, however. Debates on what exactly is meant by 'the explosion of culture' have been revived in the wake of the spectacular success of the *Centre Pompidou* whose futuristic glass and metal architecture in the historic heart of the city attracts millions of visitors from all countries and backgrounds. Provincials and foreigners discover Paris from the top of escalators encased in glass across the west façade; local school-children rush to their audio-visual workshop; Parisians young and old visit the Public Information Library, the Museum of Modern Art's permanent collection, one of the many temporary exhibitions, the Centre of Industrial Creation or the Experimental Music Department (*IRCAM*) directed by Pierre Boulez. Everything cultural is under one roof, with permanent fairground activity outside: is it culture made available to the masses, a catalyst for artistic development, or a supermarket of culture? In its five years of existence, the *Centre Pompidou* has become a leading landmark on the tourist route from the Eiffel Tower to Notre-Dame.

Bibliography

Ardagh, J., *The New France* (revised edition). Harmondsworth, Penguin Books, 1970. A very comprehensive study, with precise examples. See Chapters IV, on farmers; VI, on provincial life; IX, on daily life; X, on youth, as the most relevant to social structure.

Bauer, G. and Roux, J.M., *La Rurbinisation ou la ville éparpillée*. Paris, Le Seuil, 1976. On the invasion of rural areas by the urban overspill which thus creates the new 'rurban' phenomenon.

Biraben, J.N. and Dupaquier, J., *Les Berceaux vides de Marianne*. Paris, Le Seuil, 1981. Analyses the failure of government incentives to increase the French birth rate.

Canacos, H., *Sarcelles ou le béton apprivoisé*. Paris, Editions Sociales, 1979. The mayor of Sarcelles and his fight against 'sarcellitis' – the malaise which became associated with the concentration of high-rise flats.

Chombart de Lauwe, M.J. and P.H. *et al.*, *La Femme dans la société, son image dans les différents milieux sociaux*. Paris, Editions du CNRS, 1977. A comprehensive survey: women at home, at work, at university; the evolution over the last fifty years.

Debatisse, M., *La Révolution silencieuse. Le combat des paysans*. Paris, Calmann Lévy, 1963. A description of the movement of the young farmers in its early days by their (then) leader.

Données sociales. INSEE (Institut national de la statistique et des études économiques), Paris, 1981. Statistical information on all aspects of social life, with an analysis of the main trends and reports on social surveys and consumer studies.

Dossiers et documents. Paris, *Le Monde*, ten issues per year. A supplement to the well-known daily newspaper, gathering together recent articles concerning social, political and economic problems. A very useful tool for the student who wants to keep up-to-date with the evolution of French society. Recent issues include: *La Sécurité sociale*, (juin 1981); *La Drogue* (novembre 1981); *Les Immigrés* (janvier 1982); *Les Jeunes et l'emploi* (mai 1982); *L'Impôt des Français* and *Le Temps libre* (juillet-août-septembre 1982).

Dupeux, G., *La Société française, 1789-1970*. Paris, Colin, 1972, and London, Methuen, 1976. See its analysis of the population structure and migrations in particular.

Esprit, 'L'administration' (Numéro Spécial). Paris, January 1970. On the administrative machine and the conditions of the civil servant – an important collection of essays.

Esprit, 'L'armée et la défense' (Numéro Spécial). Paris, October 1975. In particular B. Kitou's inside view as a conscript, and the analysis of the 'malaise de l'Armée'.

Lenoir, R., *Les Exclus*. Paris, Seuil, 1973. On the poor, the old, the handicapped, and all those who never gained entry to the consumer society.

Le Roy Ladurie, E. and Vigne, D., *Inventaire des campagnes*. Paris, J.C. Lattès, 1980. The first part traces the history of 'peasantry', the second presents the *paysans* in a series of live interviews. Both informative and enjoyable reading.

Mallet, S., *La nouvelle classe ouvrière*. Paris, Seuil, 1963, and Nottingham, Spokesman Books, 1976. On the changes in working-class life and consciousness.

Mendras, H. (eds) *et al. La Sagesse et le désordre: France 1980*. Paris, Gallimard, 1980. An excellent collection of articles including social and institutional aspects of contemporary France.

Minces J., *Un ouvrier parle*. Paris, Seuil, 1969. Two long interviews with a working-class militant, before and after May 1968.

Reynaud, J.D. and Grafmeyer, Y. (eds), *Français, qui êtes-vous?* Paris, La Documentation Française, 1981. A collection of articles on social classes, the industrial world, the institutions and intellectual life, with very useful, up-to-date statistics. Most informative.

Sue, R., *Vers une société du temps libre*. Paris, PUF, 1982. A study of the changing patterns and importance of leisure in contemporary society.

Syndicat de la Magistrature *Justice sous influence*. Paris, Maspero, 1981. An examination of the judicial system by judges who analyse the evolution of the system and discuss the balance between social control and individual liberty.

Vaughan, M., Kolinsky, M. and Sheriff, P., *Social Change in France*. Martin Robertson, Oxford, 1978.

A very comprehensive collection of government *Reports* was published in 1982, the result of the surveys carried out by commissions appointed to study the state of the country at the time of the Socialists' return to power in 1981. Well-informed, comprehensive, up-to-date, programmatic as well as analytical. Among them:

La France en mai 1981, forces et faiblesses (with its five volumes of Appendices), by the *Commission du Bilan* under the chairmanship of F. Bloch-Lainé, a report to the Prime Minister.

Démocratie culturelle et droit à la différence, by H. Giorfan, a report to the Minister of Culture.

Le développement du tourisme social, by J.B. Grosborne, a report to the Minister of Leisure.

L'Insertion professionnelle et sociale des jeunes, by B. Schwartz, a report to the Prime Minister.

Les Tableaux de la solidarité by C. Blum-Girardeau, a report to the Minister of National Solidarity.

They are all published by *La Documentation française*, together with many other books and reviews, among which are *Les Cahiers français*, five issues per year. Recent issues were devoted to *La Fonction publique* (nos 194 and 197), *Le Monde urbain* (no. 203), *La Décentralisation* (no. 204).

All these publications are available from *La Documentation française*, 29-31 quai Voltaire, Paris, which also houses a well-stocked documentation library.

Two

Political parties

Eric Cahm

Introduction

François Mitterrand's coming to power in May 1981 has brought about a dramatic change in the position of the political parties in France. For the first time in its history, the Socialist Party (PS) dominates the political landscape. Mitterrand, the man behind its revival in the 1970s and the outstanding figure in the party, is ensconced in the Elysée Palace as President for a seven-year term. The party has an absolute majority in Parliament until 1986 (285 seats out of 491), and has no need there of the support of the Communist Party (PCF), now reduced to only forty-four seats, half the number it gained in the 1978 election. The Communist Party, for many years the leading party on the Left, which could command the votes of over 20 per cent of the electorate, has now been reduced to the status of a docile junior partner in government, obliged for the most part to dance to the Socialists' tune. Its share of the electorate slumped to 16.1 per cent in 1981.

The 1981 parliamentary election turned the tables on the two former majority parties, Jacques Chirac's RPR (*Rassemblement pour la république*) and the Giscardian UDF (*Union pour la démocratie française*). These parties of the Right, which had made up the bulk of the parliamentary majority for twenty-three years, provided France with presidents and enjoyed the fruits of governmental office, now found themselves in the unaccustomed situation of parties in opposition, the RPR with only eighty-five seats in Parliament and the UDF with only sixty-four.

It is the emergence of the Socialist Party as by far the largest party in France, and the fact that the Left is now in government and the Right in opposition, which have done so much to transform the circumstances of French party politics.

However, the basic pattern which emerged during the presidency of Giscard d'Estaing with these four major parties, the Socialists and Communists on the Left, and the RPR and UDF on the Right, as the main contenders in the political struggle and the only credible sources of presidential candidates, remains unchanged under Mitterrand. It has if anything become more pronounced. The four parties shared the mass of the votes in both the 1978 and 1981 parliamentary elections:

The four major parliamentary parties in the 1978 and 1981 elections

	Left		Right	
	Communists	*Socialists*	*UDF*	*RPR*
percentage of votes cast on first ballot 1978	20.6	22.6	21.5	22.6
percentage of votes cast on first ballot 1981	16.1	37.4	19.2	20.8

It can be seen from the above that the four major parties obtained 87.3 % per cent of the votes in 1978; they took all but seventeen of the seats in Parliament. In 1981, however, they did even better, with 93.5 per cent of the votes and all but thirteen of the parliamentary seats. So that although there are parties in France other than the big four, notably the MRG (*Mouvement des radicaux de gauche*) and the PSU (*Parti socialiste unifié*) the four major parties share the votes of most of the electors and virtually monopolize their parliamentary representation.

The host of minor parties, whether of the extreme Left or the extreme Right, have lost ground electorally in the 1970s and are forced more and more to operate outside the parliamentary sphere. It is also worth noting that while party politics is dominated today by the gang of four, there is a persistent mood of disenchantment with all the parties, and with politicians in general, which has not been affected by the change of majority. An opinion poll in the autumn of 1982 showed that, as in January 1981 before Mitterrand's election and the Socialist landslide, only 29 per cent of the French felt confident in politicians in general, and only 22 per cent felt confident in the political parties in general (*Le Nouvel Observateur*, 30 octobre 1982).

Of course political parties in France originated in Parliament, which dates back to 1814, and ever since the nineteenth century, the mainstream parties of Left and Right have been based on the representation of the French electorate in the Lower House. It has always been the characteristic of revolutionary parties, whether of the extreme Left or the extreme Right, that they have been opposed to the current political system and have had, apart from the Communists, only a toehold inside Parliament.

To understand the French political parties, what they stand for, and how they relate to each other, it is essential to grasp something of the significance of the terms 'Left' and 'Right', something of the history of each party, and of how all the parties have been affected by the political system of the Fifth Republic. In this system, power has become concentrated in the hands of a President elected for seven years by direct universal suffrage, and the old unstable majorities of the Third and Fourth Republics, made up of shifting coalitions of parties, have been replaced by majorities made up of the same two or three parties, which now last throughout a Parliament.

Left and Right

Originally, at the time of the 1789 Revolution, the men of the Left got their name because they sat to the left of the President in French parliamentary assemblies; the men of the Right were those sitting to his right. This initial distinction between Left and Right reflected a difference of opinion about the Revolution, and to this day the difference in political attitudes between left-wingers, who broadly support the principles of the 1789 Revolution, and right-wingers, who reject them, still forms the ultimate basis of the distinction between the two. Even in 1966, a radical spokesman did not hesitate to refer to the party's determination to 'donner force et vigueur aux conquêtes de la Révolution'. 'Left' has thus continued to imply support for the French Revolution, 'Right' to mean rejection of it. Throughout the nineteenth century, the men of the Left continued to believe, with the Revolution, that all men were born free and equal, both as regards rights in society and political rights. No king, no individual or group, they held, could claim by birth any social privilege, any absolute right to govern others; all political power stemmed from the people alone, and any popular government must take the form of a Republic based on universal suffrage. Likewise, the authority of the Catholic Church in state and society was an affront to individual freedom and must be destroyed by the separation of Church and State and the abolition of Catholic education. The Right, on the other hand, remained monarchist, believing in the need for authority in Church, State and society, which could be reasserted by a return, if this were possible, to the system of the *Ancien Régime*, based on absolute monarchy, a social structure dominated by a privileged upper-class minority and a Catholic Church enjoying both religious monopoly and unchallenged control over men's minds.

By the beginning of the twentieth century, the principles of the Left had apparently triumphed: universal suffrage had come to stay in 1848, the monarchy had been permanently replaced by a republic in 1871, non-religious State education had been introduced in the early 1880s, and the Church was separated from the State in 1905.

However, Left and Right continued to represent conflicting viewpoints regarding the issues raised by the 1789 Revolution, which were not yet closed, despite all the progress which had been made towards putting the ideas of the Revolution into effect. Men of the Left stood not only for the defence of the new Republican institutions, they could still look forward to the further extension of Republican ideas in the direction of popular control of government and a more wholly secular society. Men of the Right could still look back nostalgically to a society in which men deferred to authority – whether of politicians, bankers or priests – and could still try to ensure that, despite the coming of the Republic and universal suffrage, French society would remain firmly under the control of a superior minority rather than the mass of the voters. As for the religious issue, it has still not lost its power to divide Frenchmen by the time of the Fifth Republic, and indeed has yet again become a political issue today, as the Mitterrand regime plans the nationalization of church schools in the pursuit of secular principles (*la laïcité*).

Men of the Right still look favourably on authority in politics, in the shape of the strong President introduced under the Fifth Republic, and still support a continuing role for the Catholic Church in French education; while those of the Left look for more individual liberty, more control of government by the voter, and moves away from church schools. In these respects, the old meanings, of Left and Right still hold good.

The twentieth-century party spectrum

The Left and Socialism

In the nineteenth century, Socialism arose out of the conflict between the owners of capital and those who owned nothing but their labour power, a conflict that had been heralded by Marx (and de Tocqueville) at the time of the 1848 Revolution. While this conflict was all too apparent in the bloody clashes between workers and bourgeoisie in the June days of 1848, the idea of a political movement aiming at Socialism, and based purely on the working class, did not become current in France until 1880.

Socialism remained for long simply a special feature of the extreme Left, inseparable from Republicanism: under the Second Empire, the Paris workers remained faithful, for the most part, to the Republican opposition. Even after the coming of the Republic in 1875, the workers continued to give their support to the Radicals, who had become the most advanced of the Republicans.

The Socialists aimed, from the 1880s however, at independent political action by a party of the working class. They aimed first at the capture of political power. This would be followed by the introduction of Socialism, achieved through the handing over to society at large of the ownership of the means of production. Now the economic issue between labour and capital was made central for the first time to a political programme. For the Republicans, economic changes had always remained very secondary to political and anticlerical measures.

French Socialism was, from the outset, internally divided. The revolutionary Marxist Socialists, who formed the *Parti ouvrier français* under Jules Guesde, held initially that the objectives of Socialism – the capture of political power and the introduction of a new economic system – could be attained at one blow by a working-class insurrection. These revolutionary Socialists regarded all struggles other than that of the working class against the bourgeoisie as irrelevant to the attainment of Socialism. The traditional left-wing struggle for democracy and secularization was, therefore, of no concern to the workers. The democratic Republic itself was no more than an instrument for the class domination of the bourgeoisie. While Parliament might be a useful platform for propaganda, there must be no alliances with bourgeois parties and no participation in bourgeois governments. The Socialist Party must concentrate on its tasks of recruitment and propaganda among the workers in preparation for a revolutionary seizure of political power, to be followed by the expropriation of the bourgeoisie. Bourgeois democracy would rapidly wither away, and the workers would be in a position to usher in a classless society. The anticipation of modern Communist ideas here is, of course, striking.

The reformist wing of French Socialism, whose ideas were finally crystallized by Jean Jaurès, believed for their part in the attainment of Socialism by democratic means. Hence the term Democratic Socialists, applied to them and to their successors in the twentieth century. They perceived a gradual movement towards Socialism already taking place within bourgeois society. Unlike their revolutionary counterparts, they accepted the usefulness to the working class of the democratic Republic, parliamentary processes and even partial reforms within bourgeois society, such as the reduction of hours of work in industry.

They were prepared to ally themselves with the Radicals,

and even, with hesitation, to enter bourgeois governments. Alexandre Millerand was the first to do this, in 1899. At the end of the development within bourgeois society towards Socialism, a final, decisive transformation of the property system would take place. The introduction of Socialism could be brought about democratically, since, in view of the continuous growth of the proletariat, there would eventually be a majority in the country in favour of the social revolution.

By the end of the nineteenth century, Socialism had thus joined Radicalism on the Left, displacing it towards the Centre in the process. The more conservative Republicans, for their part, had already moved into the Centre. These drifts to the centre form part of a frequently described process in the history of the French parties: beginning in opposition on the Left, they eventually gain power, carry out their programme, and then settle down in the Centre to defend their achievement, both against the Right, who would like to go back to the *Ancien Régime*, and against new men of the Left, clamouring for further changes. The Republicans went through this process after 1880; the Radicals and the Democratic Socialists have gone the same way in the twentieth century.

At the beginning of the present century, the basic party divisions in France were beginning, as a result of the changes just described, to fall broadly speaking into the pattern which was to be characteristic of the whole period up to 1958.

The twentieth-century Left, properly so called, was to be made up of the two wings, revolutionary and reformist, of the Socialist movement. The Socialist Party enjoyed a period of uneasy unity from 1905 to 1920, then divided irrevocably at the Tours Congress of 1920. The revolutionary wing now set up the French Communist Party, which was soon turned by Moscow into a faithful agency for the interests of international Communism, as Moscow saw them. The old objective of the attainment of Socialism by revolution remained, distant though this might often seem, and the party's organization, centralized and authoritarian, became the strongest of any party in France.

The Reformists, or Democratic Socialists of the SFIO (*Section française de l'internationale ouvrière*), were rebuilt into an effective party by Léon Blum after the 1920 split, attaining power for a time in the Popular Front period, when Blum himself became Prime Minister.

The Centre

The last two decades in the nineteenth century had seen the decline of the old monarchist and Bonapartist Right and Centre, a move into the Centre by the right-wing Republicans, known as *opportunistes*, and the emergence of the Radicals as the newest representatives of the Republican Left. However, as we have seen, Radicalism itself was being displaced towards the Centre by a new force, Socialism.

The twentieth-century Centre included a number of parties. Traditionally considered left-wing because of their strong anticlericalism, the Radicals formed themselves into a party in 1901, came to power in 1902, and were responsible, as members of the left-wing *Bloc des gauches*, for measures against the religious orders, and for the separation of Church and State (1905). It was at this point that, having achieved all their old programme, they settled in the Centre, becoming a party of the *status quo*, ready to defend the Republic against the Right, but wary of any substantial social changes. They became, in the twentieth century, so completely identified with the political system of the Third Republic that they described their party as 'l'expression même de la démocratie française'. Their position in the political Centre was brought out clearly by their views on the issue of Socialism. While remaining, in principle, attached to the idea of private property, they were prepared to envisage measures of social welfare such as old age pensions. But they were more hesitant on such reforms than the Socialists.

The conservative Republicans equally belonged, at first, to the Centre. Descended from the old *opportunistes*, they formed two branches in the twentieth century. Their left wing consisted of the *Alliance démocratique*, founded by Waldeck-Rousseau in 1901, which remained faithful to the alliance with the Radicals and to the ideas of the Centre, namely preservation of the political and religious *status quo* after the separation of 1905, and the maintenance of the rights of private property. Their right wing formed itself into the *Fédération*

républicaine in 1903, which looked for a more authoritarian
Republic, remained attached to economic liberalism, and
aimed at a rather nationalistic foreign policy. With the gradual
abandonment by this group of its anticlericalism, followed by a
reassertion of Christian values, conservative Republicanism
completed its shift to the Right after 1945. The conservative
Republicans had been discredited during the war, but in 1954
they set up the *Centre national des indépendants*, the
ancestors of the Giscardians.

After the First World War, the Christian Democrats emerged
politically as a consequence of the gradual renunciation by a
small number of Catholics of their old hostility towards the
Republic and democracy. The small inter-war Christian
Democratic Party, founded in 1924, was known as the *Parti
démocrate populaire*. Its insistence on the rights of Church
schools led commentators to place it on the Right, on the
traditional religious criterion. On the other hand, its economic
ideas were more progressive than those of the Radicals. By the
time the Second World War and the Occupation had engulfed
France, the Christian Democrats had evolved somewhat nearer
Socialism and the Left. Their ideas were based on the conception of democracy, which they sought to extend from Parliament to industry, and on the ideal of cooperation between
capital and labour. At the Liberation, the Christian Democratic MRP (*Movement républicain populaire*) took its place
among French parties, rivalling the Communists and Socialists
in the first years of the Fourth Republic.

The Right and free enterprise

Right-wing ideas first reappeared in the twentieth century in a
violent form: the nationalism of the extreme Right. This
extreme Right was largely the creation of the Dreyfus Affair.
With the virtual disappearance of the old monarchist Right and
Centre, national defence against the German threat took over
from a restoration as the chief rallying cry of the Right. Since
Dreyfus had been accused of betraying military secrets to
Germany, the extreme Right, at the beginning of the twentieth
century, seized the opportunity to claim that it was the
spineless Republican regime that was ultimately to blame.

Maurras and Barrès looked for a firmer, more authoritarian political system, which could support more vigorous diplomatic and military measures against Germany. 'C'est une vérité générale', Maurras remarked, 'que la politique extérieure est interdite à notre Etat républicain.' Under the threat of a German attack, which became ever more real to many Frenchmen after the Kaiser landed in Tangier in 1905, the nationalist ideas of the extreme Right revived in the years before 1914, and brought with them a revival of the classic themes of counter-revolution: reverence for tradition and authority in state and society and, in the case of Maurras, the idea of monarchism itself. Right-wing organization has always been loose in France, and the anti-Republican Right centred on Maurras's newspaper, the *Action Française*, which became a daily in 1908. Street agitation was carried on by the young bloods of the *Camelots du Roi*. This tradition of anti-Republican agitation was carried into the more or less Fascist Leagues of the 1930s, which organized massive anti-parliamentary demonstrations on 6 February 1934, and were only banned when the left-wing Popular Front came to power in 1936.

More moderate right-wing ideas were seen in the Republican Right, which, as has been noted, grew up in the twentieth century as the most conservative of the Republicans completed their return to the ideas of the past, political authoritarianism and Catholicism, and espoused the defence of the interests of the small farmer and businessman.

Traditionalist ideas of the Right were able to stage a temporary come-back under the regime of Marshal Pétain in 1940. And, while de Gaulle defied Pétain in 1940, in founding the Gaullist Resistance he was reviving the essentially right-wing Bonapartist tradition, aiming at authoritarian government from the Centre, on the basis of a movement embracing the forces of both Left and Right on a national platform. The Gaullist movement dates from de Gaulle's London broadcast of 18 June 1940, in which he called on all Frenchmen to unite round him in resistance to Germany. Because of France's continuing divisions, de Gaulle was able, at least in times of crisis like 1940, 1947 and 1958, to create a broad national movement, which he saw as an expression of the will of the whole French people. Gaullism claimed to transcend existing party divisions, which were seen as harmful to France, and the General, standing above the parties, sought to draw his power directly from the people. There is in Gaullist doctrine an amalgam of ideas of Centre and Right. The notion that the head of state should be elected democratically by the whole people has a Centre flavour, as have the other schemes, for profit-sharing and workers' participation in industry, proposed by left-wing Gaullists; on the other hand, Gaullism's insistence on a strong executive and an independent foreign and military policy for France are authoritarian and nationalist, and are more suggestive of right-wing principles. Despite the appeal to the Left, the main emphasis remains more right-wing than centrist, and the practice of Gaullism has been essentially authoritarian.

The Second World War and after

The party divisions of pre-1939 France, which, as we have seen, largely took shape in the very first years of the twentieth century, appeared to have been considerably transformed at the Liberation in 1944. The conservative Republican and right-wing groups, though not all had collaborated with the Germans, seemed compromised with Vichy. The Radicals had become discredited with the old Third Republic, of which they had always been the main champions. The Second World War and the German Occupation had set off a massive left-wing reaction: Socialism was in the air, and the Communists and Socialists shared a virtual monopoly of French political life with the now substantial MRP until 1947. This three-party period was dominated by the issues of post-war reconstruction, and by the introduction by the Left and the MRP of measures of nationalization, economic planning and social welfare. General de Gaulle saw no place for himself in the reviving party structure and resigned at the beginning of 1946.

It was only with the coming of the cold war and the halting of social reform that the party system began to fall back into a more traditional pattern. From 1947, the threat to France from international Communism seemed to overshadow somewhat the traditional threat from Germany. The Communist Party, being identified with the external menace emanating from Moscow, could no longer be tolerated as a governing party: it went into permanent opposition, breathing fire and flames against 'bourgeois' democracy, which it now denounced as a tool of American imperialism. Its period of identification with the French struggle against Fascism, and even with the Republican idea, was ended. It reverted to its old revolutionary language, which had been put into cold storage during the Popular Front period, and throughout the period since 1941, when Stalin threw world Communism into the struggle against Hitler. The French Communists once again laid emphasis on their long-term theoretical aim, a violent seizure of power by the workers, to usher in Socialism via the dictatorship of the proletariat. In the short term, they distorted the political system in two ways: since the Communist deputies were permanently in opposition, all government majorities had to be formed by parties to *their* Right, thus narrowing the margin of manoeuvre in Parliament for the other parties; and the party sterilized thereby the votes of a large section of the working class, who voted for the Communists as the most 'progressive' party.

The other left-wing group, the Socialist Party or SFIO, began to move towards the Centre, chiefly under the impact of the cold war. It came to accept as permanent the political and economic *status quo* of the Fourth Republic, which it sought to defend against Communism and Gaullism. It began to give up, in practice if not in theory, its belief in the ultimate objective of Socialism, and some saw it, indeed, as a new party of government – a sure sign of movement towards the Centre. The MRP, despite its own movement towards the Right, lost ground and met a serious setback in the election of 1951.

At the same time, the older parties of the Centre and Right reappeared on the scene. The Radicals staged a come-back as the political habits of the Third Republic once more took over and the constitution of the Fourth Republic came to seem more and more like a carbon copy of that of the Third. Even the conservative Republicans emerged once again, to set up, at the parliamentary level at first, the *Centre national des indépendants* (1948). The CNI later became the CNIP (*Centre national des indépendants et paysans*) when a small peasant party merged with it.

The most dramatic development of the period was the meteoric rise of the Gaullism of the RPF (*Rassemblement du peuple français*) from 1947. While the regime of the Fourth Republic came under fire from the Communist Left, de Gaulle launched his own campaign, which came close to the appearance of an attack from the Right. He denounced the Constitution and political system of the Fourth Republic as 'le régime des partis', and in place of these called for a structure in which the executive would be directly responsible to the people, in keeping with the Gaullist ideology. The RPF, he claimed, would also unite France in defence against the Communists. The RPF soon claimed 1 million members, and the Fourth Republic seemed threatened from both flanks. However, the storm was weathered, an electoral system was devised for the 1951 elections to weaken the hold of Communists and Gaullists, and by 1953 de Gaulle had once again retired from the political scene.

The party system after 1947 was thus affected by two new factors: firstly the rightward drift of the Socialists and the Centre groups, Radicals and MRP; and secondly the emergence of a Gaullist movement, claiming to stand above party and represent the whole nation.

The party system in general

With the removal of the RPF from the political scene, the pattern, on the whole, reverted to something like what it was before 1939. The mid-1950s, therefore, provide as good a vantage-point as any from which to survey a number of general features of the system, which remained largely unchanged before 1958.

The first of these is the multiplicity of the parties. This multiplicity, as we have seen, stems from the political and religious divisions created by the French Revolution, which are cut across by the division between bourgeoisie and working class, created by the growth of modern large-scale industry.

It can now also be clearly seen that, despite the multiplicity of the parties and the bewildering variety of party labels, the parties do in fact fall into ideological groups within which the continuity of attitudes over the years is striking.

Apart from their multiplicity, the other feature most note-worthy to the British eye about the French parties is that they have included such powerful anti-parliamentary groups, including the forces of the extreme Left (the Communists and the post-1968 revolutionaries), and the whole of the extreme Right. In Britain in the twentieth century, all the major parties at least have accepted the framework of parliamentary demo-cracy, and anti–democratic parties have remained on the poli-tical fringe. In France the picture has been very different. The threat to democracy from the Fascist Leagues was taken very seriously by the Left in the 1930s, and it was widely believed that the right-wing demonstration of 6 February 1934 might lead to the fall of the Third Republic. And after the Second World War, not only the Poujadists, but de Gaulle himself, led attacks on the parliamentary system.

Equally, from its beginnings in the late nineteenth century until the 1960s, the revolutionary wing of the Socialist Move-ment as represented first by the Guesdists of the *Parti ouvrier français*, then from 1920 by the *Parti communiste français*, for the most part remained opposed to the parliamentary system. Both parties saw parliamentary democracy as a mere tool of the bourgeoisie, and their aim – at least on paper – remained, until 1968, to wrest political power from the bourgeoisie by insurrection and set up a purely working-class government. While the possibility of revolution seemed remote in France from the end of the last century until 1968, the Communist Party never ceased to regard itself as revolutionary, with the result that most of the time it remained in a political ghetto, isolated from the main body of French political life and unwilling to take part in, or even support, the majority of French governments. Only during the periods of its tactical alliance with democracy against the Right – as during the Dreyfus Affair and during the years of Fascist threat (1934 to 1947) – was revolutionary Socialism in France prepared to fit in with the Republican system. And only since 1968 has it shown itself more and more ready to come to terms permanently with parliamentary methods, and renounce revolution. Meanwhile new revolutionaries have emerged, and the inability of both reactionary and revolutionary groups to co-exist amicably within the parliamentary system has continued to produce a degree of extremism in politics that has not been paralleled in Britain.

The third important general feature of the party system in pre-1958 France was the relative weakness of the parties. Apart from the Communists, few were strongly organized like their British counterparts, with annual conferences and a network of branches. On the whole they were weak, with low memberships. Maurice Duverger his book *La Démocratie sans le peuple* (1967), has drawn attention to this point in vivid terms:

> La première originalité de nos partis politiques, c'est leur faiblesse, leur infirmité. On appelle 'partis' chez nous des états-majors sans troupes, des comités sans militants, de petits groupes de notables locaux, des poignées de politiciens professionnels ou semi-professionnels, sans rapport avec les grandes organisations populaires qui portent ce nom dans les nations voisines. Seul notre parti communiste avec 400,000 adhérents fait figure internationale. Nos autres partis sont extraordinairement faibles par rapport à leurs homologues étrangers. La SFIO n'atteint pas 90,000 membres alors que la social-démocratie allemande en réunit 620,000. . . . A droite et au centre, les différences sont encore plus saisissantes. Nos indépendants se réduisent à quelques milliers de notables, alors que le parti conservateur britannique compte plus de deux millions d'adhérents individuels. Le MRP ne réunit pas dix mille adhérents alors que la démocratie chrétienne allemande en groupe 280,000 et la démocratie chrétienne italienne un million et demi.

Many 'parties', it should be added, were impermanent, being no more than electoral alliances, which collapsed immediately after the election campaign that brought them into being. This brings us to the question of the nature of party alliances – yet another general feature of the system. It is a basic fact of political life in France that no party can afford to neglect electoral alliances if it is to get its candidate elected as President or win the maximum number of seats in an election. With an electoral system based on a second ballot, at which the weaker candidates, who have polled the lowest number of votes on the first ballot, withdraw from the contest, the parties are forced to come to agreements with each other for the second ballot, to stand down in each other's favour if their candidate comes off badly at the first. Only in 1968 and 1981 has a single party obtained an overall majority in Parliament. Alliances therefore inevitably spring up at election times between parties whose ideas are closest together, and who are ready to sacrifice some measure of ideological purity in order to join forces. The whole process of the formation and dissolving of party alliances in France can be seen as a result of the pressure of electoral systems on the parties; if that pressure becomes strong, and ideas are compatible, there will be an alliance; if the pressure eases off, or ideas are too far apart, the alliance will not be possible. The *Fédération de la gauche* is a case in point: founded in 1965, it brought together a large part of the non-Communist Left, under the impact of the system for the election of the President of the Republic introduced in 1962 (see below). Because Communists and Socialists could not yet work together, it remained a rival to the Communist Party. And when the invasion of Czechoslovakia in 1968 revived cold war attitudes of hostility to the Soviet Union and Communism, the Radicals deserted the *Fédération*, simply on the grounds that the Socialists were *too close to Communism*. Ideological incompatibility is not an unchanging factor.

De Gaulle against the parties under the Fifth Republic

Theoretically, the coming of the Fifth Republic should have done much to alter the pattern of twentieth-century party politics in France which has just been described. For, in their traditional form, the political parties were part and parcel of the parliamentary system of government that de Gaulle had condemned as 'le régime des partis' and replaced by the system of the Fifth Republic. The essence of the parliamentary system lies in the responsibility of governments to Parliament, and so to the majority parties in that Parliament. De Gaulle's Fifth Republic was based on quite different principles: he maintained that since governments in France before 1958 depended on constantly shifting majorities based on the parties, they were weak and unstable; they must, under the Fifth Republic, be responsible in the first place to the President. This would bring about governmental stability. It was the President who was to appoint the Prime Minister; the latter was then to submit his list of ministers to the President's approval. The support of a parliamentary majority, under the Fifth Republic, came to seem, for governments, more and more of a formality.

Parties under the parliamentary system

How should this have affected the role of the parties? The fact is that it ought to have undermined their whole purpose, for in a parliamentary democracy such as France was before 1958 it is the parties who are the basic claimants to political power, rival organizations vying with each other at elections and in Parliament to get into a favourable position to form or support a government, either alone, or in a combination with others.

At election times, their aim is to obtain support from the electors for their candidates and a more or less specific programme, and any party winning the support of an overall majority in Parliament would expect to use its control of Parliament to set up a government to translate its ideas into action. Such a situation, though normal in Britain with its two large parties, has been rare in France. There the smaller parties can at best hope to combine their parliamentary strength to form a composite majority, obtain only a share in governmental power and see only some of their aims incorporated into the government's action. The parties, in a parliamentary democracy, can thus act as a means whereby the conflicting programmes, with which the electorate are asked to show their agreement at election time, can be channelled into coherent action. Political parties under a parliamentary system, in so far as their election programmes reflect the wishes of varying sections of the electorate, can provide a means by which the conflicting ideas and interests of various groups among the electorate can be channelled into government action.

The Gaullist alternative

De Gaulle always denied the effectiveness of the French parties in carrying out this task. He held that the parties simply could not channel the interests of the French people as a whole into coherent action: the French were too volatile, too easily led into superficial bickering that ignored the people's real wishes. The parties in Parliament represented nothing but themselves, and so parliamentary democracy was incapable of solving France's problems. Under the Fifth Republic, he believed, both parliamentary democracy and the traditional parties had become obsolete; he dubbed the latter 'les partis de jadis'. These parties, he declared in 1962, 'lors même qu'une commune passion professionnelle les réunisse pour un instant, ne représentent pas la nation'. The governments of the past, 'ne représentant jamais autre chose que des fractions . . . ne se confondaient pas avec l'intérêt général', he asserted in 1958.

It was not the parties, or the squabbling professional politicians that led them, who could represent France; it was de Gaulle himself. The Fifth Republic was based on the notion that the ideas and interests of a France which was at bottom really united could only be channelled into action through a direct link, over the heads of the party politicians, between the French people as a whole and the person of their President. He was to become the living embodiment of national unity, as he had been in 1940. Rule through governments beholden to the parties in Parliament was to be replaced by the rule of a President, who, being responsible to the people as a whole, could appoint governments, and in times of need consult the people, by dissolving Parliament or holding a referendum. In such a system, the parties ought to have become superfluous.

Parties and clubs under the Fifth Republics

What, in fact, happened after de Gaulle came to power in 1958? In the first place, a new Gaullist movement was set up, the UNR (*Union pour la nouvelle république*), to fight the 1958 and subsequent parliamentary elections. The UNR, in keeping with de Gaulle's principles, claimed to be something quite different from a party. It was officially described in about 1963 as a 'union', 'un rassemblement de familles spirituelles diverses, animé par une conception commune du destin de notre pays'. Its aim was to organize support for de Gaulle and the new constitutional system on a nationwide basis.

As for the traditional parties, de Gaulle seemed at first to have succeeded in his campaign to discredit them. While the new Gaullist movement moved electorally from weakness to strength, support drained away from Communists, Socialists, Radicals and MRP. The total number of votes gained by all the traditional parties taken together fell from 15.6 million in 1958 to 11.8 million in 1962. The decline of the old parties was widely commented on, and there was talk of 'depolitization' in France, a decline of interest in politics itself.

But political discussion continued, at any rate on the Left: its focus shifted from the parties to the political clubs that multiplied after 1958.

But how far had the pattern really changed by the end of the 1960s? We have noted one important development resulting from the new Constitution: in view of the continued presence of pro-Gaullist majorities in Parliament from 1958, the old pattern of shifting majorities in Parliament had been replaced by that of a regular majority, together with its corollary, a regular opposition. Parties could now be classified according to whether they belonged to the majority or the opposition.

However, the Gaullists, despite their protestations, had developed into a normal party, in so far as they fought elections and exercised political power under de Gaulle's aegis. Indeed they were, from the early 1960s until 1974, the main party of government.

Enthusiasm for Gaullism had begun to ebb, though, by 1965, and the Gaullists' claim to represent the whole nation was wearing thin: economic difficulties marred the picture of continuous economic expansion and prosperity which they projected, so that the parties of the Left experienced a revival. The new institutions in fact helped in this revival when the election of the President by universal suffrage took effect in the presidential election of 1965. The left-wing parties were allowed television time during the election campaign, and the French launched into political discussion on a scale unknown since 1958. The total poll (85 per cent) was unprecedentedly high, and it showed clearly that the 'depolitization' which had been spoken of since 1958 was a myth. The parties of the Left rediscovered something of their old role, if not yet as aspirants to government, at least as useful vehicles of protest. By 1965, de Gaulle's success in taking over in person the role of the parties in representing the citizens and selecting governments, was waning. In the presidential election he was forced to a second ballot by Mitterrand, and only got back in on the second ballot by 55 per cent against 45 per cent for his left-wing opponent.

The new system for electing Presidents was, however, affecting the relations between Left, Right and Centre. The need to form political groupings round the two candidates who could hope to oppose each other on a second ballot was having the effect of grouping the political forces of the non-Communist Left around the SFIO, and the Right and part of the Centre around de Gaulle. The Centre candidate, Lecanuet, was eliminated on the first ballot in the presidential election, and the Centre votes split on the second ballot between de Gaulle and Mitterrand. A new phenomenon was thus emerging to displace the old domination of the Centre in French politics, a polarization between Left and Right, together with a splitting and squeezing out of the Centre.

This polarization process continued to dominate the political scene in the period before the 1967 elections. The Socialists, Radicals and clubs began to organize their joint forces for the elections in the *Fédération de la gauche*, originally formed to support Mitterrand in 1965. The *Républicains indépendants* (RI) of Valéry Giscard d'Estaing found themselves bound by the logic of polarization to maintain their conditional support for the orthodox Gaullists, which was expressed in the famous formula 'Oui-mais'.

The party political pattern was beginning to fall into the present-day form described at the beginning of this chapter, in which the polarization between Left and Right keeps RPR and UDF together, and forces Socialists and Communists into alliance, with the result that the old forces of the Centre have disappeared from the scene. In other words, there has been an *extension of the Right towards the Centre*. This pattern of polarization, between a mainly right-wing majority and a mainly left-wing opposition, was at its most intense in Parliament immediately after the 1967 legislative elections, when, because of the narrowness of the Gaullist majority, both majority and opposition for a time experienced the pressures towards party discipline in what some thought was really at last beginning to move towards a *de facto* two-party system.

At last it seemed that those who had talked so earnestly since 1958 of a simplification, a regrouping of the French parties into fewer units, could hope for real change. Alas, this was a vain hope. For, as we have seen, even when parties do come together in France, it is mainly as a result of electoral pressures: when these pressures die down between elections, the alliances break up, and the parties naturally fall back into their basic ideological groupings, which have the power to persist from decade to decade. When the French have been and continue to be so divided on such fundamental issues as the nature of their political regime and their economic system, party divisions are likely to remain deep, and co-operation between different political movements a tender plant. While parties will come together, if ideologically compatible enough, for short-term electoral advantage, ideological cleavages may revive, elections may fade into the distance, and in any case the attachment of political leaders to the individual identity of their own formation is a powerful obstacle to any permanent fusion. All these factors were at work when the *Fédération de la gauche* after 1968 not only failed to turn itself into a party, but melted away, leaving the Radical Party ready for a take-over bid by Jean-Jacques Servan-Schreiber, and the Socialists in splendid isolation as they founded a 'new' party and started a debate with the Communists, which after many hesitations culminated in the drawing up of a joint government pro-gramme for the elections of 1973. The electoral 'need' for the Socialists to combine with the Radicals disappeared, while affinities grew with the Communists, as the latter gradually shed the last of their reservations over parliamentary methods. The division between the Communists and the non-Commu-nist Left, which had been a deep one ever since the split of 1920 now seemed on the way to being healed, as a result of internal changes in the Communist Party. Progress in the 'de-Stalinization' of the party had been slow, certainly; Thorez, the old guard leader, remained in office until his death in 1964, and the new party statutes introduced in that year hardly marked a great step towards internal democracy in the party. On the other hand, doctrinal moves towards the acceptance of a 'passage pacifique au socialisme' seemed to point to a retreat from revolutionary violence, as did the new readiness to accept that Democratic Socialism might be allowed to coexist with Communism through the whole period of change-over to Socialism. The fears of the Socialists of the SFIO that to collaborate with the Communists could only be a prelude to being completely absorbed by them were somewhat allayed, and an electoral pact was signed between Communists and Socialists at the end of 1966, after the first top-level talks since 1947. At the time of the 1967 elections, the new softening of the Communist line was accompanied by declarations of readiness to accept governmental responsibilities. Declarations such as these were taken quite seriously by the French public, which was preparing, for its part, to welcome the Communists back into the fabric of French political life. A turning-point in the process of reintegration for the Communists came during and after May 1968, when they fought shy of revolution. By 1970-2, the Socialists had shed all their hesitations and a new alliance was born, one with infinitely greater electoral attractions than that represented by the *Fédération*, and one that seemed now within the limits of political compatibility.

On the eve of the Events of May 1968, the political parties seemed, in short, to have changed very little, despite the coming of the Fifth Republic and a new Gaullist movement; many of the factors governing their relations were the traditional ones which have been described. As for the 'modernization' which had been talked of, the Gaullists' ideas were not all that much different from those with which the General had launched the RPF in 1947. The Communists were changing, it is true, but for the non-Communist Left 'modernization' seemed to mean no more than a growing acceptance, with reservations, of the political system of the Fifth Republic, and a coming to terms with the mixed economy, part publicly owned, part capitalist. This was in the hope that social inequalities could be ironed out within the existing system through the rises in the standard of living created by an ever greater expansion which resulted from economic planning. This 'modern' policy seemed, from a Socialist point of view, closer to conservation than innovation; it was an attempt to arrest the growth of public ownership at the point it had reached in 1945.

A new dimension of economic and social conflict

As 1968 approached, however, fundamental social changes were beginning to foreshadow the arrival of a new factor to complicate the party political pattern anew: the re-emergence of anti-parliamentary groups, in the shape of a new extreme Left, threatening to outflank the Communist Party on its left, as it became integrated into the system, much as the Socialists themselves had outflanked the Republicans at the end of the last century, when they settled down as Conservatives to defend the system.

What were these social changes? As some sociologists were beginning to point out, managerial authority, in the large-scale industrial units that multiplied in post-war France, had become a more immediately oppressive feature than mere ownership. The old conflict between worker and factory-owner, which had been at the root of the division between left-wing and right-wing parties for many decades, was being complicated by a newer conflict between worker and manager. This change in the nature of social conflict was hastened by the proliferation of large bureaucratic structures outside the sphere of production: in the professions and education, in business and administration, in the parties and even in trade unionism. The individual at the base more often than not found himself or herself in conflict with remote and impersonal authority.

The revolt of 1968 constituted an attack, spreading from the students to professional people – teachers and others, and even to some of the younger workers, directed against authoritarianism throughout the economic and social structures of society. In politics, it meant a reaction against central State authority, and the bureaucracies that traditional political parties, even of the Left, had increasingly developed. Whereas Socialism and Communism on the old pattern were prepared to accommodate to the central State, indeed to capture and use it to introduce Socialism, the political movements thrown up by May 1968 reverted to older traditions of libertarian Socialism, even anarchism, in rejecting authority and looking for a new economic system based on management of the firm by the workers themselves, or *autogestion*, which implies the removal of central State authority as well. Despite the variety of labels, the *Parti socialiste unifié*, the Trotskyist *Ligue communiste* and other Trotskyist and anarchist groups constituted in the years after 1968 a small but vigorous extreme Left, united at least in opposition to the central State, to party hierarchies and to bureaucracy, and wedded to libertarian forms of Socialism, based on workers' management and spontaneous forms of popular action. As the hope of revolution has faded, the new movements have increasingly thrown in their lot with specific campaigns, such as that on the nuclear issue, on the rights of women and on those of national minorities. They remain a source of ideas for the major parties. Close to them are some of the ecologists, whose appeals on behalf of the environment are often accompanied by a libertarianism which places them also on the extreme Left.

The Socialists, and even to a tiny extent the Communists, have not remained unaffected by the ideas born of 1968, as will be seen below, but though they may have adopted some of the language of *autogestion*, their strong party machines and their acceptance, and now exercise, of central State authority keep them quite distinct from the libertarian extreme Left. Meanwhile, during the late 1970s, the French political system continued to be dominated by the big battalions of the Right and of the moderate Left, so that today the RPR and the UDF, forced into opposition, and the Socialists and Communists as governing parties, occupy the bulk of the political stage. But, as the 1979 European election demonstrated, mainstream French politicians can never afford to ignore the forces of extremism waiting in the wings. As old extremism is absorbed into the system, new extremism emerges with a new challenge.

The parties of the Right since 1968

After 1968, the parties of the Right continued to govern France until 1981. Among them, the Gaullists at first remained the dominant element. They enjoyed, indeed, an absolute majority in the *Assemblée nationale* after their landslide victory in the legislative elections of 1968. Even de Gaulle's departure after his referendum defeat in April 1969 did not at first affect the leading role of the Gaullist party. Another of its leaders, Georges Pompidou, replaced de Gaulle as President, and the party, now called UDR (*Union des démocrates pour la Ve République*), remained essentially an extension of the President and his policies: it had no leader other than him and little function other than mustering electoral support for him.

The question was now frequently asked as to whether the movement could survive without de Gaulle: apparently it could, as long as it controlled the presidency and the main levers of power. But under de Gaulle's successors, the nature of the party was changing: it was losing some of the working-class support the general had always enjoyed, and from a large party of Right *and* Left, which could dominate French politics, it was becoming a smaller, more narrowly conservative party, much more a party of the Right. Faced by a challenge from the united Left (see below) the Gaullists went into the 1973 legislative elections talking of 'movement' and the modernization of France; however, they only obtained 23.86 per cent of the votes on the first ballot: electoral decline was setting in. They now lost their absolute control of Parliament, though they still dominated the parliamentary majority with 183 deputies against the 73 favourable to Valéry Giscard d'Estaing.

In 1974 came a much more serious reverse when Giscard d'Estaing, a non-Gaullist, was elected President, after the Gaullist, Jacques Chaban-Delmas, scored only 15.1 per cent on the first ballot. The loss of the Elysée was followed in 1976 by the loss of the post of Prime Minister, when Jacques Chirac, who was a Gaullist, found himself obliged to resign as Prime Minister because he could no longer work with Giscard. The Gaullists were losing their grip on power as they lost electoral ground. The downhill trend was arrested somewhat when M. Chirac took over and revitalized the party at the end of 1976, renaming it RPR (*Rassemblement pour la république*), but its score in the 1978 legislative elections was only 22.5 per cent on the first ballot. By 1979, it had even lost its place as the leading group of the majority, scoring only 16.1 per cent of the votes. Chirac obtained 18.02 per cent on the first ballot in the

1981 presidential election. Gaullism has thus survived the loss of its historic leader and its loss of political power, but its level of support has now become stabilized at only half what it was in the heyday of the General, and the party is more conservative.

The Giscardians, however, have proved slow to supplant the Gaullists as the leading political force on the Right. In 1973, they were still no match for them, and Giscard d'Estaing, when he captured the presidency in 1974, was still lacking in one essential attribute for political success which both his Gaullist predecessors had had, namely a united party loyal to him which could dominate Parliament and ensure presidential policies were embodied in legislation. He was, as Mitterrand remarked, 'in a minority in his own majority', and reliant at times on the votes of the Left. Giscard had to base his whole political strategy on the vain hope of extending his majority towards the Centre so as to outweigh the Gaullists: the hope was vain because, under the pressures of polarization described above, one Centre group, the CDP (*Centre démocratie et progrès*), led by Jacques Duhamel, had already joined the majority in 1969. Lecanuet and the CDS (*Centre des démocrates sociaux*) joined in 1974. So that when Giscard came to power in 1974 the extension of the right-wing majority towards the Centre was already far advanced, and there was little scope left for strengthening himself in this direction: it only remained for one wing of the Radicals to come in in 1976. Giscard's single possibility was to unite his own supporters and those former political forces of the Centre which had now joined the majority into a new formation to try to counter-balance the Gaullists and form the nucleus of the presidential party he was lacking. He did not begin to achieve this until 1977, when the UDF (*Union pour la démocratie française*) was created in time for the 1978 legislative elections. The UDF brought together the Giscardians of the PR (*Parti républicain*), the followers of Jean Lecanuet in the CDS and the Radicals. The UDF polled only 21.4 per cent on the first ballot in 1978 against the Gaullists' 22.5 per cent though it did overtake the Gaullists in the European election of 1979 (27.4 per cent against 16.1 per cent). It was, and remains, an uneasy alliance of three groups, jealous of their own identities. All attempts to turn it into a single party have so far failed: traditional causes of division, ideological differences and personal rivalries between its leaders, Giscard and Raymond Barre, have prevented any real fusion.

In the years between 1978 and 1981, the forces of the right-wing majority remained divided into two rival groupings, RPR and UDF. They were forced to collaborate within the majority, but old ideological differences, and the increasing personal rivalry between their leaders as the presidential election approached, envenomed the atmosphere. Chirac adopted a violently polemical tone, and went to the very brink of breaking up the parliamentary majority, in an attempt to assert the distinctiveness of the RPR. He stood against Giscard in the 1981 presidential election, and by failing to offer Giscard firm support for the second ballot, materially helped Mitterrand to win. Giscard talked of treachery, and as the Right was forced into opposition in 1981 it was demoralized both by its defeat and by the exacerbation of its divisions. The Giscardians turned on their defeated leader, he withdrew from the scene for several months, and in the June elections the RPR stood the test better than the UDF (20.9 per cent as against 19.16 per cent). With the Left firmly in power, the parties of the Right have now begun the task of healing their divisions and finding new leaders and policies. The modest unity achieved in the 1983 municipal elections has not brought an end to the *guerre des chefs* between Chirac, Giscard and Raymond Barre.

The parties of the Left since 1968

The Socialist Party (SFIO) in the late 1960s seemed to be an ageing and fast-dwindling party: it reached its lowest ebb when its candidate, Gaston Defferre, polled only 5 per cent in the presidential election of 1969. But in the years which followed it went through a process of rejuvenation and radicalization. It was refounded as the *Nouveau Parti socialiste* In 1969 and by its Épinay congress of 1971 it had acquired a new policy, a new leader and a new strategy. In place of the old compromises with capitalism (and colonialism) which, for many, had discredited the SFIO, the *Parti socialiste* (or PS as it is now called) reasserted its commitment to extending public ownership, while at the same time adopting some of the language of 1968, talking of *autogestion* and decentralization; François Mitterrand became party secretary, and he brought with him a new strategy, that of alliance with the Communist party as the only possible road to power for the Socialists. On these new foundations, the party entered negotiations with the Communists, which led to the adoption of the joint government programme, or *programme commun*, referred to above, which forms an astonishing anticipation of the programme Mitterrand has set out to put into effect since May 1981: it included nationalizations, the extension of workers' rights within companies and measures of decentralization. The rump of left-wing Radicals, forming the *Mouvement des radicaux de gauche*, joined the Socialists and Communists in support of the programme, and so from 1972 the right-wing majority was faced by a new, broad, left-wing alliance, *l'Union de la gauche*.

The Mitterrand strategy paid off handsomely for the PS which went from strength to strength, obtaining 19.04 per cent on the first ballot in the 1973 legislative elections, close behind the Communists, who polled 21.4 per cent, then pulling ahead of them as the main victors in the cantonal elections of 1976, and polling 22.8 per cent as against the Communists' 20.6 per cent in the first ballot of the 1978 legislative elections. In 1978, the Socialists overtook the Communists for the first time in a legislative election since the Second World War.

This growing success of its rival represented a severe challenge to the Communist party, which had grown accustomed to its role as the leading party on the French Left, which seemed to confirm the party's vision of itself as the vanguard of the French working class. From as early as 1974, the party saw with growing dismay the Socialists reap all the benefits of left-wing unity. Its militants complained that they were no longer the vanguard. Once the Communists saw they were losing their leading position, they bridled, and began attacking the PS.

The Communists' position was not made easier by the recent ideological development of the party. For to attack the Socialists from a sound base would have meant in theory returning to the old revolutionary stance, to acceptance of violence and the ideas of Lenin, and to unquestioning loyalty to Moscow. Whereas the whole of the party's recent ideological development had been towards acceptance of peaceful democratic norms, alliance with the Socialists, and growing independence from Moscow: in 1976, the party actually jettisoned the last of the old Leninist dogmas, the dictatorship of the proletariat. So the party was hoist with its own petard. It could neither reverse over a decade of ideological development, nor tolerate an alliance in which it now felt condemned to become the junior partner. So it had to part company with the Socialists without a firm revolutionary stance: the alternative would have been to continue along the democratic road until the party became indistinguishable from the Socialists. That way lay eclipse, loss of identity, the risk of fading away into being a mere appendage of the PS. The party must at all costs preserve its identity, even without a firm ideological stance. And so it indulged, in the late 1970s, in a variety of incoherent tactics, some frankly demagogic, such as calling for the departure of immigrant workers. After its brief period of 'Eurocommunism', marked by a sudden concern for human rights and some direct criticism of Moscow, it turned on the PS, accusing it of 'veering to the Right', broke off negotiations for the updating of the common programme in September 1977, and in effect abandoned the alliance for the 1978 legislative elections. The prospect of coming to power in the coat-tails of the Socialists horrified the Communists.

The Left in 1978 was thus as divided as the Right. The common programme of 1972 had created a popular *élan*, and given many left-wing electors a real hope of victory in the legislative elections of 1978. Certainly, the parties of the majority feared a left-wing victory till the Communists broke up the alliance. In the event, the Right retained a parliamentary majority, and the fact that the Socialists scored higher than the Communists ensured that Communist attacks on the Socialists would continue.

As the presidential elections of 1981 approached, the Left remained divided. The PS was internally divided into currents, one of them led by Michel Rocard, who had come into the PS in 1974 from the PSU and represented for some a Socialism closer to 1968, more committed to decentralization and *autogestion*, as well as less certain about the Communist alliance. Rocard became Mitterrand's chief presidential rival within the PS, but after a false start by his rival, Mitterrand became the party's candidate. Predictably, the Communist Georges Marchais stood against him.

Paradoxically, the Communists' continuing attacks helped Mitterrand by reassuring voters of the Centre, and he won a clear victory in May 1981, while Marchais was reduced to a humiliating 15.48 per cent on the first ballot, the Communists' lowest score since 1936. Between the two ballots, the Communists threw in their lot unconditionally with Mitterrand, and so delivered themselves into his hands. They now found themselves precisely in the position they had striven so hard to avoid. In the landslide legislative elections they lost half their parliamentary seats while the PS obtained an absolute majority. And they are now in government only by grace and favour of Mitterrand, who granted them four Ministries as a recompense for their (last-minute) electoral support.

The two parties of the Left have thus now replaced those of the Right as governing parties of the majority. The PS has taken on the mantle of a party of government. After helping the President rush through at breakneck pace the bulk of his Socialist programme, the PS now finds itself in the unenviable position once held by the Gaullists: that of a governing party reduced to being a mere extension of the President and his policies. As Mitterrand is forced increasingly to take unpopular measures to contend with the severe problems of the economy, measures which seem right-wing to grass-roots Socialists, and as he concentrates power increasingly in his own hands, so tension grows between the party's left wing, with its Socialist aspirations, and a President and party leadership drifting to the Right, towards authoritarianism and the management of the *status quo*. The party seems poised to complete its drift to the Centre, which parallels that of the Republicans and Radicals when they eventually came to power in 1880 and 1905 respectively. The question for the future is whether the Left of future decades will emerge from the extreme Left of today or from the more libertarian currents in today's PS.

The Communist Party, for its part, now seems unable to stem its electoral decline, and is clinging firmly to its governmental role as one of its few remaining assets. It will remain in government and loyal to its giant Socialist partner until it sees scope for an alternative independent role. To many observers, its decline seems both historic and irreversible. There is less and less room in France's post-industrial society for a revolutionary party of the industrial working-class, and there seems little likelihood of any renewal of the Left coming from this direction.

Bibliography

General

Siegfried, A., *Tableau des Partis en France*. Paris, Grasset, 1930. Translated as *France: a Study in Nationality*. New Haven, Yale University Press, 1930. Offers the best overall historical introduction to French politics since 1789.

Goguel, F., *La politique des partis sous la Troisième République*. Paris, Le Seuil, 1946. Outstanding treatment of French party politics before 1939.

Chapsal, J., *La vie politique en France depuis 1940*. Paris, PUF, 1966, and the same author's *La vie politique sous la Ve République*, Paris, PUF, 1981, together provide a full historical narrative of French politics from 1940 to the end of 1980, with extensive bibliographies on the parties. The last chapters of *La vie politique sous la Ve République* should be essential background reading for any study of French political parties today.

Wright, v., *The Government and Politics of France*. London, Hutchinson, 1983 (second edition). A penetrating and no-nonsense account of the realities of French politics by a leading British specialist. The best introductory book for the student, now updated.

Bell, D., *Contemporary French Political Parties*. London, Croom Helm, 1982. An up–to–date study in English.

Duhamel, A., *La République giscardienne*, Paris, Grasset et Fasquelle, 1980, and *La République de M. Mitterrand*, Paris, Grasset et Fasquelle, 1982, should be read as the most brilliant and accurate accounts of French politics in the years before and after the election of Mitterrand, with ferocious pen-portraits of party leaders.

For chronological accounts in French of recent party politics see the annual volumes of *L'Année politique* and the annual supplements to the *Encyclopaedia Universalis*, covering calendar years, which appear with remarkable promptness. Such accounts form an ideal lead-in to detailed research in the back numbers of *Le Monde*, or *Le Matin de Paris*, or in the press-cutting collections of the *Institut d'Etudes Politiques*, 27, rue Saint-Guillaume, 75007 Paris, or the Documentation Française, 8, Avenue de l'Opéra, 75001 Paris. The *Annual Register of World Events* includes, each year, an invaluable essay on France, as does *Report on World Affairs* (quarterly), and *Keesing's Archives* provide useful, reliable and up-to-date detail in English.

There is also a constant daily stream of up-to-the minute news and comment on party politics on French long-wave radio stations. Reception of these is often excellent in Britain. The following is a guide to what is available:

RTL: (1271m – 236kHz) Philippe Alexandre's gossipy but incisive political commentary, full of inside information (weekdays 7.45 a.m. – all times given are *French*) and the *Grand Jury RTL–Le Monde*, Sunday 6.15 p.m. (an interview with a politician).

Europe 1: (1648m – 182kHz) *Club de la presse*, interview-debate, usually with a leading politician, Sunday 7 p.m. Political commentaries by Claude Imbert of *Le Point* and Serge July of *Libération*, Saturday 8.30 a.m. *Face à face* – political discussion between Alain Duhamel and Jean-François Kahn, Sunday 9.15 a.m. News at 8 a.m. and 7 p.m. daily; Yvan Levaï's press-review and *Expliquez-vous* 8.20 and 8.30 a.m. Monday to Friday.

France-Inter: (1829m – 164kHz) News at 8 a.m. and 7 p.m. Monday to Friday followed by a political discussion among four journalists, Friday, 7.20 p.m.

A full listing of all regular radio and television programmes is given in the weekly *Télérama*, which should also be used to locate political interviews on television.

Parties

Among the shorter groups of essays on the parties the most satisfactory are in Duverger, M., *Institutions politiques et droit constitutionnel*, 2. *Le système politique français*, Paris, PUF, 1982 (sixteenth edition), which includes very full bibliographies on the parties; and in Goguel, F. and Grosser, A., *La Politique en France*, Paris, Colin, 1981 (new edition), which gives 1981 election statistics. Borella, F., *Les partis politiques dans la France d'aujourd'hui*, Paris, Seuil, 1981 (fourth edition, up-to-date as at 1 January 1981) is essential for its solid analysis of the parties and the party system.

Cahm, E., *Politics and Society in Contemporary France 1789–1971: A Documentary History*. London, Harrap, 1972. Traces the evolution of the parties through documents in French. Introductory essays in English and bibliographies on each party. Some more recent documents in the French edition, *Politique et Société: la France de 1814 à nos jours*. Paris, Flammarion, 1977.

Duverger, M., *Constitutions et documents politiques*. Paris, PUF, 1968. Reproduces the statutes of the political parties and gives full electoral statistics for the twentieth century.

On individual parties and groups see:

Anderson, M., *Conservative Politics in France*. London, Allen & Unwin, 1974.

Avril, P., *UDR et gaullistes*. Paris, PUF, 1971. Useful documents.

Charlot, J., *Le Phénomène gaulliste*. Paris, Seuil, 1970. Translated as *The Gaullist Phenomenon*. London, Allen & Unwin, 1970. Basic on Gaullism as are the documents in the same author's *Le Gaullisme*. Paris, Colin, 1970.

Chiroux, R., *L'Extrême-droite sous la Ve République*. Paris, LGDJ, 1974.

Gombin, R., *Les Origines du gauchisme*. Paris, Seuil, 1971. Translated as *The Origins of Modern Leftism*. London, Penguin Books, 1975.

Guidoni, P., *Histoire du nouveau parti socialiste*. Paris, Téma, 1973.

Hauss, C., *The New Left in France: The United Socialist Party*. Westport, Conn., Greenwood Press, 1978.

Journal of Area Studies, no. 4 (autumn 1982) special issue on France. Obtainable from School of Languages and Area Studies, Portsmouth Polytechnic, Hampshire Terrace, Portsmouth, PO1 2BU.

Kriegel, A., *Les Communistes*. Paris, Seuil, 1968. Translated as *The French Communists: Profile of a People*. University of Chicago Press, 1972.

Lavau, G., *A quoi sert le parti communiste français?* Paris, Fayard, 1981. Outstanding on the Communists.

Lecomte, B. and Sauvage, C., *Les Giscardiens*, Paris, Albin Michel, 1978.

Nicolet, C., *Le Radicalisme*. Paris, PUF, 1967.

Nugent, N. and Lowe, D., *The Left in France*. London, Macmillan, 1982.

Pfister, T., *Les Socialistes*. Paris, Albin Michel, 1977.

Portelli, H., *Le Socialisme français tel qu'il est*. Paris, PUF, 1980.

Rémond, R., *Les Droites en France*. Paris, Aubier Montaigne, 1982. Replaces and updates his classic *La Droite en France de la Première Restauration à la Ve République*, 2 vols, Paris, Aubier-Montaigne, 1968 (third edition), which was translated as *The Right Wing in France*. London and Philadelphia, Oxford University Press and Pennsylvania State University Press, 1968. Fundamental on all aspects of the Right.

Robrieux, P., *Histoire intérieure du parti communiste français*, 3 vols. Paris, Fayard, 1980–2.

Rocard, M., Martin, J.-P., Martinet, G., Sandoz, G. and D'Almeida, P., *Qu'est-ce que la social-démocratie?* Paris, Seuil, 1979.

Servan-Schreiber, J.-J. and Albert, M., *Ciel et terre: manifeste radical*. Paris, Denoël, 1970.

Simonnet, D., *L'écologisme*. Paris, PUF, 1979.

Tiersky, R., *French Communism 1920–1972*. New York, Columbia University Press, 1974.

For reviews of the latest books on French politics and on all aspects of France since 1789, see the quarterly *Newsletter* of the Association for the Study of Modern and Contemporary France. Details from Peter Morris, Department of Politics, University of Nottingham, Nottingham NG7 2RD.

Three

Trade unions

Richard McAllister

Introduction

'La fête du travail symbolisera avec éclat la division syndicale. Le fait d'avoir un gouvernement composé de communistes, de socialistes et de radicaux de gauche n'y a rien changé.' Thus *Le Monde* announced the continued disunity of the trade union movement as the first May Day under the Mitterrand Presidency and the Left government approached.

There was nothing very new about such disunity. The main trade union confederations had also paraded separately on May Day in 1980 and 1981. But equally, there had been occasions in the past (as with the Popular Front government of 1936) when the elusive unity of the working class had appeared closer, at least on May Day. Such relative unity was the exception, not the rule, however. Awkward and difficult relations have been much more typical for French trade unions.

When, in 1982, President Mitterrand asked his Cabinet why, in view of the government's programme, its relations with the trade unions were so bad, he should not, perhaps, have been too surprised at the answer. In France, disunity, effective weakness, verbal and occasionally physical militancy have reinforced each other. They have been evident in all the relations in which the trade unions are involved: with each other; with political parties and governments; with management; with their rank and file. This chapter seeks to examine why this has been so, and how far, if at all, it has changed.

Background

When Giscard was elected President in 1974, one of the first things to be commissioned was a report on reform of enterprises, the Sudreau Report. It traced the origins of the 'crisis of confidence between the social partners' back to the d'Allarde decree and the Loi Le Chapelier of 1791. The latter, in particular, had prohibited members of any trade or profession from combining on the basis of their 'supposed common interests'. Reform of this situation was a long time coming, grudgingly given and limited: the recognition of unions (significantly, *syndicats*) by the law of 1884 did not give them the freedom to operate within individual plants, and most public services (including the railways) were prohibited initially from unionizing. The right to organize union sections in the workplace did not finally arrive until a law of December 1968, in the wake of the 'Events'.

Divisions were apparent almost immediately after the passing of the 1884 law. Indeed, despite changes of name and on occasion of stance, it is remarkable how closely the original lines of division match those of much later times: revolutionary and reformist; 'confessional' and secular. Right from the start, the divisions between the main strands of Socialism in France found their echo in the industrial organizations. The strategy of political action – the need to conquer the machinery of State to better the workers' lot – was represented by the Marxist *Fédération nationale des syndicats*, founded in 1886. A different approach, seeking originally to 'domesticate' the labour movement, the 'self-help' and self-improvement strategy, was represented by the *Bourses du travail*, combining employment-exchange with educational and friendly society functions. These formed a national federation in 1892. *The Confédération générale du travail* (CGT), founded in 1895, was to become the most important national organization. It preached industrial action; but, although it commanded the loyalties of the majority of the militant working class in the period up to the First World War, it has never succeeded in uniting all the main unions. Almost as if following the Leninist precept ('split, split and split again!') it has itself split three times – in 1921, 1939 and again in 1948. Yet another contrasting strain was 'social-Catholic' in origin, pre-dating, in the *Cercles ouvriers* of the 1870s, the actual legalization of unions; but given a powerful push by the Papal Encyclical *Rerum Novarum* of 1891. This urged Catholics to become actively involved in the problems of workers.

At various points during the last century, a greater degree of unity in the trade union movement has seemed possible; but at each point it has been overwhelmed by the forces making for disunity. Lack of unity was no surprise in the swirling tides of the generation that followed the Paris Commune. But it seemed that, when the different strands of French Socialism came together in 1905 to form the *Section française de l'internationale ouvrière* (SFIO), this might lead in turn to greater unity in the trade union movement. It did not do so because the CGT at that time was dominated by revolutionary syndicalists who believed that a revolutionary general strike was essential and despised those who became embroiled in parliamentary charades. The other principal occasion when unity seemed possible was the electoral victory of the coalition of the Left, the Popular Front, in 1936. For three years, indeed, the CGT was reunited: but the 'Muscovite' allegiance of its leading Communists was clear (not for the first or last time) in their support of the Nazi-Soviet pact in 1939, and again a split occurred.

The Second World War brought great repression and suffering to all trade unionists, and this, together with the important part played by a number in the Resistance, helped to recreate a sense of solidarity. Once again, it proved short-lived. The Fourth Republic was only a couple of years old when cold war tensions once again caused a split which has so far proved enduring.

The main divisions in the French trade union movement date from this period. Since then, there have been three large confederations, as well as two other important bodies and a host of minor ones. The biggest (though the extent of its dominance has never again reached its apogee at the Liberation) was, and continues to be, the CGT. Its two main rivals were the *Confédération générale du travail-force ouvrière* (CGT-FO) and the *Confédération française des travailleurs chrétiens* (CFTC). The CGT has been, throughout its recent history, very closely allied indeed to the French Communist Party (PCF). It has always retained token non-Communists in certain positions, but the key offices are nowadays virtually monopolized by PCF Members. It was precisely to counter this obedience to the PCF line – and behind it, it was usually thought, the Moscow line – that the CGT-FO was set up in 1948. It was mildly Socialist, and reformist in outlook and tactics. The CFTC was much older: its roots were in the social-Catholic tradition of the nineteenth century already mentioned; but it was actually set up in 1919. Although both Catholics and Protestants could be members, it was of course predominantly Catholic. As time went by, it generally became more radical; in doing so, it exchanged the earlier suspicion felt towards it by other unions (that it was 'yellow', a creature of the *patronat*) for the suspicion of many Church leaders that it was a tool of Communist and Socialist revolution – even *if* an unwitting one. As this strain grew, it gradually lost its Church links, and these ended finally in 1964. It then split; the great majority marking the shift by a change of name to that which it bears today: *Confédération française démocratique du travail* (CFDT). Only about a tenth opted to retain the 'Christian' formula and the old name, CFTC, thus creating another, minor, breakaway confederation.

In addition to the 'big three', certain other organizations should be mentioned. Next largest is a trade union federation which is specific to a particular sector, and thus not affiliated to a confederation: the *Fédération de l'education nationale* (FEN), which has grown rapidly in line with the expansion of education since 1945. Next in importance is the *Confédération générale des cadres* (CGC), founded in 1944, representing precisely those 'cadres' of its name – managerial, technical and scientific personnel who disliked the political affiliations of the other confederations and wished to defend their status and income differentials. There are other minor groups as well –the *Confédération des syndicats indépendants*, the *Confédération des syndicats autonomes*, and so on.

The fragmentation and division of the French trade union movement goes hand in hand with its weakness, which is still marked. It is both a cause and an effect of that weakness, whose various aspects we shall examine later. Nor is this sort of fragmentation uncommon in western Europe. There are united trade union movements in Britain and West Germany for example; but in Belgium, Holland, Italy, Spain, Switzerland, the situation is more like that in France.

Such division is but one aspect of deep political cleavages. These may be based on any or all of social, ideological, or geographical factors. In such a situation the political Left is almost always split too (though this is less true of Holland), and this holds whether or not there are close organizational links between parties and unions. In France a number of factors in the general environment of the trade unions have tended to heighten or sharpen divisions between them. The most important appear to have been: the revolutionary tradition; the religious factor, and the pattern of economic development of the country over the last century and a half.

The tradition of seeking fundamental change through revolution is well known. In both the late eighteenth and the nineteenth centuries, the lessons to be derived from seeking social change by revolutionary means have been much contested in France. This was no less true of the blood-bath of the 1871 Paris commune than of earlier episodes, and sharpened the divide within the working class between reformists and revolutionaries. Likewise with the religious question: despite the existence of 'progressive' Catholicism, religion was regarded as fundamentally reactionary by much of the Left. In France, religious practice has for long been regionally differentiated; and has been strong in, amongst other places, several of the parts of the north and east which have also become main industrial centres. The religious question dominated political debate in the first years of the present century, and has helped sustain a major division within the trade union movement since.

The pattern of economic development in France has also enhanced and sustained division within the trade union movement. Although rapid economic change occurred patchily in most countries, it was particularly patchy in France, and the places most affected by the new developments – including the development of an industrial working class – were often physically far removed from each other. Local conditions, too, were very diverse: again, not conducive to the growth of a unified and powerful mass movement with a sense of common cause underpinned by similarity of experience and relative ease of communication. The main industrial concentrations were around Paris, and in the north and east; there were patches (for example in mining areas) elsewhere. The result was a ghetto mentality: the industrial working class was aware of being in a minority; and in addition, often worked in relatively small plants and factories harder to organize than large units; and local conditions, including wage-rates most notably, differed strikingly until quite recently.

Recent economic changes have been numerous, but their effects somewhat ambiguous. By the mid-1970s, it was clear that twenty-five years of rapid economic growth were coming to an end. During that period, France had become a much more industrial country, and in some ways, more of a mass society than ever before. By the late 1970s, however, the talk was of de-industrialization. The high growth period was itself marked by one major explosion, in the tradition of 'drame révolutionnaire' – the Events of May–June 1968. This produced quite considerable changes in industrial attitudes – on both sides of industry. The period also saw the growth to a dominant position in the economy of a number of large firms: some already nationalized, such as Renault; some originally not, but nationalized under Mitterrand (such as Rhône-Poulenc); and some remaining in the private sector (Peugeot-Citroën). Questions not merely of ownership, but of how firms should be run, came more to the fore. France from this period has become much more urbanized, and has experienced a very large growth of salaried employees. Despite this, in general the number of trade unionists has declined; French trade unionism remains numerically weak as well as organizationally divided. And despite the many changes under the Fifth Republic, the influence of the more distant past continues to weigh heavily.

The trade unions and ideology

The influences of ideological differences upon the French trade union movement appear to be many and varied, but are in practice hard to evaluate. Two points stand out. The first is that it is not always the *same* beliefs or ideologies which have been prominent. The second is that there has always been an element of ideological competition: a tendency for some groups to indulge in leapfrogging with others in the escalation of demands (a phenomenon not limited to the unions), and for other groups to distance themselves deliberately from this process. An interesting question, but a hard one to answer, is whether ideology has had any 'independent' effect on members or non-members of trade unions in France: whether it can be said to have attracted or repelled them, or to have shaped their perceptions of the world and how they relate to it.

The ideologies that have had prominence have changed; or a particular trade union grouping has sometimes changed its ideological attachment. Revolutionary syndicalism, the belief in a great general strike to bring about massive societal change, though it remains present, is now the belief of rather few (though often influential) people. It was the original credo of the CGT at the end of the nineteenth century; and it was especially influential around 1900–10. It was not a single, self-consistent doctrine but rather a reflection of an attitude and a mood. Thus its most famous expression, the Charter of Amiens adopted by the CGT Congress of 1906, talked about improving the workers' lot in essentially reformist ways, but added that complete emancipation required the expropriation of the capitalist class; this would be brought about by a general strike which would establish the *syndicats* no longer as mere 'resisters' but as the basis of the new social order. Revolutionary utopianism was therefore very much part of the credo too.

These years were perhaps the high watermark of revolutionary syndicalism. But in 1908, a sharp increase in unemployment was followed by severe repression by the authorities of the syndicalist movement. In the very next year, 1909, the CGT leadership was taken over by one of the hardiest perennials ever of the French trade union movement, Léon Jouhaux. He remained its general secretary from 1909 to 1947, when, logically according to one of his views, he transferred his allegiance to the CGT-FO. It was he who converted the CGT to a much more reformist approach.

This approach, however, was directly challenged by the

Russian Revolution of 1917 and events immediately following it. A growing body of opinion looked to the Soviet model of a successful revolution: others favoured continuing along a parliamentary road to Socialism. This divide showed itself first in the political parties, leading to the setting up of the PCF at the Tours Conference in 1920. But its effects did not stop there, for the Leninists of the PCF believed that the trade unions required the lead of a revolutionary political party with a high degree of class consciousness; and that these unions should be subordinate to the party which should infiltrate and control them, since, left to their own devices, they would concentrate only on the narrow sectional interests of their members and could achieve little. This view was totally opposed to that of the social democrats and reformists: the conflict came to a head in the violent 1921 Lille Conference which culminated in the expulsion of the Communists. At this point the Communists were in the minority, and set up their own organization, the CGTU (*Confédération générale du travail unitaire*).

This episode has left a deep legacy of hatred between Communists and non-Communists, within both parties and the unions. Only on certain occasions since were the PCF and CGTU willing or able to associate closely with non-Communists on the Left, notably during the 1930s when the Soviet Union, alarmed at the rise of Fascism and National Socialism, was prepared to back the Popular Front. But the events, first of the 1930s – deep economic depression, and the fight against Fascism – and then of the Second World War, served to increase the appeal of the Communists. Their excellent organization helped them in the Resistance: in turn, their excellent Resistance record gave them a dominant position in the immediately post-war trade union movement. At the CGT 1946 Conference, the Communists could count on about 80 per cent of the vote to go their way.

For a short while all seemed workable: Jean Monnet's proposals for planning looked to trade union involvement; even de Gaulle's Bayeux speech had looked to increased functional representation. It did not last long. The tensions of the cold war period reached very directly into French politics: after the expulsion of the Communist members of government

in 1947, the CGT called a wave of strikes which were widely
described as 'insurrectionary' and certainly seemed aimed at
bringing government and the economy to its knees. Non-
communists within the CGT became more and more alarmed;
an unease increased by the Prague coup of February 1948
which confirmed the worst fears of many about Moscow-
inspired methods. Once again there was a split; but this time,
with the Communists firmly in the majority, it was most of
the non-Communists who left CGT to set up the CGT-FO in
1948. The bitterness of this period marked relations between
the two groupings for a long time thereafter, even though the
seriousness of subsequent conflicts was generally not as great.
The new union, CGT-FO, sought to distinguish itself from the
CGT by concentrating directly on issues of 'relevance' to its
membership, rather than honing them for the wider political
struggle, or, indeed, as CGT did, taking up cudgels on behalf of
the non-unionized in an effort to widen its constituency. In its
turn, CGT-FO was also very much a child of the cold war: it
was widely reported to have not only the (domestic) support of
SFIO, but that of US Unions and the CIA as well.

The third main confederation had, as we have seen, a very
curious history. CFTC drew much of its membership from the
lower middle classes and from women; it was rather despised
by the other confederations, yet its membership was greater
than that of CGT-FO for much of the time. Post-war, its
original ideological position may be described as 'liberal-
Catholic'. As with other French trade unions, however, it
claimed for itself independence of all political parties, and,
with the shift to the Right of the Christian Democratic MRP
and of economic policy, CFTC took its distance. The final
victory of its Reconstruction group led to the split and
formation of CFDT in 1964. From that point on, as we shall
see, events (and Events) took over: the CFDT went through an
'ultra-radical' phase, before swinging rather more recently to
trying to find a middle-way between social democracy and
Marxism. Its successes during the 1970s and early 1980s owe
not a little to the influential General Secretary of the period,
Edmond Maire, to whom we shall return.

The fact that a number of different ideologies and
perspectives arc catered for in the unions might be thought

conducive to overall numerical strength. The opposite is the case. France is virtually at the bottom of the European league in the proportion of the workforce unionized. In Switzerland, that proportion is about 90 per cent; the EEC average is some 43 per cent, with West Germany, Italy and the UK all near or above the 40 per cent level. In France the figure has been falling, steadily if not dramatically, to about 23 per cent. Thus, despite the range of ideology, there is a real problem about the 'representativeness' of trade unions in France which, when added to the hostile instincts of the *patronat*, especially at plant level, has made for prickly and difficult relations between the two sides.

Organization and record

The picture that emerges then, is one of underdevelopment and weakness. French trade unions have had an uphill struggle to be taken seriously by the *patronat*, by government, and by the mass of workers. There have been surges in their numerical strength: after the First World War, after the Popular Front victory of 1936; following the Second World War, and following the Events of 1968: but there have also been relapses.

The unions have usually been regarded by employers as unreliable partners: as unable to make a settlement stick with the shop-floor and even as unable to control strike action. The Sudreau Report commented on the tendency of the grass-roots to 'spontaneous' action. The trade unions as such have generally been seen as being only one of a number of channels for contact, negotiation and management of industrial relations – and, depending upon the situation in the particular factory or plant, by no means always the preferred one. There are also the *délégués du personnel*, finally confirmed in law in 1936. In addition, there are the *comités d'entreprise* (or works councils) set up after the Second World War in all undertakings with a staff of fifty or more. The *délégués* have generally been the more effective 'grievance' channel; the *comités* (chosen by the staff from among candidates usually nominated by the unions), which deal with welfare and social activities, and are supposed also to act as a channel for information and advice between management and workers, have usually been less effective. Unions have also had to vie with each other to obtain the status of 'most representative' union. This status confers important rights (of negotiation and representation), is conferred by the State, and may be – and has been –challenged in the administrative courts.

The organization of trade union activity in France is both territorial and functional. Most main bodies are confederations, with a decentralized and usually rather weak structure. The CGT, for example, has both a geographical structure (*unions locales*, *unions départementales*) and a professional (or occupational) structure (*sections syndicales d'entreprises*, *syndicats*, *fédérations nationales*) together making up the *confédération*.

The total membership of French trade unions is small, almost certainly between 4 and 5 million. All confederations have habitually claimed more adherents than their paid-up membership. The CGT probably has about 1.25 million paid-up members and the numbers fell quite substantially from 1978 to 1981, mainly in response to the perceived 'wrecking tactics' of the Communists over the 'united-left' negotiations and the 1978 legislative elections. The CFDT's membership is estimated at from 900,000 to 1 million; it grew substantially following its radical stance in the Events of 1968. That of CGT-FO is between 700,000 and 900,000; it also has grown, partly as its 'moderate' stance of co-operation with management found some echoes among the more reformist and innovative sections of the *patronat* during the 1970s. FEN probably has about 0.5 million members and CGC between 300,000 and 500,000.

All the organizations suffer from limited financial resources and consequently limited numbers of paid headquarters staff. At 'confederal' level, CGT and CFDT each have headquarters staffs of only between one and two hundred: FO well below a hundred. Constituent organizations, with small budgets of their own, also support very small staffs. There is heavy reliance upon unpaid 'militants' at local level, which in turn decreases the control between the various levels. Nor do the confederations have the kind of substantial strike-funds to support a prolonged strike, and one result is a marked preference for token one-day stoppages, work-to-rule, go-slow and rotating lightning-strikes, affecting one plant after another unpredictably. Action at the plant level is very often unsuccessful, even if spectacular (occupations, locking-in of management and so on). Negotiations frequently have to be referred to much higher and usually national level if they are to succeed.

Such has been the tradition. There is also evidence of change. Characteristically, that change seemed to require the extraordinary catalyst of the Events of May–June 1968 to set it in motion.

The Events and their aftermath

It is generally agreed that the Events took most people, and certainly much of the union leadership, by surprise. The CGT was especially alarmed at the outbreak of 'spontaneity' (demands for a transformation of work-relations and so on) and sought to alter and limit demands and to channel them into the traditional mould – rates of pay and hours, benefits and so on. Although they succeeded in doing this to some extent, in other ways the Events did signal a long period of reflection and reconsideration, on all sides, of the role of trade unions and their relationships both with employers and with the activities of the State.

From the point of view of the union leaderships, the grievances that had appeared at the time of the Events were not novel. They felt left out in the cold by government economic policy; victims of a 'reform' of the social security system in 1967 in which they had not been involved and which appeared to combine higher contributions with unchanged or diminished benefits. Unemployment was rising, and real wages were held down in the name of 'competitiveness' and the wider 'financial rigour' by which France in the late 1960s sought to build a substantial balance of payments surplus which could be turned – literally – into gold; transported to the vaults of the Bank of France, hence forcing the 'Anglo-Saxon profligates' – the United States and Britain – to mend their ways. The protests began at the grass roots; they were not directed by union leaderships. They were directed, most of all, at antiquated social relationships, rigid and outdated attitudes especially of management. Much of what happened, too, was in imitation of the students – the occupation of factories in particular – even though no united front between students and workers was established.

At the time, it was claimed that the general strike peaked with some 9 million involved. Though this was almost certainly an exaggeration, the government was badly shaken and at one time looked as if it might fall. But the longer chaos continued, however, the stronger the reaction to it became, as the massive Gaullist victory in the election a month later proved.

The main forces involved differed sharply in their reactions at the time, and in their attitudes afterwards. The CGT, along with the PCF, declared that a revolutionary situation 'did not exist'. Regardless of the ability of the government to 'defend the Republic' by military means (de Gaulle was absent, endeavouring to reassure himself on this point, at the height of the crisis) it was fairly clear that there could be no 'revolutionary situation' if the CGT and PCF declared that there was not. The CGT settled for accommodation in the Grenelle agreements – mainly involving an across-the-board 10 per cent pay increase and a one-third rise in the minimum wage (SMIC – *Salaire minimum interprofessionnel de croissance*), which also served to reduce differentials. They had no intention of seeking 'transformations' of work–relations which might take the edge off class antagonism and alienation. For all this, Georges Séguy, General Secretary of CGT, was heckled and booed for his acceptance of the Grenelle agreements. Not a few of the rank and file were seeking – realistically or not – much wider changes of outlook and regarded Grenelle as a betrayal.

This was truest in the CFDT, which was quite deeply affected by the Events, confirmed in the more radical course announced by the 1964 split. At its 1970 Congress, it linked the call for collectivization of the means of production and exchange to more novel demands which distinguished it from the other confederations. These were calls for democratic planning (as opposed to merely 'technocratic') and *autogestion* (workers' self-management). It was in the years immediately following the Events that the CFDT seemed most hostile to the existing order. Under Edmond Maire, its General Secretary from 1971, it generally returned to the pursuit of immediate benefits, but without dropping calls for long-term and radical change. Although its membership has grown, it is clear that this membership does not necessarily share the more radical visions of some of its leaders.

The response of FO was distinctly confused, but in general it emerged even more 'moderate', anti-Communist and anti-gauchiste than before. Despite its animosity to the CGT and PCF, FO, under its General Secretary André Bergeron was a crucial backer of the Grenelle agreements, thus helping to ensure that 'reform' – mild at that – would be the outcome.

Promises and sounds of sweeping change were fairly rapidly diminished. The 'wilder' schemes of René Capitant (briefly Couve de Murville's Minister of Justice, charged with preparing a new labour code) died the death, stifled by the combined hostility of CGT and *patronat*. Although participation was severly limited, a number of changes were made. Profit sharing, introduced in very modest degree in 1967 and opposed by the unions, was given some boost; and the role of the *comités d'entreprises* was modestly strengthened. Most significant was the recognition, at long last, of union rights to organize and operate within the plant. There were more diffuse and less concrete changes, of attitude and of mood. For a period (1969–72) the government (under Chaban-Delmas) talked of *politique contractuelle*, the involvement of representatives of labour in a fuller and more organized way at national level in economic decisions – a process of tripartite consultations which, if it fell far short of corporatism, yet seemed to move in that direction. Union membership rose, modestly; the number of *sections d'entreprises* grew much more rapidly, on the back of the 1968 law. There began a process which, with varying success, continued through the 1970s and early 1980s – of the more active involvement of workers in the organization of work-patterns and practices, and active consultation of them, much favoured the by FO. The glacial attitude of the *patronat*, too, showed signs of change, especially when François Ceyrac became its President in 1973. Between them, Ceyrac and Edmond Maire may be taken as talismen of the new mood.

Union relationships

Relations with each other

Enough has been said to show that the main confederations differ amongst themselves not merely over economic strategy and issues, but over political issues also, and over the relationships between the political struggle and pursuit of economic aims. FO takes a basically non-political approach, in the sense of distancing itself from all the parties, and stressing the independence and *separation* of political action from the 'rightful' aims of trade unions. CGT believes both in the political role of trade unions (or at any rate of itself as the largest, generally in support of the PCF though it occasionally takes a tactical and tactful distance), and also in the 'Statist' tradition, placing main emphasis upon the role of the State in intervening, and of State ownership along traditional lines. CFDT, although generally sympathetic to the PS, is by no means so close to it organizationally as CGT is to the Communists, and tends to favour economic changes which rely far less exclusively upon the State. It is hardly surprising, therefore, that even in terms of general policy and orientation, relationships between them are strained.

But there are at least three other sources of difficulty. The first concerns personalities and styles. The second is that, broadly, the three have rather different characteristic 'constituencies', different areas of strength and weakness both in terms of economic sectors and regions. Third, and notwithstanding this second factor, the three are ultimately in competition, not just to poach members from each other (which happens on a small scale) but rather to obtain the allegiance of some substantial part of the great majority of French workers – non-unionized. To do this, they believe they need to maintain a degree of 'product-differentiation', to appear distinctive and different from the others.

Georges Séguy was for a long time General Secretary of CGT, until replaced in June 1982 by Henri Krasucki. He was very much a tough, if on occasion genial, worker who saw the CGT through a number of important shifts of policy in the 1970s. In the days of the common programme of the Left after

1972, the CGT generally showed its 'liberal' face: later, it obediently followed the PCF in making a united Left victory in 1978 virtually impossible. There were those who, after that, hoped the CGT could be opened up, and its tight control by PCF activists and its role as recruiting sergeant for the party loosened. In the event exactly the opposite has happened. Henri Krasucki is regarded by most as very much a Stalinist amongst the party faithful. By contrast, Edmond Maire, CFDT General Secretary since 1971, has proved an influential and reflective individual, his manner quiet and rather shy, combining realism about what is immediately achievable with longer-range idealism, or in some eyes utopianism. Though himself a PS member, he also proved probably the government's most influential critic in 1981 and 1982, asserting too that it was a duty of trade unionists to speak truths which the parties did not dare, concerning the government's policies and the country's economic options. CFDT had proved also ready to enter a 'real dialogue' earlier, with the Giscard-Barre government from about 1978 to 1981.

CGT's great strengths lie in much of heavy industry, in public sector industrial activities, and in such areas as the automotive sector. FO's has been in the lower and middling echelons of the public service, (including white-collar) and also frequently in establishments where the *patronat* made clear its disapproval of the other confederations. CFDT's is spread more evenly throughout activities and industries, but without a heartland of support of the kind that both CGT and FO have. It has attempted to attack CGT strongholds, especially where the CGT's attitudes have alienated immigrant workers.

Competition for the allegiance of the non-unionized seems to fly in the face of what evidence there is about the preferences of most workers themselves. Surveys suggest that a majority believe the existence of several confederations damages workers' interests and weakens the movement. In general, relations between the main confederations have grown worse since the late 1970s, and, unlike the parties of government, few formal arrangements for co-operation bind them together.

Relations with the political parties

The trade union confederations are almost always at pains to assert their independence from all political parties. They are just as regularly accused by the bulk of French workers of having too close affiliations with one or other party. The CGT-FO goes farthest in avoiding partisan party allegiance, not suprisingly since a significant minority of its members are supporters of parties of the Right and Centre. At the other end of the scale comes the CGT, practising the Leninist principle of overlapping membership, with party membership as the determinant of suitability for a union job. All secretaries of CGT *unions départementales* are said to be PCF members, as well as 90 per cent of heads of the CGT's industrial federations. The CFDT rides a little uneasily between these two situations, and has felt it of great importance not to be seem to be the spokesman of the PS majority within the government. Indeed, its identification with the Rocard faction inside the PS has helped guarantee that it will not be, as has Maire's frequently scathing criticisms of government policy. However, it should be noted that, in 1980 for example, the then leaders of all three of the biggest union organizations after CGT were PS members: Maire of CFDT, André Henri of FEN (prior to becoming the delightfully titled Minister for Free Time) and André Bergeron of FO.

What of the link between union membership and political allegiance or preference for the ordinary rank-and-file union member? The trends which appear are hardly startling, and difficult to identify, but we may note two in particular. First is family background: it appears that workers from backgrounds voting for the Left are considerably more likely to join the CGT than are others. Second, the question of level of political commitment: whilst fairly apathetic Right- or Centre-leaning workers may be prepared to join CGT, those more politically interested are much less likely to do so; also political interest among left-wing workers seems still to incline people strongly to joining the CGT.

Relations with government

From the unions' point of view, relations with government

have not depended merely upon what particular governments were trying to do, important though this has been. A good deal has depended on how they have felt themselves to be received and regarded by the various organs of the State and the admin-istration. Traditionally, they have not been held in high esteem most of the time. Initial attempts to involve them in the planning process were at best only a slight success. The CFDT showed itself the most willing to be involved for the longest time, but finally it too felt it should indicate displea-sure at not being able to influence inputs and priorities in time to have much impact. The attempts of the Left coalition to put planning back on centre-stage may receive some cautious support, but the CGT in particular is likely to resist any *engrenage* which appears even to question gains already made or promises given.

In general, the unions are aware that the administration, in framing legislation or in seeking advice or sounding out opinion, distinguishes rather sharply between what it sees as professional associations, who are carefully cultivated and listened to, and mere lobbies or interest groups, who are usually not thought able to contribute much (apart from requests or demands) to the process of policy-formulation or implementation. For most of the Fifth Republic, trade unions have been uncomfortably aware of being labelled as the latter. They have, indeed, an even longer history of regarding the doings of government with suspicion, and the tradition will be hard to overcome. On the one hand, the unions have watched with interest and some pride as a number of their leading figures were taken on board by government: André Henri, of FEN, Michel Rolant of CFDT, put in charge of the Energy Control Agency. But on the other hand, it remains true that most (especially the rank and file) trade unionists are suspicious of the 'intellectuals and technocrats' of the government and links remain rather tenuous. The 1982 wage-and-price freeze was a case in point. Its introduction coincided with the CGT Congress at Lille: while union leaders gave a mixed response to government economic policy, the rank and file's response was distinctly chilly.

Nor has this just been true of 'bread-and-butter' economic issues, or promises of the thirty-five hour week. For a long while (under Pompidou and Giscard), public service and local government workers provided strong opposition to the various decentralization proposals. Teachers were particularly strong in resisting major change. It is probably no accident that, in the proposals initiated in 1982 for 'rolling devolution' (by 'slices'), the last slice in time, scheduled for 1985, is education. The response of the unions to the proposals is likely to prove crucial to their implementation.

In the recent past, under Centre-Right governments, the unions were alternately wooed (in the period of the *politique contractuelle* and ignored (with the introduction of the Barre 'stabilization' and austerity proposals). This still appears the likely pattern, though with the difference that the CGT may well be used to make life more difficult for the government, and as a warning signal of the probable departure of the PCF members of the government. A series of compromises in the first two years of the Mauroy government tended to keep the unions wary of too close a relationship. These included compromises over the Auroux proposals reforming the labour code. On one key issue, that of forms of industrial democracy including workers' councils in the private sector, the government announced that it would give the 'social partners' three years to discuss the alternatives. Clearly it was hoping for a workable initiative from the unions. It did however declare the nationalized industries a 'privileged sector for social initiatives' in the hope of sustaining some momentum of reform. The CGT and CFDT unions have given voice on other fronts to their fears that a Left government was compromising too far in favour of the *patronat*: early examples were the arguments over the incidence of additional social security contributions, and the need to bale out the troubled unemployment fund, UNEDIC (*Union nationale pour l'emploi dans l'industrie et le commerce*). They have seen a more 'vigorous' and aggressive line pursued by the *patronat* since 1978, and believed this confirmed when Yvon Gattaz succeeded François Ceyrac at its head in 1982. Equally, FO and other 'moderate' groupings showed themselves wary of any experiments in 'direct democracy'.

Relations of union leaderships with the rank and file

It is well known that French workers express greater resentment and a general sense of grievance and social injustice than, for example, similarly placed British workers. Why this is so is a more difficult issue. It is sometimes suggested that the unions themselves are the most important agents shaping the attitudes of the working class. But in France, where union membership is so low, it appears that the direct effect of the unions may be limited. It seems, rather, that the unions have played a major part in reinforcing a climate of antagonism and division inside French factories; but that this may be as much the result of their sense of weakness and inability to influence decisions as it is the result of conscious policy on their part. The resentment about their position, and about social inequality in general, seems much more the result of the actual climate of French industrial relations in most factories (at least until very recently) combined with the acknowledged high degree of inequality of income and wealth in France – higher than in almost all other west European countries.

Further, it appears that there is no very strong correlation between the opinions of leaders of any particular union organization, and the opinions of that organization's rank and file. For example, on *autogestion*, a main hallmark of the CFDT leadership in recent years, the rank and file were less in favour of it than rank and file FO or CGT members. Further, it has not seemed to matter a great deal whether individuals were unionized or not: *all* French workers, unionized or not, appeared to have a greater sense of resentment and grievance than comparable groups in several other countries.

The legitimacy accorded to the union organizations by most workers appears low. A SOFRES (*Société française d'enquêtes pour sondage*) survey in October 1979 indicated that whilst in general terms it was thought to be useful to be a union member, there was much more scepticism about unions' efficiency in defending their members' interests. Low membership figures are only one indicator of low legitimacy. The CGT in particular has recently seemed out of step: it suffered substantial loss of membership between 1978 and 1983. In addition, in 1979, CGT members in the steel industry accepted redundancy terms which the confederation, negotiating for them, had rejected. The elections to membership of the bipartite industrial tribunals (the *prud'homme* elections) of

December 1982 appeared to substantiate these findings: reduced turnout was combined with a diminished share of the vote for the CGT, stagnation for CFDT and FO, and some advance for CGC and CFTC.

Relations with management

French management has been characterized as 'at best paternalistic and at worst thoroughly autocratic'. This situation has been to a large degree sustained by both union and management attitudes and circumstances. Many major milestones of union rights and recognition have either been very late in being reached, or have yet to be reached. Yet in certain respects the opposite is true: labour practice is quite evolved, and legislation is strong on the protection of workers – over dismissal and compensation, retraining, maternity and other leave. Alongside this, however, has been a situation where, in many plants, the idea of regular bargaining and consultation is a real novelty.

The unions have often found that they were only consulted in times of crisis – be it the 'global' one of the Events of 1968, or an acute sectoral crisis such as that in steel from 1979.

A main purpose of the proposals which Jean Auroux, as Minister of Labour, introduced in 1982, was to achieve a massive update of the labour code by revising about a third of it. The proposals showed that much that was already supposed to be in operation – notably in the field of *délégués du personnal* and *comités d'entreprise* – had simply not up to that time been applied. Speaking for the large employers of the *Confédération nationale du patronat français* (CNPF), Yves Gattaz appeared ready to enter into a dialogue with the government. In many respects, however, it was in smaller firms that basic workers' rights seemed farthest from realizations; and here it was not the writ of CNPF which was most influential, but that of the increasingly militant SNPMI (*Syndicat national de la petite et moyenne industrie*), whose 'neo-Poujadist' guerilla warfare, under its leader Georges Deuil, seemed intended to sabotage the Auroux reforms. Nor was SNPMI any longer a tiny and insignificant minority: the organization notched up considerable success in the 1982 *prud'homme* elections on a ticket of obstruction of workplace inspections, non-payment of contributions to UNEDIC and much more of that sort.

Conclusion

The present position and prospects

In mid-1982, Finance Minister Jacques Delors declared, 'The Socialist experiment cannot succeed without the support of the trade unions.' It is equally clear that the attitude of the trade unions depends upon their perceptions of the government's economic record.

Both are operating in a distinctly difficult environment. Unemployment in France, about 2.1 million by the end of 1982 and projected to go somewhat higher during 1983, was clearly one of the central issues. Although very bad, it was less bad than in the UK; and, more to the point in terms of a traditional French yardstick of self-esteem, the forecast was marginally less bad than for West Germany. Keeping those figures down was one acknowledged motive in the reduction of the working week and plans for work-sharing. It was clear, however, that these plans had been poorly co-ordinated, and were leading to under-utilization of plant and stagnating productivity. Social security and unemployment budgets were buckling under the strain of demands on them, and re–equilibrating them seemed likely to involve additional contributions from the workers, whether direct or indirect. Similarly, the modernization of industrial relations shows every sign of being a long and difficult haul.

The government had begun by talking about reflation and a 'dash for growth'. Redistribution of wealth through the tax system and the minimum wage, job-creation especially in the public sector, and the 'reconquest of the internal market' were some of the key themes. A year later, the fight against inflation had predictably assumed a higher priority, and the dash for growth had been quietly replaced by targets which were broadly in line with those of other west European countries. Sizeable deficits on the trade account, in the national budget, in the accounts of most nationalized industries and of unemployment and health funds, were causes for concern.

CFDT had been particularly critical, charging the government with having first ignored the inflationary, and later the employment, consequences of its policies.

One great unknown concerned the role which the trade unions wished to play. Clearly, in the eyes at least of the Socialist and MRG members of the government, it should not be a 'resistance' or obstructive one, and they favoured involving and 'incorporating' the unions much more in government policy. The response to this seemed likely to remain divided. The CGT made it clear that, in negotiating with the government, it was not prepared to surrender any *acquis* in order to gain concessions: the CFDT did not make this a precondition. Almost every instinct of the trade unions is against being incorporated, though again this is most obviously so for the CGT, whilst CFDT and FO have shown more willing.

For the trade unions, the picture appears much more one of continuity with past traditions and attitudes than of drastic change. They have become numerically weaker, and are most unlikely to reverse this dramatically. They are most unlikely to unite, or even to act in a much more united way. They are not likely to be sucked far into a 'corporatist' dialogue with the government; nor to settle for a cosy *Mitbestimmung* role on the model of the West German tradition. The main union groupings retain characteristically different approaches. Despite their weakness, they have it in their power to make life very difficult for a Left majority, one of whose boasts has been that it had massive union support. Yet the impression remains that their bark is worse than their bite, and that revolutionary rhetoric is a substitute for revolutionary action.

Bibliography

Adam, P., Bon, F., Capdevielle, J. and Mouriaux, R., *L'Ouvrier français en 1970*. Paris, Colin, 1970. An opinion and attitude survey of over a thousand workers.

Andrieux, A., and Lignon, J., *Le Militant syndicaliste d'aujourd'hui*. Paris, Denoel, 1973. A survey of the motivations and attitudes of trade union militants.

Ardagh, J., *France in the 1980s*. London, Penguin, 1982. See in particular Part 2: The Economy, modernized but menaced.

Johnson, R.W., *The Long March of the French Left*. London, Macmillan, 1981.

Lefranc, G., *Le Mouvement syndical de la libération aux évènements de mai-juin 1968*. Paris, Payot, 1969. An excellent history of the trade union movement in this period.

Nugent, N., and Lowe, D., *The Left in France*. London, Macmillan, 1982.

Reynaud, J. D., *Les Syndicats en France*, 2 vols. Paris, Colin, 1975 (second edition). A comprehensive introduction with documents and bibliography.

Sudreau Report. *Rapport du comité d'étude pour la réforme de l'éntreprise*. (Présidé par Pierre Sudreau.) Paris, La Documentation Francaise, 1975.

West European Politics (Journal), vol. 3, no. 1 (January 1980). Special issue on trade unions and politics in western Europe, ed. J. Hayward. See in particular the section on France by D. Gallie.

Four

Immigrants

Brian Fitzpatrick

Introduction

The most recent official estimate, provided by the Ministry of the Interior in January 1982, indicates that there are about 4.5 million foreigners living in France. Foreigners therefore make up 8 per cent of the total population of the country. While this figure includes some 142,000 political refugees as well as people residing in France for specific and short term purposes and foreign nationals who have chosen to spend their retirement in the country, the vast majority are immigrants who have settled in France in order to earn a living. For purposes of comparison, such immigrants currently constitute roughly 5 per cent of the population of the United Kingdom and 6 per cent of that of West Germany, the two other European countries which have experienced immigration on a large scale since the 1950s. Unlike the United Kingdom and Germany, however, France has long been accustomed to a relatively large foreign population on her soil. Her tradition of harbouring and integrating exiles dates from the *Ancien Régime* – the Irish and Scottish Jacobites, for example – and it was reinforced by the Revolution of 1789 which extended the status of citizenship to foreigners who sympathized with its ideals while presenting France as a haven for the enemies of despotism. This tradition was firmly established by the late nineteenth century when Paris was the *métropole* of exiles from all over Europe. It was broadened, too, by economic development which often relied on immigrant labour – chiefly from Italy, Spain and Belgium, and generally seasonal in

character although industrial centres like Alès (Gard) were
becoming increasingly dependent on a permanently settled
workforce recruited in Piedmont. As a result of the gradual
accumulation of these variously motivated immigrants, the
foreign population of France was proportionally almost as large
in the early 1930s as it is today. Previously, however,
immigrants did not play the role in France's demographic and
economic growth which they do today. Nor did they constitute, as they currently do, a social problem of national
proportions attracting the attention of political parties, trades
unions and, of course, governments.

Since 1945 the number of foreigners living in France has
almost doubled. The increase has not, however, followed a
steady rhythm. It has, rather, fluctuated according to the
economic climate in France and in those countries which have
provided the source of immigration. This irregular pattern
underlines the short–term aspect of the French demand for
more labour and also the overriding motivation of those who
flocked to the country when permits became available – the
search for work of almost any kind. Both these aspects of
immigration have contributed to what is now called *le
problème des immigrés*, although there is a third factor which
must be considered, namely official immigration policy which
was originally remarkably idealistic but has left France with a
particularly thorny problem in recent years. In general terms,
immigration has been noticeably higher during the Fifth
Republic than during the Fourth Republic (1946-58), and a
peak was reached in 1970 when almost half a million immigrants entered France legally. Immigration has also had a
profound effect on the country's overall population growth
since the end of the Second World War. Between 1945 and
1979 France experienced a net population increase of some 12
million. Immigrants contributed 20 per cent of that increase,
and in more recent years their share of the overall increase has
augmented: 21 per cent between 1956 and 1965; 30 per cent
between 1966 and 1976, for example.

While these figures reflect an accelerated rate of immigration from the mid-1960s to the mid-1970s – a trend which
appears to be on the wane in the 1980s – they also draw
attention to a rising immigrant birth rate at a time when the

overall birth rate in the country is declining. Children under
the age of fourteen account for some 25 per cent of the
immigrant population while the same age group forms less
than 22 per cent of the entire population. One million of the 12
million pupils currently attending French schools are the
children of immigrants.

The immigrant population is generally younger than the
French population as a whole: 52 per cent of the immigrants
are aged between twenty-five and sixty-four years against 47
per cent of the entire population of France. This is not really
surprising as emigration for the purpose of seeking work or
better prospects is usually characteristic of younger rather than
older people. All the same, the immigrant population is
showing signs of ageing: in the immediate post-war period
nearly 70 per cent of immigrants were in the twenty-five to
sixty-four age group. Again, this ageing process is not
remarkable but reflects a certain gradual integration on the
part of some immigrants. Many of these have settled permanently in the country where they sought work as young
men thirty years ago or more.

A final general observation concerns the composition by sex
of the foreign population of France. While there is a fairly even
balance between the sexes in the population as a whole, male
foreigners are more numerous – about 64 per cent. This feature
points yet again to the chief motive for emigrating: work.
Single men are generally more mobile than married men
although there are many of the latter among the immigrant
population. However, for a variety of reasons, economic,
cultural and administrative, many of these have chosen or
have been compelled to leave their family behind in their
home country. Striking visual evidence of this feature of the
immigrant community is to be found at any of France's large
airports in the summer holiday season when men far
outnumber women in the queues for charter flights to places
like Ankara, Algiers, Casablanca, Tunis, Abidjan and Dakar.

Sources of immigration

Since the end of the Second World War the racial and national
composition of France's foreign population has undergone pro-

found changes. Before 1940 immigrants were almost exclusively European and Catholic; today almost half of them
come from Moslem, Black African and Asian countries. This
marked departure from the earlier pattern of immigration has
been brought about by changing political and economic
circumstances in the post-war world rather than by any change
of policy on the part of successive French governments.

In the early decades of the twentieth century France had an
obvious appeal to emigrants who were not inspired to leave
Europe altogether in order to start afresh. She could claim to be
one of the most liberal industrial nations in Europe and usually
in need of manpower. Besides, her tradition of sheltering exiles
combined with the widespread use of French in diplomatic
circles and a high level of investment in countries like Russia
and the Balkan states to project a favourable image of France in
many parts of Europe. Before the First World War France, more
than any other European country was *à la mode*. After the war,
she was the only important continental nation to survive the
political and economic turmoil of the 1920s and 1930s as a
liberal democracy with a relatively high level of prosperity.
Understandably, then, many of the victims of major political
upheavals congregated in France: White Russians, Poles,
refugees from Mussolini's Italy, Hitler's Germany and, of
course, Franco's Spain. This politically-inspired immigration
complemented a more traditional, economically-motivated
pattern. For generations, Spaniards and Italians have travelled
to and from southern France while, in the north, the border
between France and Belgium has been a less real frontier than
the linguistic boundary which divides Belgium herself. By
1930, Italians and Poles together made up half of the foreigners
living in France.

In the aftermath of the Second World War population
movements in Europe were far greater than those which had
followed the wars of the late nineteenth century or, indeed, the
First World War. But they took place in a very exceptional
context. Eastern Europe was quickly lost as a source of immigration, and those refugees who fled before the advancing Red
Army in 1944 and 1945, and the relatively small numbers who
left Hungary in 1956 and Czechoslovakia in 1968 have tended
to settle in Austria and West Germany or else to seek entry to

more distant countries like the United States, Canada, Australia and Israel. Such countries exerted a strong pull on people seeking to put behind them the psychological scars inflicted by the war or simply to escape from the shattered economies of victors and vanquished alike, and they continue to act as magnets for refugees from repressive regimes.

Patterns of migration within Europe were also modified by the growth of the European economy in the years following the war. Greater prosperity in many countries removed the pressures to emigrate in search of work, and as western Europe's industrial core has spread outwards the sources of immigrant labour have become more distant from its centre. As we shall see below, these transformations occurred precisely at a time when France was obliged to look to immigration in order to assure her own economic future. Consequently, she has increasingly accepted immigrants from the southern and south-eastern fringes of Europe and from Africa.

Immigrants from European countries now account for no more than 51 per cent of the foreigners living in France (against 60 per cent in 1975). Within the European immigrant population, the numerical preponderance has also shifted. The 'older' national groups have declined, sometimes quite dramatically – Poles down 30 per cent since 1975; Spaniards down 15 per cent. This decline in numbers is due to a variety of factors: naturalization, a logical step for those immigrants who have integrated easily into French society over the decades; the mortality rate which naturally affects long-established groups; voluntary repatriation – usually after retirement but, in the case of a number of Spaniards, stimulated by the death of Franco in 1975. As a result of these factors, Poles and Italians who, in 1930, made up half the foreign community in France now account for barely 13 per cent of all immigrants.

By far the largest national group at present are the Portuguese who make up nearly 21 per cent of the foreign population with nearly 860,000 men, women and children living and working legally in France. Immigration from Portugal was negligible before the early 1960s when Brazil closed her doors to immigrants with few or no qualifications. This measure coincided with a period of economic expansion in France, and the demand for French entry visas rose dramatically in Portugal. Between 1962 and 1965 the number of Portuguese living in France increased fourfold to 50,000. At the same time illegal immigration from Portugal reached massive proportions with bus and lorryloads of aspiring immigrants being smuggled across Spain to the Pyrenees frontier, boat-loads being landed on remote French beaches or in small ports where they were left to their own devices, having paid exorbitant sums for the hazardous journey. Such was the impact of Portuguese immigration that formal agreements were signed by the two countries concerned in an attempt to control the influx and to provide appropriate advice and reception centres in major French cities. 1970 was the peak year for immigration from Portugal when a new agreement between the two governments admitted 89,000 workers and 47,000 dependants. In the period 1975 to 1981, in spite of the recession and in contrast to the declining numbers of other European immigrant groups, the Portuguese community in France increased by some 13 per cent.

After many years in third position as far as their numerical strength was concerned, Italians are now the second largest European contingent in France, albeit by default: their numbers have been maintained at a fairly constant level in contrast to the decline in Spanish immigrants. The 470,000 Italians currently residing in France and who constitute just over 11 per cent of the immigrant population compare with the 463,000 of ten years ago who formed 13 per cent of the foreign population. The pattern of Italian immigration has been largely determined by opportunities in other European countries and also by Italy's own economic development. After four years of quite substantial emigration to France after the Second World War (170,000 between 1946 and 1950), Italians were wooed away by better pay and conditions in Switzerland and West Germany. The creation of the EEC in 1957 tem-porarily reversed this trend, but in the long run Germany has proved to be a more tempting proposition for Italians seeking work abroad. In Germany they are manifestly temporary *Gastarbeiter* with no prospect of settling permanently – it appears that few of them wish to emigrate permanently – and the strength of the Deutschmark enables them to accumulate savings in Italy rapidly. Since the 1960s, then, the number of

Italians entering France has fallen to around 5000 per annum. Still, the tradition of Italian immigration and the size of the Italian community in France continue to produce a distinction in population statistics between *Italiens* and *autres CEE*.

Besides the Poles, whose decline has reduced them from nearly 3 per cent to 1.5 per cent of the foreign population, the Spaniards are the other old community to drop in relative importance. Spanish immigration is not a recent phenomenon. In the 1930s Spaniards were already as strongly established proportionally speaking as they are today – around 11 per cent of the foreign population. That level was swollen by refugees who crossed into France after Franco's victory in the Spanish Civil War, and who numbered more than 200,000. Nevertheless there was a marked upsurge in immigration from Spain in the late 1950s. Between 1957 and 1969 nearly half a million Spanish workers and 195,000 dependants settled legally in France. In the 1970s, however, Spanish immigration has fallen off significantly and the size of the Spanish community in France has dropped by 15 per cent from nearly 498,000 in 1975 to fewer than 425,000. This decline is due to the expansion of the Spanish economy, to the changed political climate in Spain since 1975 and to sharper competition for jobs in France from Portuguese, North African and Turkish immigrants who have been prepared to accept lower rates of pay.

France's newest immigrants have come from the south-eastern edges of Europe – Yugoslavia and Turkey. In 1965 France signed an immigration agreement with these countries which were already supplying West Germany with unskilled labour. After the agreement, Yugoslav immigration doubled to 11,000 entries within a year, and very quickly the annual intake reached 13,000. After 1969, when almost 71,000 workers and their dependants had settled in France, immigration from Yugoslavia levelled off at 10 – 11,000 entries per annum. In 1975 there were still only 71,000 Yugoslavs in France, and since than their numbers have declined to the present figure of 68,000.

Turkish immigration on the contrary has increased. While only 500 Turks entered France in 1965, nearly 17,000 arrived in 1973, by which date the Turkish community had grown to 48,000. Since 1973 the Turkish population in France has quadrupled and currently numbers 104,000 legally registered immigrants, some 2.5 per cent of the total foreign population. Moreover, in 1980 alone when unemployment and restrictions on immigration were severe, the Turkish contingent in France increased by 50 per cent in contrast to the decline in immigration from other countries.

The most striking long-term aspect of immigration to France since 1945 is the increase in the size of the North African community – Algerians, Tunisians and Moroccans. No more than 2 per cent of immigrants in 1946, these now make up 34 per cent of the foreign population of France. Algerians, of whom there are currently more than 800,000 in France, are by far the most numerous. They have constituted a special case in the history of immigration to France, enjoying the same free-dom of movement and residence as Frenchmen between 1947 and 1962, the year of Algeria's independence from France. Consequently they escaped for many years the controls and supervision which normally applied to immigrants. After inde-pendence, the French and Algerian governments co-operated to regulate population movements between the two countries. An agreement made in 1968 confirmed the special status of Algerian immigrants by granting them ten-year residence permits instead of the three-year permits usually delivered. At the same time, the French authorities reserved the right to impose a quota each year and to repatriate Algerians who failed to find work within nine months of their arrival in France. This agreement broke down in 1973 when the Algerian autho-rities, concerned at the rising level of anti-Arab feeling in France, suspended the issue of exit visas for France. A subse-quent agreement, reached in 1980, is more concerned to protect the rights of Algerians already established in France even though the automatic renewal of residence permits is reduced to three years and three months, and to encourage qualified Algerians to return to Algeria, where their expertise is sought.

The volume of Algerian migration has been enormous – 4.5 million entries recorded for workers alone between 1947 and 1973. But the growth of the Algerian community in France has fluctuated considerably, almost on a year-to-year basis. The most extreme examples of this fluctuation are offered by the year 1951 when a massive crop failure in Algeria caused the Algerian population in France to increase by 55,000, and the year 1958, the height of the Algerian war, when the same population decreased by 14,000. The past ten years have seen an increase of some 14 per cent in the number of Algerians in France, and they currently represent 20 per cent of the total foreign population.

The early 1960s witnessed a marked increase in immigration from Morocco and Tunisia as well. Both countries had been firmly within the French sphere of influence since the mid-nineteenth century. Seeking more labour for a rapidly expanding economy, the French government signed agreements with the two countries in 1963 and immigration rose immediately: 12,000 Moroccans arrived in 1963, 39,000 in 1973; and the 4000 Tunisian entries in 1963 increased to 25,000 per annum ten years later. Since 1975, both national groups have continued to grow rapidly – Moroccans by 62 per cent; Tunisians by 30 per cent – to their respective present sizes of 421,000 and 182,000. Nevertheless, together they still account for a much smaller proportion of the immigrant population (14 per cent) than the Algerians.

Black Africans constitute roughly 4 per cent of the foreign population. However, like the Portuguese, Africans were involved in illegal immigration on a large scale in the 1960s and 1970s, and the real figure may be much higher. The principal nationalities present in France are the Senegalese (27–28,000), Malians (18,000), Cameroonians (12,000) and Ivorians (11,000). Immigration from Africa followed three broad phases. The first Africans to settle in France in numbers were former colonial troops who chose to reside in France after their demobilization in 1945 and after the Indo-China war. These were followed in the later 1950s by Africans who had lived, studied and worked in French Africa's Europeanized cities – Abidjan, Dakar, Libreville, Douala and Yaoundé. After the disintegration of the French Union and the creation of a much looser association of former French possessions, the Community, many Africans took advantage of the immigration agreements France signed with the member States. Most of these immigrants came directly from the interior of their countries and had little experience of city life.

It is important to remember that a considerable part of France's black population is not 'foreign' at all but consists of French citizens born in the *Départements d'outre-mer* (Guyane, Guadeloupe, Martinique, La Réunion) and the *Territoires d'outre-mer* (New Caledonia, French Polynesia, Mayotte, Wallis and Futuna). More than 120,000 DOM/TOM citizens are currently living in France, the majority of whom have come from Guyane and La Réunion.

French immigration policy since 1945

It is clear from the introductory comments that the presence of over 4 million foreigners in the country is not accidental nor simply the consequence of France's colonial past. On the contrary, immigration has been an essential part of French economic development since the end of the Second World War, and the authorities have pursued an active immigration policy for much of the period in order to obtain the labour force needed to sustain or expand the economy. Since it was formulated in 1945 immigration policy has, however, changed in practice from the admission of foreign workers and their dependants with the intention of encouraging their integration into French society, to a less idealistic acceptance of foreign labour as a hired commodity which has to be accommodated but which should, as often as possible, remain amenable to repatriation. By 1980 the German concept of the *Gastarbeiter* had almost completely replaced the original French concept. This change in attitude has come about gradually. It can be attributed in part to changing economic conditions which have affected the whole of western Europe, in part to the political ideologies of the various French governments which have overseen the change, and, finally, to the character of the immigration which France has experienced since the end of the Second World War.

In 1945 the *Commissariat au Plan* advised the government that the economic growth proposed by the *Plan Monnet* to reconstruct the devastated country could not be achieved by French manpower alone. The target set, 125 per cent of the 1929 production level to be achieved by 1951, required the employment of 1.5 million immigrant workers. Moreover, sustained economic growth would be made easier if immigrant workers could be induced to settle in France and raise families, thereby boosting population growth and stimulating demand on the home market. Consequently the French government formulated an immigration policy based on four principles: immigration would be massive; it would be carefully organized; the State would have the sole right to recruit the immigrants; immigrants would be integrated into French society. This last point is crucial. It represented the intention to extend to immigrants the principle of assimilation which had pervaded French colonial thought, the dream of turning peoples of different races into children of France, and it distinguished French immigration policy from that of the other main continental labour-importing countries, Switzerland and West Germany, where a rigid distinction has been maintained between nationals and immigrant workers.

It is important to understand the context in which these points were elaborated. The ordinance of November 1945 which still forms the basis of French immigration policy was drawn up in the heady atmosphere of the Liberation. It was written and promulgated by idealists who solemnly reaffirmed the 1789 Declaration of the Rights of Man and of the Citizen in the preamble to the Constitution of the Fourth Republic and who, condemning colonialism, sought to replace the French Empire with a Union in which there would be no juridical distinction between the French and the 'overseas peoples'. Contradictions inherent in many of the measures drawn up at the time quickly combined with trends beyond the control of the French to distort an immigration policy which was intended to be both generous and efficient.

Appropriate government agencies were created to oversee immigration: the *Ministère de la Population et de la Santé publique* (January 1946) and the *Office nationale de l'Immigration* (ONI, March 1946). These bodies were established with the purpose of recruiting immigrant labour from those places which had traditionally furnished France with acceptable immigrants. First and foremost immigrants were to be sought in European countries with which France enjoyed long-standing good relations and whose people had already shown that they could integrate easily into French society. It was assumed that many of the immigrants would come from peoples which spread across France's borders in some manner: Belgian Walloons, French-speaking Swiss, Basques and Catalans. The greatest immigrant contingent was expected from Piedmont and Savoy in northern Italy. On the other hand immigration from North Africa was to be discouraged. At the time, although Algeria was technically part of France, Moslem Algerians were effectively second-class citizens and the planners were, in spite of the idealism of their Constitution, reluctant to encourage an influx of unskilled workers from a non-European background.

In 1947, however, immigration policy was upset by a vote in the French Parliament which utterly changed Algeria's position in relation to France. The Algerian Statute admitted the 'non-assimilated' Moslem population to full civil rights, including the right to move freely to France. Consequently the work of the ONI was largely undone, for hundreds of thousands of Algerians could, and did, seek employment in France without having to submit to the controls of the immigration authorities. Between 1947 and 1949 just over half of the 500,000 immigrants who settled in France came from Algeria against all the intentions of the French authorities. The other 240,000 immigrants were Italians (67 per cent), Germans (14 per cent) and stateless persons (13 per cent). The influx of Algerians cannot, however, be solely blamed for the failure of French immigration policy from the outset. The French government was obliged to admit that many of the Europeans it had hoped to attract to France did not wish to settle there. The United States, Canada, Australia and, in Europe itself, Switzerland opened their doors to immigrants and offered better prospects and pay than France where, paradoxically, the authorities were trying to attract immigrants to a relatively penurious and inflationary economy with a very low standard of housing. Once American aid became effective, West Germany, too, proved to be a more desirable choice for the potential emigrant.

Algerians dominated immigration until the late 1950s. By 1955 111,000 immigrant workers had settled in France through the procedures set up by the ONI. In the same period, net Algerian immigration increased by 155,000. Thus an unforeseen trend began almost as soon as immigration commenced and it continued in such a way that France's foreign labour force was drawn more and more from parts of the Mediterranean world to which the planners had assigned only a marginal role. In the 1960s French governments began to modify immigration arrangements but they were doing little more than trying to patch up a breached dyke by regulating more carefully the admission of immigrants, less with a view to selecting the most desirable immigrants than to limiting the number of illegal immigrants from whatever source. Indeed, little could be done to change the pattern of immigration radically as the demand for imported labour remained strong until the 1970s. The Fifth Plan (1966–70) required an increase in the workforce of at least 500,000. Such an increase could be met only partially (30 per cent) by natural population growth. Almost three-quarters of the extra manpower was to be supplied by an annual immigration of 130,000 workers. The Sixth Plan (1971–5) originally aimed at obtaining an annual intake of 75,000 immigrant workers, but the increased cost of energy and the related economic crisis after 1973 altered the plan's perspectives. This constant and pressing demand for immigrant labour and the strong competition from West Germany and Switzerland for available European labour obliged France to accept immigrants from an ever wider range of countries: Spaniards, Portuguese, Moroccans, Tunisians, Black Africans, Yugoslavs and Turks were recruited as the ONI extended its activities.

Faced with the need to maintain immigration on the one hand and with a high level of illegal immigration on the other (it is thought that nearly half the immigrants who arrived in France in the 1960s did so illegally) the French authorities sought to control immigration by means of agreements made with the governments of the labour-supplying countries. By so doing, France hoped to delegate part of the responsibility for vetting applicants to the relevant governments and to obtain their assistance in the imposition of annual quotas of immigrants. The first of these agreements was made with the Algerian government shortly after Algeria became independent. The agreement became the model for subsequent agreements with Morocco, Tunisia, Mauretania, Mali and Portugal in 1963; with Senegal in 1964; and with Yugoslavia and Turkey in 1965. By its terms, the Franco-Algerian agreement of 1962 enabled the French and Algerian governments to establish a mutually acceptable annual immigration quota, and all intending immigrants to France were processed in the first instance by the *Office national algérien de la main d'oeuvre* (ONAMO) which delivered the necessary certificates of good health and exit visas. In 1968 this agreement was revised and the French acquired more powers including the right to determine the annual quota of immigrants and to repatriate Algerians who failed to find work within nine months. Broadly similar revisions were made to other immigration agreements in order to standardize the controls on those foreigners who sought to enter France for purposes of residence and work. In 1971, all Black Africans were required to have a valid certificate of health and a written offer of employment, and in the same year a quota system was applied to Portuguese immigrants.

Also in the late 1960s the first measures were taken to curb illegal immigration. Until 1968 illegal immigrants were encouraged to regularize their status if they had found steady employment and a permanent abode. It was still more economical to encourage successfully employed workers to seek recognition than to engage in expulsion or imprisonment procedures. According to official estimates a high proportion of illegal immigrants took advantage of this policy: perhaps 82 per cent of the immigrants in France in 1968 were legally registered against 77 per cent in 1966. Nevertheless, as part of its more stringent control of foreign workers, the government decided in 1968 to take action against those immigrants who had entered the country illegally. In this case, too, the practices governing Algerian immigration became the norm. In no circumstances would a temporary, tourist visa, valid for three months, be exchanged for a residence permit which entitled the holder to seek work. Any 'tourist' found to have outstayed the validity of his visa was liable to expulsion. In this way, one of the most popular forms of entering France by the back door was made extremely risky. There is no way of telling accurately, however, the extent to which the trade in forged papers increased, nor of gauging the boost the measure gave to the black market in illegal labour, where the wages paid had no resemblance to the legal wage, nor even to the cost of living. The extent of the black labour market is only now becoming apparent.

The 1970s witnessed a marked acceleration in the authorities' efforts to control immigration and to modify the terms on which immigrants could remain in France. The economic recession of the 1970s affected the French economy as it affected the rest of the industrialized world, and it inspired many French people to question the policy of importing labour and of permitting non-productive foreigners to remain in France while the unemployment level soared. Yet even before the unexpected consequences of the 1973 Arab-Israeli war had been felt, moves were under way to check immigration more thoroughly than before.

The year 1970 marked the peak of immigration since 1945. 174,000 workers entered France, bringing with them 81,000 dependants. But 1970 was only the culmination of three years of massive immigration. Between 1968 and 1970 altogether 1.25 million immigrants entered France. After a decline until 1972, numbers rose again with 347,000 entries in 1973. That year the Messmer Cabinet issued two circulars (the Fontanet and Marcellin circulars) which indicated plainly that the government intended to subordinate immigration to the short-term fluctuations of the labour market. Immigration quotas were to be regulated to protect the 'travailleurs appartenant déjà à notre marché national du travail'. This clearly meant French workers, but might also include immigrants already in France had not the second circular announced the end of *a posteriori* regularization of illegal immigrants irrespective of how long they had been in France or how good their employment record had been. Had they been implemented, the two circulars could have led to the repatriation of some 10 per cent of the foreign workers in France as well as closing the frontiers to further immigration. They were, however, overruled by the *Conseil d'Etat* as abuses of administrative power.

After the election in May 1974 of Valéry Giscard d'Estaing as President of the Republic, a Secretariat of State for Immigrant Workers was created. One of the first measures announced by the new department was the immediate suspension of immigration. The labour-supplying countries accepted this as a temporary measure in a time of crisis to 'stabilize' the immigrant population in France and to improve its material circumstances. In fact Algeria had already decided to restrict visas for France because of a widespread and particularly vehement wave of racism which affected France in 1973. The suspension of immigration was presented as an important aspect of the Chirac government's social programme which was to deal with wages, social security and the length of the working week. In the spring of 1975 plans were announced to improve housing for immigrants and to help integrate immigrants by providing specialized education programmes and by dispersing the ghettos which had grown up in most industrial French cities. These benefits for those already in France were accompanied by measures which made entry into France more difficult (by denying or delaying entry permits to dependants, for example) and by the offer of financial incentives to immigrants willing to leave the country (*l'aide au retour*). At the time, there were some 87,000 unemployed immigrants – 12 per cent of the total number of unemployed. Once again the government's intentions, particularly the proposal to exclude workers' dependants, were challenged by the churches and the trades unions, and in July 1975 immigration was resumed, including that of dependants.

In 1977, Raymond Barre's government, faced with unemployment reaching 1.25 million, renewed the efforts to halt immigration and to encourage repatriation in an economy in which new jobs were not being created. Any immigrant who had been in France for five years or who was unemployed was offered 10,000 francs to return 'home' and not to seek readmission to France. Some 2000 immigrants were said to have accepted the *prime au retour* between its introduction in April and the month of September. Once again plans were announced to suspend the immigration of workers' dependants for three years – it was hoped that the delay would discourage potential immigrants from seeking entry. Once again, the legality of these measures was challenged in the *Conseil d'Etat* on the grounds that they infringed human rights, and the government was again forced to relent.

The repressive legislation concerning immigrants reached its peak in 1980 with bills and circulars introduced by the

Minister of the Interior, Bonnet, and Secretary of State for Labour, Stoléru. The Bonnet proposals were designed to allow the government to expel without appeal the estimated 30,000 illegal immigrants and any other foreigners accused of being a threat to public order. In effect this meant that legal and long established immigrants could be singled out for repatriation if, for example, they were identified at demonstrations for immigrants' rights. It was also intended that no foreigner be permitted to enter France even on a tourist visa without proof that he or she had sufficient means of support for the duration of the proposed sojourn or a return ticket. Such a measure clearly prohibited the typical immigrant who sought entry to France precisely because he had no means and wished to earn money as a result of his emigration. Stoléru's proposals modified the terms of residence for those already in France. Immigrants were to have a residence and work permit valid for three years. It was not to be renewed automatically even if the immigrant was in employment. Instead, every application for renewal would be scrutinized at the local *préfecture* in the light of unemployment in the area. In effect, no immigrant would be able to look more than three years ahead (unless he was a wealthy exile whose presence in France was considered desirable).

If implemented, the combined measures of Bonnet and Stoléru would have had a dramatic effect on immigration and on the fate of thousands of immigrants living in France, threatening them with the breakup of families and the summary expulsion of young people whose knowledge of their country of origin was often as patchy as that of a French adolescent. The aim of the proposals was to make the position of the immigrant temporary and insecure – they represented the clearest reversal of the principles on which immigration policy was founded in 1945. The measures must be seen in the context of the high unemployment which had arisen in France (nearly two million) and the temptation of an easy solution: 'deux millions de chômeurs, c'est deux millions d'immigrés en trop' – a solution which was not without a certain appeal to the French Communist Party when it was seeking to strengthen its electoral support. In the event, the Bonnet/Stoléru proposals were modified by Parliament and by the *Conseil d'Etat* in favour of the immigrants. Nevertheless, the year from the autumn *rentrée* of 1980 to the elections in the spring and summer of 1981 was a most depressing and uncertain time for France's immigrant population.

During the campaign before the presidential election of 1981 the immigrants, having no vote, were silent onlookers as candidates spoke of immigration as an economic problem, paying only scant attention to its human aspects. Most of the leading candidates, including Giscard d'Estaing, Chirac and Marchais, stated openly that immigration would be halted if they were elected, and some said they would encourage voluntary repatriation – statements, however veiled, which did little to diminish the feeling of vulnerability already widespread among the immigrants. It is not surprising that immigrants figured in numbers among those who rejoiced at the election of François Mitterrand on 10 May: the programme of the Socialist Party, based on the slogans 'Peace, Liberty and Democracy' appeared to offer them more than the other programmes put to the electorate.

The Mitterrand government has reversed a number of the more obviously repressive measures voted by its predecessors and has offered more security to many immigrants. The twin pillars of its policy are selective and limited immigration on the one hand, but on the other, the amelioration of conditions for immigrants already in France. In this sense, the policy represents an attempt at a compromise between the original integrationist ideal and the acceptance of recent economic pressures. Already the measures taken and proposed have come in for criticism from immigrants and their spokesmen as being less liberal than the interested parties had hoped.

The most dramatic changes introduced since the summer of 1981 concern the conditions for the expulsion of immigrants and the amnesty granted to illegal immigrants. The earlier Bonnet legislation made expulsion easy, virtually a police affair only. Now it is much more difficult to expel a foreigner. The immigrant has to be accused of constituting a grave threat to public order. That is to say he or she must to all intents and purposes be involved in criminal activities, and the case for expulsion must be heard in public before a tribunal which includes judges and representatives of the social services as well as those of the Ministry of the Interior. Legal aid is available to the accused so that his case can be made as eloquently as possible. Moreover, certain categories cannot be expelled in any circumstances. These include immigrants of less than eighteen years of age and immigrants who can prove that they have been resident in France for fifteen years or since the age of ten, whichever is appropriate.

Concerning the amnesty granted to illegal immigrants, whose numbers were guessed to be around 300,000 in 1981, any immigrant who could prove that he or she was in France before 1 January 1981 and was in employment (unless the dependant of a breadwinner) could register with the local authorities and receive automatically a temporary residence and work permit (*Autorisation provisoire de séjour*) and the opportunity to regularize his or her legal position without the threat of prosecution. The offer was not as generous as it perhaps seemed at first. The APS was valid for three months only, and the submission of the formal application (*dossier*) for a regular permit did not guarantee that this would be forthcoming. Each *dossier* was to be scrutinized rigorously in order to assess the applicant's long-term employment prospects. For each *dossier* received, a receipt was given to the applicant which guaranteed his or her right to live and work in France until a decision was reached on the *dossier*. By 31 December 1981, when the amnesty ended, no more than 140,000 APS had been issued, and by 15 April 1982, when the task of scrutinizing the *dossiers* was completed, only 75,450 of these had been submitted by immigrants, and only 57,100 regular work permits had been issued. Thus, the problem of illegal immigrants is far from resolved, and those who remain in France illegally continue to be liable to deportation.

Immigrants and the French economy

The importance of immigration in the growth of the economy can be seen clearly in the regular inclusion of a desirable quota of foreign workers in government planning forecasts. Immigration has been officially described as 'une donnée structurelle irremplaçable'. What, then, has been the contribution made by immigrant labour?

Immigrants occupy the lowest rungs of the social ladder. Over 80 per cent of them are employed in a manual capacity, and two-thirds of these are unskilled or semi-skilled; 40 per cent work in building and public works, and a further 20 per cent in the steel and automobile industries. To these figures one must add some 10 per cent in the service industries – catering, sanitation, cleaning, parks and gardens. The contribution of the newer immigrant groups to this manual category is striking: 95 per cent of the Turks, 90 per cent of the Moroccans, 88 per cent of the Algerians, 85 per cent of the Portuguese.

As one moves up the social ladder, the reduction in the number of immigrants is significant: only 5 per cent in low-grade clerical positions and jobs in the wholesale and retail trade; the minority of foreigners who have jobs in middle management or the professions (less than 3 per cent) come from the EEC countries or from Switzerland, and fewer than 1 per cent of the immigrants discussed in this chapter are employed in these categories.

For those who do succeed in rising above the category of manual workers, the majority become self-employed. Thus, some 6 per cent own their own businesses – generally small shops and cafés which cater for the immigrant population itself. There are notable exceptions as anyone knows who has visited the *quartier Saint-Michel* and the *rue Mouffetard* in Paris where the oriental restaurants and shops are aimed essentially at tourists.) In Paris, over 12 per cent of the cafés and 20 per cent of the *épiceries* are now owned by immigrants from North Africa. In most cases, immigrants acquire shops and cafés which the French *commerçants* reject because the turnover is relatively low. The immigrants tend to stay open much longer and to forgo holidays in order to maximize profits and pay off costly loans obtained in many cases from fellow countrymen in France or from sources in their country of origin. Commerce has always provided a living for many members of France's relatively small south-east Asian community, of whom there are currently only 23,000.

The concentration of immigrants in the least prestigious and lowest-paid jobs illustrates the main function of immigration: the provision of a source of cheap and plentiful labour which is not intended to be in competition with French labour. The predominance of immigrant labour in certain sectors of the economy has undoubtedly enabled the authorities and employers to keep wages down in those sectors: municipal cleaning, the factory production line, for example. The repetitive or menial nature of the tasks performed would only attract French labour at significantly higher rates. Moreover, by channelling the almost exclusively unskilled immigrant labour into manual employment which requires little or no training, successive French governments have succeeded in making immigrants economically productive at virtually no cost to public finances. Indeed, immigrants remain the only socio-economic group which contributes far more to the treasury than it takes from it. Most of them are young and healthy; many are single; others leave their families in their home country and so constitute only a minimal drain on welfare facilities. At the same time they pay taxes and social security contributions, including a contribution to a retirement pension which is forfeited if they leave France – as many have done – before the age of retirement. Even the limited range of accommodation made available by the State has been financed largely out of immigrants' taxes. In every respect, the common accusation that the immigrants in employment 'mangent le pain des Français' is manifestly untrue.

Apart from the financial benefits France has gained from the use of foreign labour – and the Sixth Plan (1971–5) costed their contribution to the economy as being equivalent to a free gift of 90,000 million francs – it is generally accepted that immigrant labour has been an essential factor in keeping many firms economically viable because the cost of replacing immigrants by mechanized processes or by more expensive French labour would have been crippling. Among such firms, car manufacturers would have been seriously affected: in the Paris region, where Citroën, Renault and Talbot have large factories, 80 per cent of the unskilled labour on the production line is foreign. This factor was recognized during the ban on immigration imposed from the summer of 1974 to that of 1975 when the *commission de dérogation* appointed to examine special cases affected by the ban ensured that two of the largest car manufacturers remained supplied with immigrants. French cars would not have remained competitively priced and production would have slowed down if the exceptions had not been made. Similarly, many of the major building and public works schemes would not have gone ahead if there had been a shortage of manpower. It is estimated that one third of all housing currently built (two-thirds in Paris) is built by immigrants.

Immigrant labour has also been advantageous to the government and to employers as far as industrial relations are concerned. In 1963, Prime Minister Pompidou told Parliament that, 'l'immigration est un moyen de créer une certaine détente sur le marché de l'emploi et de résister à la pression sociale'. In the view of this conservative politician, immigrant labour had clear advantages. It enabled governments to maintain a differential between the unskilled and poorly paid immigrants on the one hand and the apparently cushioned French workers on the other. At the same time, the use of immigrant labour in the least acceptable jobs reduced the risk of confrontation between employers and the workers – very few immigrants were unionized, and even fewer understood the issues. According to the *Agence nationale pour l'emploi* (ANPE), one of France's leading car manufacturers ruthlessly exploited the ignorance and docility of immigrant labour in the 1960s and early 1970s. Refusing whenever possible the workers referred by ANPE, recruitment teams went to countries like Turkey and provided immigrants with all the necessary papers to secure their admission to France. A batch of immigrants would be employed on the production line and kept in ignorance of their rights for as long as possible. Every six months or so, an 'internal rationalization of personnel' would take place, and those immigrants who had shown some tendency to make demands would usually be laid off or split off from workers whom they might influence. Such practices are quite illegal but, according to ANPE, it is not difficult for determined employers to fabricate employment requirements which permit them to turn down ANPE approved labour.

Apart from these systematic and sophisticated attempts to exploit an ill-informed and docile workforce, there is a much cruder method of cutting labour costs and reducing industrial disputes. This involves the use of illegal immigrants and it is still widespread among smaller firms. Illegal immigrants have no rights at all. Consequently, those who choose to employ them have been able to set their own wages and terms. Apart from the savings on the wages paid, the employers make no contribution to the social insurance of the employee, and they are perfectly free to fire the illegal immigrant without fear of reprisals. The Mitterrand government has introduced legislation which penalizes such employers with heavy fines, imprisonment and the confiscation of their plant in an attempt to eliminate the use of illegal labour, but the estimated proportion of illegal immigrants who continue to work on the black labour market – 35 to 40 per cent not counting those who have crossed the frontiers illegally in 1982 – indicates that the measures have by no means resolved the problem.

With the birth rate falling again in France yet with ever clearer moves towards a greater use of technology in all sectors of the economy, the long-term value of immigrant labour is perhaps less evident than it was twenty years ago. Certainly, for many years to come, building and cleaning will employ immigrants, but the needs of these and other sectors of the economy can be met by those already present in the country. In the industrial sector, it is more than likely that those firms which continue to rely on immigrant labour, legally or illegally brought into the country, will be forced out of business by competitors who have made their factories more efficient and productive by adopting modern processes and equipment. France's commitment to nuclear energy will certainly revolutionize industry further, and it seems unlikely that the economy will ever revert to the type which required large-scale immigration. It may well be that the era of imported, unskilled labour is over.

Immigrants in French society

Le problème des immigrés has been acute for a decade. Although many Frenchmen expressed reservations about immigration when it commenced in the 1940s (54 per cent of an IFOP (*Institut français d'opinion publique*) poll opposed it in 1945, 63 per cent in 1948), immigrants received little attention in the years of economic expansion. Algerians were the exception, but the passions they aroused related essentially to the Algerian war. The circumstances changed quite dramatically in the early 1970s. By then, immigrants had established a foothold in France, and their numbers had reached saturation point just before the apparently boundless expansion of the economy turned suddenly into a recession. Since the early 1970s immigrants' rights, living conditions and life style have been the increasingly vexed and emotive subjects of debate. Clearly the recession and the high level of unemployment it has inflicted on France has aggravated the question and has led many people to seek the simplest solution, that of removing a foreign population which is perceived increasingly, however unjustly, as a burden on the State. But the present agitation is related also to the conditions in which immigrants live and work, to the vast gulf which separates them from the majority of French people. They are omnipresent but unknown except when they appear in the newspapers as statistics or as the accused in the criminal courts. The present isolation of the immigrant community owes as much to the accumulation of past practices and trends as it does to the response of governments and public opinion to the effects of the recession.

It has been noted that the immigration policy formulated in 1945 explicitly offered the possibility of integration to immigrants. At the same time, the majority of those who entered France were not of the kind expected by the authorities: they were neither European nor Christian, but North African and Moslem. To overcome the fundamental cultural differences created by these circumstances, an active integration policy would have been necessary. Such a policy did not exist, largely because the ONI had insufficient funds at its disposal, but also because it had no jurisdiction over the Algerians who formed the bulk of the immigrants. Consequently, the majority of immigrants entering France were left to their own devices. Even in the best material conditions, it is unlikely that a *laisser-faire* policy of settlement would have worked because of the cultural and linguistic obstacles involved. Material conditions in French cities were far from good, however, because of the acute housing shortage which has dogged France since the end of the Second World War. The consequence has been the rapid growth of immigrant ghettos in the most insalubrious parts of French cities where the immigrants have been the victims of crooked landlords and have been encouraged by their isolation to cling to their own customs and practices, often translated directly from the villages of the Maghreb and Africa, instead of coming to terms with the French way of life.

Housing has remained a major problem. More than 75 per cent of immigrants live in cramped and sub-standard conditions while barely 15 per cent are deemed to enjoy housing of a standard acceptable to the French themselves. The *bidonvilles*, collections of corrugated iron and timber huts which mushroomed on waste land around most French cities in the 1960s and which housed large numbers of illegal immigrants, have now all but disappeared, bulldozed by the authorities in the mid- and late-1970s in an attempt to do something about the dire housing conditions of the immigrants. In 1968 some 75,000 immigrants were thought to have been *bidonville* dwellers.

Now the majority of immigrants live in rented accommodation in and around the cities. More often than not, their rooms and flats are to be found in shabby and dilapidated tenement buildings where the rents charged – often by immigrant landlords –are out of all proportion with the amenities offered: bare rooms, a cold tap and a lavatory on the landing. Paris, with the largest immigrant population, typified these conditions in the mid-1970s. According to the prefect of Paris, there were 400,000 immigrants in the city in 1975. Of these, 3500 lived in unhealthy slums, 5000 in run-down hotels and a further 1000 in sub-standard hostels. 'Au total,' concluded the prefect, 'il faudrait reloger 7,000 à 8,000 immigrés, et il ne s'agit là encore que des travailleurs célibataires'. Since then, efforts have been made to improve the immigrants' housing conditions, but they have not often proved adequate. Purpose-built hostels were put under the management of a publicly funded body, SONACOTRA (*Société nationale de construction pour travailleurs*), whose aim was to make the hotels pay their way. All too often the immigrants living in the hostels have complained of high rents, poor facilities, little repair work and an authoritarian form of management. In a number of hostels rent strikes were begun and the police were called in to evict the strikers. More immigrant familes have been relodged in public housing, the *Habitations à loyers modérés* (HLM), but here again the operation has been less than successful. New ghettos have been created in the high-rise flats of the working-class suburbs as a result of the conflict between the immigrants' life styles – 'ils font du bruit la nuit', 'leurs odeurs de cuisine sont insupportables', 'ils vivent à dix dans des appartements faits pour quatre' – and those of their reluctant French neighbours has become worse. Gradually the latter move out so that tower blocks, even whole *cités* are inhabited by immigrants. The consequent problems are serious. Most of the HLM complexes are on sites completely devoid of the most basic leisure amenities – lawns, gardens or playgrounds. The young have nothing to distract them except the buildings themselves. Vandalism and petty crime have become more common in these barren settings which frequently have the added disadvantage of being far from the immigrants' place of work. Fatigue at the end of a long day often encourages parents to leave their children to their own devices. The rising level of youth unemployment, particularly high among the children of immigrants, is adding to the feelings of hopelessness and frustration experienced in these new ghettos. The bitterness and frustration which has built up in the *banlieues* where the immigrant population has increased considerably reached a climax in December 1980 and January 1981 when the Communist mayor of Vitry, south-east of Paris, led an attack on a hostel which was to house African immigrants. With the aid of a bulldozer, the hostel was put out of commission on Christmas Eve on the grounds that the local population simply would not tolerate the imposition of this extra burden on the municipality. In the following month, the PCF was involved in another anti-immigrant movement at Montigny-lès-Cormeilles (Val-de-Marne), this time concerning the drug problem. The two incidents demonstrated plainly how close to the surface racism had come, and the extent to which a major social problem could be exploited for political purposes.

Material conditions are not the only aspect of *le problème des immigrés*. Vocational training, schooling and adult literacy facilities have never been adequate, and their lack condemns most immigrants to a future as unskilled, poorly paid labourers; their children to unemployment. At present, in only nine schools in Paris are subjects taught in Arabic as well as French in an attempt to ensure that schooling is more than just a formal process in which most of the material taught passes over the heads of the pupils from immigrant backgrounds.

Indeed, it is the 'second generation' which is potentially the bleakest aspect of the entire saga of immigration to France. There are now about 1.5 million children whose parents are immigrants, and of these nearly 30 per cent are of Algerian extraction. Immigrants' children, particularly north Africans, leave school sooner than French children, they have fewer qualifications, a higher unemployment rate and a higher delinquency rate than their French peers. Even though many were born in France after 1963 and are able to claim French citizenship, for the general public they are still *bougnoules*, *zincos*, or, in less openly crude circles *des gens typés*, and they carry with them a handicap and, increasingly, a chip on their shoulder. To begin to rectify the situation would require massive sums of money and a form of positive discrimination which, in the current economic climate, would certainly be unacceptable to the French taxpayer and would mean political suicide for any government proposing such a measure.

Conclusion

The present French government has inherited an extremely complex and delicate problem where immigration is concerned. So far, it has tackled the most obvious – and the easiest – aspects of the problem. It has stopped further immigration and has attempted to consolidate and extend the rights of immigrants in France. Yet even in this domain it has held back somewhat. While immigrants now have the right to form their own associations without the prior permission of the Minister of the Interior, the right to vote in local elections, something which the immigrants' spokesmen had been seeking quite responsibly for a number of years and which François Mitterrand defended in his election campaign, has been postponed indefinitely.

In one sense, the matter of voting rights, even in local elections, raises the question of permanence and integration. It may be that the French, like the Americans, will decide that only naturalized citizens should have full civil rights. Is it likely, however, that many of the immigrants will eventually become sufficiently integrated into French society to seek naturalization? There have been barely a million naturalizations since 1948, and half of the immigrant population has chosen to return to its country of origin since post-war immigration began. Even among the second generation, while many adolescents would not consider exchanging European city life, however deprived, for the patriarchal structures of an African or Maghreb village, for unemployment in Algiers or Ankara, they seldom believe that their generation will ever be able to integrate fully into French society – 'ce n'est pas une carte d'identité qui te changera la gueule', one youth reflected bitterly. Far from being torn between their origins and France, they often feel rejected by both, and can look forward to little more than an existence as cultural half-castes. Their predicament more than anything else demonstrates that too little has been done too late to promote effective integration in the last quarter of a century. No amount of material assistance is now likely to demolish the wall of intolerance and prejudice which keeps immigrants apart from the 'Français de souche française'. Prejudice is being articulated more and more loudly by the groups and movements which have mushroomed on the extreme Right of the French political spectrum and which play on the fears of the 'Français moyen'. At the same time, the intolerance is increasingly translated into direct action, usually in the form of random attacks on individual immigrants and organized commando raids against immigrant HLM complexes.

The immigrants are not without friends. The Churches and trades unions lobby on their behalf and provide advice and assistance. There are also specialized, voluntary organizations like the *Fédération des associations de solidarité avec les travailleurs immigrés* (FASTI) and the *Mouvement contre le racisme et pour l'amitié des peuples* (MRAP) which offer legal advice and seek to mobilize public opinion. Ultimately, though, the politicians who alone can effect changes in the law are likely to remain more sensitive to the mood of the electorate than to the plight of a disenfranchised and unloved minority.

There are no simple solutions to the many and complex problems which form part of the legacy of France's immigration policy. In fact France has been a multiracial society for two decades at least: Islam, with some 3 million adherents, is the second religious denomination. Neither the lawmakers nor society as a whole has accepted that fact, however, and several million immigrants and their children are effectively second-class citizens. They are likely to remain so for years to come.

Bibliography

Both the *Institut national d'Études démographiques* and *La Documentation française* have published a series of studies on different aspects of contemporary French demography and society including a recent and important study of the 'second generation':

Marangé and Lebon, *L'Insertion des jeunes d'origine étrangère dans la société française*. Paris, La Documentation française, 1982.
More general studies of immigration and immigrants include:
B. Granotier, *Les Travailleurs immigrés en France*. Paris, Maspéro, 1976.
A. Le Pors. *Immigration et développement économique et social*. Paris, La Documentation française, 1977.
J. Minces, *Les Travailleurs étrangers en France*. Paris, Seuil, 1973.
G. Tapinos, *L'Immigration étrangère en France de 1946 à 1973*. Paris, PUF, 1975.

Le Monde has three items of relevance in its series 'Dossiers et documents': nos 29 (March 1976) and 87 (January 1982) on immigrants, and no 49 (March 1978) on racism. These consist of extracts from the daily edition of *Le Monde* which undoubtedly presents the most comprehensive and informed facts and opinions.

The view from the moderate Left may be most conveniently found in the weekly *Le Nouvel Observateur* and the daily *Le Matin*, while the weekly *Minute* reflects right-wing opinion quite accurately.

The racial conflict aspects of immigration can be seen in:

F. Bernardi and J. Dissler, *Les Dossiers noirs du racisme dans le Midi*. Paris, Seuil, 1976.

J. Brunn, *La nouvelle Droite*. Paris, Nouvelles Editions Oswald, 1979.

Five

Foreign policy

Alan Clark

Introduction

The Gaullist heritage. The essential principles of de Gaulle's foreign policy in the 1960s were few and uncomplicated. The vital initial postulate was the paramount importance of national independence, the re-establishment of which would enable France to regain its previous, traditional position of international eminence. In independence France would be free to enter into multiform co-operation with other nations and thus fulfil its historical 'vocation' of the promotion of peace and of certain civilized values. On the other hand without independence, valid international co-operation would not be possible since it would inevitably involve the subordination of one of the co-operating partners. National indignity apart, such co-operation-in-subordination would in practice be bound to fail.

From 1958 French foreign policy quickly became *le domaine réservé* of the President of the Republic who accorded it prime importance, determining its major orientations and deciding particular, often crucial issues. De Gaulle conducted a personal policy in an individual fashion. It has been suggested that his foreign policy was characterized more by the originality of its diplomatic style than by the solidity of its achievements and it is as well to distinguish the two aspects. Yet, substantial or more intangible, important changes in French foreign policy certainly did take place under de Gaulle. Following the broadly successful and relatively rapid decolonization of France's African possessions and the settlement of the Algerian war, de Gaulle had worked to establish national independence on the only basis that, in his mind, was valid: French control of an effective national security system. This led him in 1966 to withdraw France from the integrated military command of a NATO dominated by the USA, and to develop a French nuclear strategy and strike capacity. As the converse of this disengagement from the American orbit, a policy of co-operation and *détente* with the USSR and the 'satellite' countries of Eastern Europe was pursued with enthusiasm.

In European affairs, French intransigence concerning the establishment in the EEC of a common agricultural policy, successful though it proved to be, took second place in de Gaulle's estimation behind his political ambition to establish a confederal association of west European states, a 'Europe of nations' in which France would resume its historical position of leader. Between and distinct from the super-powers of East and West, de Gaulle's western Europe was to have been indispensable to world stability. But after his best efforts (the Fouchet Plans, 1961-2, and the Franco-German Treaty, 1963) had failed to impress the Community partners, his political Europeanism was of necessity reduced to an unshakeable opposition to any proposals which might lead to the emergence of supranationalist Europe, more or less aligned with the USA. Fear of such 'Atlanticization' of Europe was prominent among the reasons for French opposition in the 1960s to British membership of the Community.

Often preached in the UN, the Gaullist gospel of the independence of nation states was appreciatively received in many parts of the Third World. France's international standing was enhanced still further by the vigorous and generous co-operation and aid policies it pursued, particularly in the newly independent African Francophone states. Nevertheless the function of arbiter in international conflicts which de Gaulle had on occasion loudly assigned to a 'neutral' France was losing credibility at least with Israel as, in the Middle East, French sympathies were increasingly seen to lie with the Arab oil-supplying states (1967 arms embargo).

For Couve de Murville (Minister of Foreign Affairs, 1958-68) de Gaulle was beyond doubt 'un homme d'une passion intransigeante et sa passion était la France'; his foreign policy pursued 'l'intérêt national au sens le plus élevé du terme'. Couve de Murville was, and remains, a prominent cultivator of the Gaullist mystique and his assessment should not be accepted uncritically. Both within and outside France numerous critics have accused the foreign policy of de Gaulle of being anachronistic, unrealistic and therefore dangerous, merely negative, or – most damning – of being the product of an old man's idiosyncrasies. In principle at least the pursuit of national independence by de Gaulle was never a matter of ignoring harsh world realities; rather he constantly affirmed the priority of the national reality as the vital precondition of international dealings. His basic position was not inevitably nationalist in the pejorative sense of the word (although many foreign commentators saw it as such) to the extent that France's 'nationalness' sought peaceful rather than aggressive relations with other nations. It could be held of course that, unlike Louis XIV, de Gaulle had little real choice in the matter.

Foreign policy under Pompidou (1969-74)

It is certain that at de Gaulle's resignation (April 1969), French prestige stood higher than at any time since 1940 and, arguably, since before the First World War. During the 1960s France had exerted a determining – not everyone would say beneficial – influence on the economic and political evolution of Europe and of a large portion of Africa. And the voice of France had been heard – if not always listened to – in far wider fields, from Washington to Moscow and in many capitals of the Third World. Foreign reaction to the new French standing in the world was doubtless an unstable amalgam of resentment and respect, envy and affection. Apart from predictable reservations concerning the expense involved in maintaining Gaullist co-operation and nuclear policies, domestic French feelings were still, in the main, ones of sympathy with the needed restoration of national dignity. That the principles and personality of the President himself had been central to this restoration was no less clear, in particular to those many Gaullists who were determined to ensure France's continued fidelity to the pattern laid down since 1958. In true French fashion, de Gaulle's death in 1970 only intensified – in some quarters, almost sanctified – that determination.

While showing little sign of wanting to depart from the main lines of Gaullist doctrine, Pompidou's foreign policy did have its points of difference, born of an acknowledgement that circumstances had changed. On the other hand the control of foreign policy remained, as in the 1960s, firmly in the control of the new President of the Republic. Indeed to the extent that it was informed by a greater awareness of France's internal economic needs and of the increasing integration of domestic and foreign interests, that control may be said to have intensified under Pompidou. His Foreign Minister Michel Jobert liked to make the distinction between *la vision* of de Gaulle's approach to foreign policy and *la gestion* of Pompidou's.

In defence policy Pompidou was faithful to his predecessor's line, maintaining the quiet modifications from the high rigidity of France's 1966 position that had been perceptible from 1968, but did not engage himself in any positive developments of that line. The cost of the nuclear arms programme began to weigh more heavily, both financially and politically. France's neglected conventional forces were by the early 1970s badly in need of more modern equipment, and several embarrassing delays in the realization of stages in the nuclear programme had to be announced to a public no longer enthralled by the General's rhetoric and more concerned to see increases in social spending. Criticism of the tiny size and doubtful efficacy of *la force de frappe* flourished: in the middle of Pompidou's presidency, France had progressed to the point where nine of a projected eighteen ground-to-ground missiles stood ready in their silos in Haute-Provence, while two of a proposed fleet of five missile-firing nuclear submarines were in service by the end of 1972. Nevertheless France went ahead with its series of atmospheric nuclear tests in the Pacific with sufficient determination to resist the campaign of international protest led in 1973 by the governments of Australia and New Zealand. A truly Gaullist President had no choice in the matter in any case. France had not signed the 1963 and 1968 international treaties on nuclear disarmament and arms control, and the agreement on the prevention of nuclear war signed between the USA and the USSR in June 1973 justified in Pompidou's eyes the earlier intransigence of de Gaulle. For France the June treaty was tantamount to the self-promotion of the two super-powers to the shared office of nuclear policeman for the rest of the world. It was, according to Jobert, a *condominium* which should not be confused with genuine progress towards international *détente*. For the French, the proof of the validity of their interpretation was seen in the joint and exclusive regulation of the October War in the Middle East (1973) by the USA and the USSR; the super-powers had decided to settle world affairs without consulting their allies. The final twelve months of Pompidou's presidency amply underlined basic Gaullist principles and attitudes relating to national security. At the Helsinki conference on European security and defence (July 1973) and elsewhere France emphasized the need both for each nation, and for a united Europe, to exercise its defensive responsibilities: subjugation to the super-powers of East or West in so vital an area as defence was not to be tolerated.

Pompidou's relations with the super-powers were however not always as difficult as they became in 1973 and were at no stage sharply marked by the temperamental anti-Americanism to which many considered de Gaulle had on occasion succumbed. However relations deteriorated considerably in 1973 when, as well as the USA-USSR treaty on the prevention of nuclear war, two major areas of discord emerged. In April the American Secretary of State, Kissinger, began a diplomatic offensive intended to ensure agreement between the USA and Europe as the latter proceeded more or less slowly towards economic and political union; in June he proposed a 'new Atlantic charter' designed to promote this Atlanticist orientation of Europe. For the USA and for France's European partners the project had its merits: quite apart from its substantial economic interests in western Europe, the USA ensured the lion's share of a NATO defensive system which sooner or later would be affected by the decisions of any politically united Europe of the future. But for France it was yet another attempt by the Americans to dominate, and this time not only the sovereignty of France but also the autonomy of a possible union of Europe were threatened. French resistance to American proposals for joint western policies was underlined again at the end of 1973 when Pompidou rejected Kissinger's idea of forming a common front of oil importers for concerted action in response to the quadrupling of oil prices by the exporting countries (October 1973). At the end of Pompidou's presidency (he died in office, 2 April 1974) France appeared again in the familiar Gaullist stance of isolated opposition to American intentions in several fields.

Pompidou continued to develop political links with the USSR in the context of Gaullist 'balanced' relations with the super-powers. Until 1973, Pompidou's exchanges with Brezhnev were cordial and progress was made in Franco-Soviet commercial and technical exchanges. There was certainly room for it: in 1970 just 2 per cent of French exports went to the USSR. By contrast *détente* with eastern European states, so loudly hailed by the General, was maintained in little more than form: state visits (Tito came to Paris in 1970) and minor trade agreements. The treaty of June 1973 and the October War demonstrated again that in matters of real importance the USSR preferred to leave France out of account and treat directly with its American rival/partner. One notable consequence of the French position with regard to the super-powers was that, on his visit to Peking (September 1973), Pompidou found himself talking the same diplomatic language as the Chinese leaders: both disapproved of the 'collusion' between the USA and the USSR. For Pompidou their joint 'imperialism' was no less potentially dangerous than had been the conflict between the two blocs in the 1950s and 1960s.

Europe offered the greatest opportunity to Pompidou for creative departures in foreign policy. Innovation in this sphere was sorely needed. De Gaulle's intransigence had had much to do with the stagnant state in the late 1960s of both the EEC and the movement towards political union. Pompidou's general desire to set Europe in motion again was evident at the European summit (held at The Hague in December 1969) which agreed to open negotiations with candidate countries, notably Britain. French opinion was not particularly enthusiastic and the British public clearly divided on the matter of entry but, in a fashion reminiscent of de Gaulle's personalized intervention in major policy orientations, the essentials appear to have been agreed in the Paris meeting between Pompidou and the British Prime Minister Heath in May 1971. A month later it was decided in Luxembourg that Britain (and Ireland and Denmark) should enter the EEC on 1 January 1973.

From 1971 the bulk of Pompidou's activity was given to the promotion of greater European union, especially in the monetary and political spheres. His efforts suffered a demoralizing political set-back from the relative failure of a referendum he held (April 1972) on the enlargement of Europe: 40 per cent abstentions (the highest rate since Napoleon!) were recorded and only 36 per cent of the electorate voted 'Yes'. It was an attempt at the grand Gaullist gesture that did not come off: Pompidou had not received the clear popular mandate he had hoped for and the French hand at the autumn summit had not been strengthened in advance. Called at the French President's suggestion, the Paris meeting of the Nine (October 1972) established a calendar for a political union that was to be achieved by 1980. Pompidou did not depart from de Gaulle's insistence on a confederal union of states, although he was more sensitive to the isolation of France that was liable to result if that policy was presented in too absolute a fashion. His temperamental preference was for progressive, concrete realizations; only ineffectual goodwill was plentiful however, and 1973 ended with Europe struggling in the aftermath of the oil crisis, still unable to agree on common monetary, energy and raw materials policies.

Not without alienating important sections of French informed opinion, Pompidou remained firm in the pro-Arab stance adopted by de Gaulle in 1967, and conducted his Middle East policy with a sure sense of national economic interests. The diplomatic position remained much as before (guarantees for both Israel and the Palestinian people and a negotiated settlement based on mutual concessions), but France's energy supplies were also involved and had to be protected. Pompidou's pragmatism became glaringly evident when, while maintaining the embargo on arms to Israel, he agreed that France should supply Libya with 100 Mirages (January 1970). Gaullist claims to impartiality fell to pieces: Pompidou's France was no longer a peacemaker but was concerned rather to exert influence and cultivate interests. French diplomats covered the Middle Eastern states thoroughly in the context of a long-term policy intended to develop French industrial, commercial and cultural interests in the region.

Pompidou's action in the Middle East should be seen within his wider policy of expanding the French role in the Mediterranean. By emphasizing southern interests Pompidou thought France could re-balance the northern predominance that would result from the Europe of Nine, and regain some of its lost importance by occupying a prominent position in the 'new' Mediterranean that might emerge. Efforts were made to implement the scheme from 1969 and met with moderate success. By mid-1970 France had developed closer contacts with Lisbon and Madrid. French determination to improve relations with the Maghreb also showed results and after the storms of the 1960s diplomatic normality was restored between France and Morocco in 1969. Algeria posed a more important and more difficult problem. The loss of French oil concessions in the Algerian nationalizations of 1971 was a heavy blow to accept as, with economic following political decolonization during the 1960s, France had witnessed the erosion of the privileged exchanges with Algeria which in 1962 de Gaulle had anticipated. The situation between the two countries was sometimes delicate: French imports of Algerian wine were stopped in 1970, the proportion of French aid going to Algeria declined steadily and, following racial tension in Marseilles, Algeria suspended the heavy emigration of its workers to France (September 1973). Pompidou nevertheless persisted in his efforts to cultivate good relations, looking to France's longer-term economic and strategic interests. His concept of an Arab-Latin Mediterranean was farsighted and perhaps feasible, but it was also not without its opportunism (at the expense of Israel) and somehow lacked the cachet of his predecessor's more loftily conceived diplomacy. It was a policy defensible as prudent manoeuvring, but one which also contained the implicit admission that France's role, after being played on the world stage, might in future be limited effectively to western Europe and the Mediterranean – and to a presence in Africa.

While President Pompidou visited at least once most of the

former French territories in Black Africa; after 1958 de Gaulle had not ventured further south than the countries of the Maghreb. The difference illustrates Pompidou's greater concern for a co-operation policy that was less paternalistic and more open to the rapidly changing circumstances of the Third World. Wherever possible the privileged relations between France and its former colonies were maintained, but Pompidou agreed readily enough to African demands for liberalizing reforms of the 1960 co-operation agreements. Although it actually increased in volume, the proportion of the French budget given to co-operation declined to 1974; aid from the private sector (banks, industry, and so on) became almost as important as public aid – and less disinterested. Further, the French co-operation programme began to spread its funds and expertise beyond its traditional African spheres of influence: in 1970, 40 per cent of French aid went to developing countries outside *la zone franc*. This modified maintenance of a relatively good co-operation record demanded a degree of political courage at a time when such expensive policies, no longer buoyed up by de Gaulle's charisma, attracted diminishing public support. It is clear that particularly as the oil crisis deepened, Pompidou saw the problems of the Third World (the stability of prices received for raw materials, trade relations with the developed world) in global, long-term perspectives and, by 1974, the familiar Gaullist thesis of an international mediatory role for France had cropped up again. France's refusal to follow the American 'common front' strategy on oil prices and her stress on the necessity for developing countries to be fully involved in all discussions which related to international trade were welcomed by the many countries of the Third World dependent on prices received for their exports to the west.

Foreign policy under Giscard d'Estaing (1974-81)

Under Giscard d'Estaing the patterns of French foreign policy, while not breaking free from their Gaullist mould, in some areas underwent modification and in others became confused and difficult to decipher. Within weeks of his election Giscard indicated three principal points of foreign policy reorientation.

An extension of French involvement in international (presumably other than bilateral) co-operation with developing countries and no less than a 'new era' of international relations based on 'le respect et l'cstime mutuels, [et] un esprit de compréhension et de liberté' were promised. The form such change might adopt was not easy to imagine from the third point: while remaining independent in its commitments and decisions, '[la France] veut désormais consacrer ses forces, son imagination et son talent à forger son avenir'. A certain tone of imprecise idealism infused to all appearances with boundless goodwill had been set.

Yet a number of features of Giscard's reputation in the field of foreign policy were widely acknowledged at the start of his term of office. He was first and foremost a convinced European and looked to a politically united Europe having its own defence, currency and foreign policy. Although he always denied it, critics (many Gaullists, most Socialists and all the Communists) accused him of Atlanticist leanings, of working for greater French and European association with the USA, particularly with regard to economic and defensive structures. By his own admission Giscard was more positively internationalist in his approach to foreign policy: problems now posed themselves on a world scale, state-to-state relations (à la de Gaulle) were no longer sufficient in many cases and what he termed *une politique mondiale* was vital, although national sovereignty was to be firmly preserved. Such a global perspective necessitated what Giscard regularly referred to as a policy of *concertation*, that is of dialogue and harmonious co-ordination rather than intimidation and conflict (*la confrontation*). To what extent an implied criticism of de Gaulle's resolute defence of (his version of) national interests was to be detected in these Giscardian emphases was of course a matter of political opinion.

But elsewhere change was undeniable, not least in Giscard's political position. As leader of the *Républicains indépendants* (RI) he was the first non-Gaullist President of the Fifth Republic and while he chose an ambitious member of the UDR, Chirac, as his first Prime Minister, it was clear from the start that in spite of their internal divisions the parliamentary Gaullists would ensure that departures, imagined or real, from their founder's principles (in particular with regard to defence and national independence within Europe) did not pass uncriticized. It might have been thought that the narrowness of his electoral victory (less than 2 per cent more votes than Mitterrand, the candidate of the combined Left) would have restricted Giscard's freedom to conduct his own foreign policy – after all he could not claim the solid majority support on which the confidence of de Gaulle and Pompidou (until the 1972 referendum) had largely rested. However, Giscard's political base expanded significantly later in his term: important gains were made by the Giscardian UDF both in the 1978 Legislative Elections and in the European elections of the following year. Presidential foreign policy in the three years to May 1981 in consequence often appeared more determinedly innovative and markedly more dynamic (or, as critics of both Left and Right would prefer, misguided and foolhardy), particularly as regards disarmament, Africa and Europe.

The parliamentary opposition on the other hand failed throughout the decade to make a decisive impact in foreign policy matters. The scanty final section of the 'common programme' (signed in June 1972 by the PCF, PS and left-wing Radicals, and formally valid until the March 1978 elections) which outlined the foreign policy of a future French government of the Left was unimpressive: in the areas of defence and European policy, for example, it posed as many questions as it supplied answers. The extreme disunity that re-emerged from the middle of 1977 both between and within the two major parties of the Left only exacerbated matters. The situation could have proved damaging: in the absence of effective challenge from a Left in impotent disarray and from a diminished Gaullist Right, the potential in 1980-1 for a neo-Gaullian abusive 'presidentialization' of French foreign policy appeared great.

Obliged until 1978 to take account of a delicate political situation at home, Giscard came to power at a time of serious and persistent international difficulties. The oil crisis of late 1973 promised to involve other raw materials and threatened shaky international financial systems. Europe was in conflict, immobile if not actually regressive. The USA was in the final throes of Watergate. The new French President's large financial experience (Giscard had been a liberal Finance Minister under de Gaulle, 1962-6, and under Pompidou, 1969-74) was expected to produce in the conduct of foreign policy an intensification of Pompidolian sensitivity to French economic interests. Complex and rapid change on all sides also encouraged Giscard to develop his predecessor's pragmatism: in a world characterized more by chaos than by order, *le pilotage à vue* and *la gestion de l'imprévisible* (the phrases are Giscard's) became the only practical attitudes to adopt. Critics nostalgic for de Gaulle's loudly affirmed basic principles and long-term strategies were reluctant to admit Giscard's constant emphasis on change and on what he called '[le] grand réaménagement des relations internationales' in the late 1970s. The same critics could have been more sensitive to the sombre underlying conflict that coloured Giscardian foreign policy: on the one hand the advocacy of a humanitarian *mondialisme*, biased towards the indispensable implementation of greater international economic justice and the needs of the developing world; on the other, the no less necessary defence of national strategic and economic interests.

Even had he wanted to do otherwise Giscard would have been under pressure, for reasons both political and technological, to adopt a defence policy acceptable to the Gaullists. Before election he promised to maintain and develop French nuclear weapons and guaranteed the absence of France from disarmament and non-proliferation talks which sought only to maintain the blocs of the super-powers. Early in Giscard's term of office, however, nuances developed which were interpreted as departures from his predecessors' resolution: nuclear tests at Muroroa were confined underground and their frequency restricted (three tests in 1975, two in 1976). Between 1974 and 1977 further perceived deviations from established defence policy occurred with disconcerting frequency. Against a background of increasing military co-operation between French and NATO forces, declarations made in 1976 by both Giscard and his Chief of Staff, General Méry, clearly implied an extension of the hitherto strictly national dissuasion policy (Méry's concept of *la sanctuarisation élargie*) and an increased degree of French involvement in NATO's military structures. Government assurances that defence policy had not changed fell on deaf parliamentary ears. In this context of distrust and ambiguity Giscard's repeated insistence on the need to modernize France's conventional forces and in particular to develop mobile, multi-purpose interventionist units was seen as symptomatic of a relative departure from de Gaulle's priorities.

Deviation in defence policy was in fact more apparent than real. Following the relative pause of 1976-8, nuclear dissuasive policy was substantially redefined along firmly Gaullist lines. Commissioned in 1979, France's sixth strategic nuclear submarine, *Inflexible*, was programmed to enter service in 1985 armed with the M4, a new generation of longer-range, multi-headed missile. Existing FOST (*Force océanique stratégique*) submarines were to be renovated and similarly equipped from the later 1980s. As a result the megaton capacity of France's strategic forces was projected to quadruple in the seven years to 1985. More specifically Giscardian emphases on flexibility and innovation were discernible in longer-term projects announced in mid-1980: mobile, landbased strategic missiles for the 1990s, the technological development of enhanced radiation weapons (the so-called 'neutron bomb'). Consequences of Giscard's energetic reaffirmation of defence policy were soon evident. Underground nuclear testing in the Pacific accelerated again: eight tests were reported in both 1978 and 1979. Not surprisingly French defence costs rose significantly: by 30 per cent in real terms between 1977 and 1981, a rate of expenditure not achieved by most European NATO countries.

Considerable international interest was stimulated by Giscard's presentation to the UN (May 1978) of a number of disarmament proposals. His address, which marked France's return to the world disarmament scene after some twenty years' absence, was characterized by a typically subtle combination of Gaullist orthodoxy and Eurocentric innovation. His efforts to regionalize and in particular to Europeanize progress in international disarmament (Giscard proposed to the UN a pan-European conference on conventional disarmament) were as idealistic as they were necessary. Not only French but west European disquiet intensified as, in a context marked by increased Soviet military power in eastern Europe, the signing of SALT 2 (June 1979) brought into question the validity of American nuclear commitment to European security. Subsequent deterioration of strategic tensions in Europe (Euromissiles, Poland) served to intensify fears in French circles, from the Gaullist RPR to the PCF, that the super-powers of East and West were effectively disposing between themselves of European security. It did not diminish the potential value of Giscard's distinctively European approach to security problems which in fact, in 1981, continued to underlie much of the work of the Madrid conference on disarmament in Europe.

Giscard's predicted determination to effect a *rapprochement* with the USA became evident in the months following his election; even before the considerable public success of the presidential visit to Washington in celebration of the American bicentenary (May 1976), a more cordial tone in bilateral political relations had been established. In the aftermath of Carter's visit to France (January 1978) relations between the two countries were, Giscard claimed, 'cordiaux, ouverts et respectueux des droits de l'autre' – that is, to a degree never previously equalled, the USA recognized France's right to pursue autonomous national policies.

Such formal assertions of the excellence of Franco-American relations became increasingly difficult to reconcile with multiplying points of conflict of a commercial or industrial nature: following 'illegitimate' tactics over replacement contracts for European NATO military aircraft (1974) and American landing-rights for Concorde (1977), effective interference by the USA in French civil nuclear sales to South Korea and Pakistan (1975-9) was resented by the bulk of French political opinion. Differences of position in the energy and security fields also became apparent. For several years Giscard pressed the USA, as an indispensable major contribution to an internationally integrated resolution of the 1970s' energy crises, to import and use less oil on the one hand, and on the other, to produce more. In vain. In mid-1979 France was prominent (for example, at the Tokyo summit of industrialized nations, June 1979) in voicing EEC resentment at the absence of a concerted American policy on oil imports. Carter's signing of SALT 2 was seen as a further indication of American indifference to European concerns.

As with the USA France's relations with the USSR from 1974 were characterized by a change in tone, although in this case the evolution occurred more erratically, in the direction of uncertainty and, especially after 1977, prolonged ambivalence. During Giscard's first year of office Franco-Soviet relations were pursued diligently and fruitfully, with France emphasizing its determination to develop still further the policy of *détente* and co-operation which, initiated by de Gaulle, had become established in the mid-1970s as a permanent feature of its foreign policy. Indeed the triple formula of *détente, entente et coopération* was still employed by France, at the end of the decade, to convey the essential of its formal relations with the USSR. Nor was this a mere diplomatic nicety, for Franco-Soviet co-operation had, by the later 1970s, become varied, substantial and, ultimately, expanding. At the end of Brezhnev's visit (December 1974) important energy and industrial agreements were concluded, together with a general agreement on economic co-operation intended to triple bilateral trade to 1980; in 1976 the value of industrial contracts signed between the two countries was the highest ever. By mid-1979 (Giscard visited Moscow in April) all seemed set fair for the next decade: wide-ranging co-operation agreements (from marine research to gas technology contracts, from sales of electronic equipment and nuclear reactors to reciprocal language education arrangements) to 1990 were signed.

More recent diplomatic relations were decidedly less smooth. After almost three years of Soviet disquiet at both the confused evolution of French defence policy and at Giscard's more conciliatory attitude towards the USA, 1977-8 was marked by a deterioration in relations so serious as temporarily to hamper commercial exchanges. Secondary areas of dispute were not lacking: Soviet rejection of the French disarmament proposals of May 1978, the Middle East, human rights, China. Central to Franco-Soviet dissension however were Moscow's virulent attacks on Giscard's African policy, and in particular its criticism of French 'imperialist' intervention against 'progressivist' forces in Zaire and Chad (see p. 139). The Franco-Soviet *détente*, then of some fourteen years' standing, may indeed (as Giscard claimed on French television in April 1979) have made a significant contribution to peace and stability in

Europe, but just as clearly no French impingement on the USSR's African strategies could be tolerated. Or, presumably, would be tolerated in the future. So vulnerable a dichotomy between *entente* and *coopération*, diplomacy and trade, constituted at best an unpredictable basis on which to build Franco-Soviet relations in the future. Giscard himself discovered this when, in 1980, he attempted to maintain traditional *détente* with the USSR while at the same time condemning the Soviet invasion of Afghanistan (December 1979): the widespread political criticism this stand incurred in France may have contributed to Giscard's defeat in the 1981 presidential election.

The numerous uncertainties of relations with both the USA and the USSR reflected the recent shift in France's foreign policy perspectives away from the bipolar world of the super-powers towards an international scene conceived, where possible, in multipolar, regionalist terms. Complex, subject to constant redefinition, it was a movement compatible both with de Gaulle's criticism in the 1960s of the hegemony exercized by the two super-powers and with his largely symbolic recognition of the importance of Third World nations. Pompidou's initiatives in Africa, the Mediterranean and the Arab world maintained the movement. In his turn Giscard attempted to co-ordinate French foreign policy more tightly than ever around the triple regional 'poles' of Europe, the Arab states, and the Third World, especially Africa.

As Pompidou had done in 1969, Giscard set out with a high determination to relaunch Europe. Even more than his predecessor, Giscard had from the mid-1970s to pit his ideals against a Europe that was retrogressive and gravely disunited: in particular, common monetary and energy policies were still lacking at a time when all member countries were experiencing more or less acute economic difficulties. Progress towards curing Europe's many defects was so rare that late in 1976 analyses of the impotent condition of the Nine flourished and French observers even speculated sceptically on the future survival of the EEC's original and still fundamental customs union.

Particularly since 1977, however, Franco-German relations materially underpinned European development, providing much needed stability and stimulus. It was, for example, a text jointly presented by Schmidt and Giscard to the European Council (July 1978) that supplied the basis for the European Monetary System (EMS) which came into operation in March 1979. If the birth was a difficult one (France suspended its participation for three months because of a disagreement with West Germany over Community agricultural subsidies), the EMS's early functioning was sound: a substantial advance in monetary co-operation had been achieved.

A European energy policy proved a more intractable problem: progress had been reluctant (Giscard met with no response in his efforts to rouse the European Council's concern for the question in November 1976), partial, and very possibly fragile since it was made only under the irresistible pressure of international circumstances. Under French presidency, the European Council called (in March and June 1979) for European dialogue with the OPEC states, announced its determination to restrict EEC oil imports until 1985 to the global levels of 1978, to co-ordinate the national energy policies of the Nine and to develop their alternative energy sources (nuclear power especially, in the case of France). It also criticized the huge increases in American oil imports since 1973. The council's energy front was impressive if less precisely quantified and far-reaching than France had wanted. If the impact of Giscardian Europeanism and of the ideal of *concertation* in international questions was clear enough, it remained far from certain that such a spirit could preserve a united approach by the EEC to the precarious world energy situation of the 1980s.

French efforts from 1974 to promote a politically more united Europe were persistent. Giscard's early tactics in this field owed much to de Gaulle's European 'union of states': the new President suggested that the nine heads of government should meet together as informally as possible, three or four times a year (the first meeting was held in Paris, September 1974), in order to discuss current or longer-term matters of European concern. Prominent among Giscard's intentions in initiating this European Council was the idea of progressively accustoming the Nine to regular political discussion from which co-ordination and perhaps, by accretion as it were, greater unity might emerge. Such a process had to be supplemented by institutional change, in particular by a European Assembly elected by universal suffrage. After initial moves in 1975–6, formal progress towards the realization of this major Giscardian ambition was made with notable smoothness, culminating in the inauguration, in mid-1979, of the first democratically based European Parliament.

In at least the short term, and from the French point of view, the first European elections were seen as a political triumph for Giscard's European policy: the firmly Europeanist UDF received the largest proportion of votes cast of the four principal political groupings in France, and therefore sent the largest number of Euro-deputies to a broadly sympathetic Centre-Right Assembly's first session in Strasbourg. The two formations most fiercely critical of presidential enthusiasm for the institutionalization of Europe, the PCF and the RPR, came third and fourth respectively in the election. While the installation of the Assembly clearly contributed significantly to European integration (after the elections Giscard justifiably stressed the importance of the existence in the 1980s of an acknowledged political expression of European opinion), it did so primarily on the abstract, institutional level: its capacity for contributing effectively to persistent, more immediate difficulties (energy; unemployment; the budgetary dispute with Great Britain; industrial and agricultural policies within the EEC) had by 1981 not been demonstrated.

In the 1979 Euro-elections almost 40 per cent of the French electorate abstained from voting, but with economic interests more pressingly at stake the next stage in the construction of Europe – the expansion of the EEC to twelve members by the inclusion of Greece (from January 1981), Spain and Portugal – was less likely to benefit from such broadly sympathetic public disinterest. Giscard's unequivocal, if not unconditional, support for the Europe of Twelve was exceptional in 1978–9: to the PCF, parts of the PS, the RPR, to farmers' groups and some industrialists in the Midi, the entry of Spain in particular would threaten French social and economic interests. If to such hostility were added both left-wing and Gaullist charges that Giscard intended to establish an 'Atlanticized', supranationalist Europe (which, according to Chirac, would result in 'l'asservissement économique [et] l'effacement international de la France'), and the necessity for sweeping institutional reform of an enlarged EEC, it seemed probable that the qualified success achieved to 1981 by Giscardian European policy would be difficult to equal, or even maintain.

For both economic and strategic reasons Giscard developed relations with the Arab world to a point far beyond that reached by Pompidou. The French diplomatic position with regard to Israel shifted in emphasis if not in fundamentals when, by late 1974, Giscard had already stressed the vital importance of arriving at a durable settlement of the Palestinian problem, a settlement which had to include the establishment of sure and recognized frontiers for all concerned, and in particular for Israel and the Palestinian people. By 1977 France maintained that Israel should withdraw to its territorial limits of 1967, while the Palestinians should have access to a homeland (*une patrie*). The need for a global settlement of the Middle East caused France to share the majority of the Arab world's anxiety and reserve about the Camp David agreements, seeing them (a further point of Franco-American dissension) as a fragmentary and potentially divisive response to a wider issue.

If relations with Israel were eventually normalized (in 1977) after France's effective recognition of the Palestine Liberation Organization (UN debate, October 1974), French identification and involvement with the Arab world expanded enormously throughout the 1970s. Such association ranged in later years from disturbingly mercenary pro-Arab reactions, typified by the Abou Daoud affair (in January 1977 Daoud, an alleged organizer of PLO terrorism, was arrested in France, but after Arab protest and in spite of Israeli demands for his extradition was rapidly released), to the promotion of dialogue between the EEC and the OPEC States, and to the elaboration in mid-1978 of an embryonic military and diplomatic axis with Saudi Arabia in an effort to respond to Soviet penetration in the Horn of Africa. But above all Franco-Arab relations were governed by economic necessity. Obliged since 1973 to pay escalating prices for its oil imports France, as other industrialized countries, strove as never before to increase its industrial and technological sales to the Arab states. The inevitable identification of French policy towards the Arab world with the promotion of commercial and strategic interests was firmly underscored by Prime Minister Barre's highly successful visit to Iraq (July 1979) only a matter of weeks after the second Geneva meeting of OPEC. Iraq undertook to guarantee up to one third of France's annual oil imports, thereby more than doubling its supply rate; in return France would sell Iraq a wide range of arms and military equipment, and a civil nuclear research centre. If in the wake of the Iranian revolution and the Gulf War France redefined some of its strategic relations in the Arab region, the perilous and fragile formula of 'oil for arms' had not outlived its usefulness, or its necessity.

France's recent relations with the Third World were characterized by an unstable combination, not unknown in de Gaulle's day, of generous intentions and imperfect realizations of those intentions. Giscard consistently presented himself as a renovator of French co-operation policy. Long-established links with North and Black African countries were to be retained, but also revised. Most importantly, the taint of imperialism was to be removed from co-operation in all its forms, technical, cultural or merely linguistic: *l'Afrique aux Africains* was the slogan Giscard regularly brandished in talks with African leaders from 1975. In consequence the numbers of French medical, teaching and administrative personnel based in Africa diminished gradually as greater emphasis was placed on co-operation through investment and the establishment of self-sufficient structures within the developing countries – formation rather than assistance.

This revamped policy did not hinder the important expansion and revival of bilateral relations in Africa and elsewhere. Complementing significant *rapprochement* with previously critical 'progressivist' states such as Angola, Ethiopia and Madagascar, Giscard's historic visit to Guinea (December 1978) definitively restored the relations between Paris and Conakry which had been ruptured in 1958 just before the start of de Gaulle's presidency, symbolized the more dynamic outgoing character of Giscardian co-operation – and promised to be highly profitable. Subsequently, unprecedented French initiatives were undertaken in former British and Portugese territories with a view to expanding and coordinating French co-operation on a broader regionalist basis throughout West Africa. Of potentially equal importance was the long overdue revival of diplomatic, industrial and economic interest in South and Central America, as evidenced by productive presidential visits to Brazil (October 1978) and Mexico (February 1979), and by various ministerial tours of Argentina, Colombia and Panama (April 1979).

Far more controversial was Giscard's policy of military intervention in Africa. In western Sahara, Chad, and the Shaba province of Zaire in particular, French military personnel and equipment were repeatedly and sometimes heavily engaged in stabilizing chaotic internal situations. But at what point did stabilizing assistance end and 'neo-colonialist interference' begin? Reactions were divided and often extremist. The USSR and 'progressivist' African States (for example Tanzania, Madagascar) were unreservedly hostile. Among Arab nations, Libya denounced French policy in Chad as archaic colonialism, while Franco-Algerian diplomatic and economic relations went into serious decline from mid-1977 in the face of French assistance to Morocco and Mauritania and after the Algerian-backed Polisario Front held several French civilians hostage. On the other hand, numerous Black African States, not invariably francophone, expressed varying degrees of relieved approval of the French supportive actions; more discreetly, the EEC, the USA and even sections of the OAU associated themselves sympathetically with Giscard's initiatives. By 1978 the risks inherent in such African interventionism were felt, not least by the French Left, to be acute: the prolongation and escalation of military involvement (in response to the civil war there, French troops in Chad were doubled to 2500 in March 1979), and the detrimental identification of France with so-called 'moderate' regimes (Mobutu's Zaire, Bokassa's Central African Empire) and unenlightened policies (continued French interference in the Comores and presence in Réunion, ambiguous commercial relations with South Africa and so on). If in 1979–81 French interventionism in Africa appeared less militarily activist, diplomatically more balanced and reserved, the longer-term coherence of what Giscard termed *la fidélité africaine de la France* was still not evident; many in France feared that the need to protect French economic and western strategic interests, as well as African security, could give rise to further piecemeal responses.

More durably innovatory was the importance Giscard repeatedly attached to the need to adopt international regionalist perspectives when responding to the situation of the Third World. While France still had a useful role to play in Africa and elsewhere, often limitedly national, bilateral action was insufficient: economic, political and strategic problems posed themselves on so complex a scale that only a multilateral approach, involving effective negotiations between industrialized and developing nations, was appropriate. Unfortunately Giscard's various proposals in this vein too often remained at the level of prestigious diplomatic initiatives, with little or no practical application. Launched in 1974 at the joint suggestion of France and Saudi Arabia, the North-South conference on international economic co-operation ended (June 1977) with the participating Third World countries disillusioned by the industrialized world's reluctance to agree to extensive structural reform of the international financial and commercial systems. It may have been true, as Giscard was prompt to claim, that a spirit of dialogue had at least been born, but fundamental problems such as energy supplies and Third World indebtedness remained virtually unchanged. Two years later Giscardian assertions of *concertation* and *interdépendance* as the keys to a more just and workable international economic order were still more numerous than effective: the fifth United Nations Conference on Trade and Development (Manila, June 1979), at which France represented the EEC, concluded in Third World bitterness at the nationally self-protective attitudes of an industrialized world fearful of global recession, while even the Lomé Convention (between the EEC and African, Caribbean and Pacific countries) was renewed only with difficulty and in confusion (May–June 1979).

Giscard's major address to the sixth Franco-African Conference (Kigali, Rwanda, May 1979) indicated the three principal interest areas of contemporary French policy, and encapsulated the undoubted farsightedness, the high ambition but also the disconcerting ambiguity of that policy. Fusing ideas of Euro-Arab and Euro-African association regularly mooted since 1974, Giscard proposed a Euro-African-Arab *trilogue*, the elaboration by carefully prepared stages of a triangular charter of solidarity. No fewer than seventy-eight States were, potentially, to be involved. Such a vast project in multilateral political and economic co-operation (technology/ raw materials/oil) would not, however, supplant Franco-African bilateral relations, nor reduce French commitment to African security. Having recently cancelled the debts of eight African states, France announced at Kigali an increase of almost 50 per cent in its co-operation budget from 1980, as well as substantial additional contributions to African development bodies. Yet a few months later the decisive role played by the French Army in the overthrow of Bokassa's tyrannical regime (September 1979), while it stabilized a deteriorating situation, exposed Giscard to charges of metropolitan manipulation of the internal affairs of former colonial territories.

The editor of *Le Monde* Jacques Fauvet came persuasively close to the truth when, in the early days of 1981, he summed up French foreign policy since 1974 as the work of '[un] diplomate ingénieux dans l'inspiration à défaut de l'être toujours dans l'action'.

Foreign policy under Mitterrand (1981-   )

The election in May 1981 of a Socialist President of the Republic roused more extreme hopes and fears for French foreign policy than had the arrival of his liberal conservative predecessor seven years earlier. Inside France rather than abroad, on the left rather than on the right, the hopes sprang from Mitterrand's and the PS's long recognized concern for European and international disarmament, for the economic and humanitarian development of the Third World and, more vaguely, for an approach to international relations that would be more firmly principled than that, for example, which Giscard had exhibited in his hesitant, undignified responses in 1980–1 to the crises in Afghanistan and Poland.

The fears were more numerous, more acute since more closely defined, and more widespread, being evident both abroad (from Washington to Moscow, from Bonn to numerous Arab and Francophone African capitals) and at home (all Right of Centre opinion, but also the PCF). In the mid-1970s both PS and PCF had after all still favoured dismantling the national nuclear strike capacity: what would happen to defence strategy under Mitterrand? The consequences for NATO and European security at a time of increasing continental tensions were potentially critical. Surely French relations with the major powers of West and East would suffer disruption, especially following the introduction, in June 1981, of four Communist ministers into Prime Minister Mauroy's Cabinet? If ideological common ground between Presidents Reagan (who took office in January 1981) and Mitterrand appeared minimal then prospects for improving co-operation in a deeply recessive European Community were not enhanced by the new French government's anomalous expansionist economic policies. Previous French policies towards Africa and the Arab world had been widely criticized as mercenary, opportunist and ineffective (according to Mitterrand, Giscard's sole diplomatic principle had been *épouser les circonstances*): what upheavals might be in store in those areas? And so on.

Not all but most of such speculations have to date (October 1982) proved groundless: certainly the more excited fears – but also the more lofty hopes – have not been realized. Although for electoral reasons both Giscard d'Estaing and Mitterrand would resent the association, France's foreign policy under its two latest Presidents has to a marked degree been characterized by incidental change coupled with essential continuity.

Since the middle of 1981 French commitment in security matters has been notably firm and clear. Having quickly reaffirmed his government's adherence to the established Gaullist line of autonomous national membership of the Atlantic Alliance, Mitterrand went further than Giscard had ever done by supporting the USA's insistence on the need to respond to the build-up of Soviet military power by establishing NATO missiles in western Europe: worthwhile disarmament negotiations could proceed only once a position of equilibrium had in this way been re-established. This apparently paradoxical *rapprochement* between Atlantic and French perspectives had little effect on the more specifically national dimensions of Mitterrand's defence policy. The nuclear dissuasive arsenal will be extended and modernized in ways that attempt to combine irreproachable Gaullist orthodoxy (a seventh strategic nuclear missile-firing submarine is to be constructed from 1985) with the more flexible, Europeanist concerns of Giscard (the 1982 defence budget proposed a new tactical nuclear missile system and a mobile intercontinental ballistic missile). Unlike the situation in West Germany and some other European NATO countriés, the continuity of French defence policy has barely been affected by popular neutralist pressures. However, problems concerned with the number, training and future role of France's conventional armed forces, and with total defence costs, continue to pose substantial challenges to the maintenance of national independence. In an economically sombre future such problems will not be easily resolved.

In June 1981 Claude Cheysson, France's Minister of External Relations, suggested that the USA would find in his country 'un solide partenaire, sinon facile'. Broadly common Franco-American international responses (to the Euro-missiles question, to the Middle East imbroglio, to the Polish crisis) have since demonstrated their solidity. A year later however Cheysson referred openly to *[le] divorce progressif* which was dividing Washington not merely from Paris, but from western Europe in general. Sharply divergent approaches to monetary and commercial policies, and the impact of these on East-West relations underlay this deterioration in Atlantic solidarity. Washington's calls for increased NATO defence spending caused resentment among European States which from late in 1980 had seen their recessions worsen as a consequence of persistently high American interest rates. Reagan's advocacy of unrestricted international trade did not extend to EEC steel exports to the USA, while active American opposition in 1981–2 to the construction of a major natural gas pipeline from Siberia to western Europe appeared to European eyes both incompatible with American cereal sales to the USSR and an intolerable infringement of European economic sovereignty. Intermittently supported in his stand by EEC nations such as West Germany and Britain, Mitterrand regularly distinguished between political and commercial relations with the USSR: while the former could not be regularized until, for example, Soviet troops withdrew from Afghanistan, the latter should continue (a massive contract for the supply of Soviet gas to France was signed, in January 1982, just one month after martial law was imposed in Poland). De Gaulle and Giscard had thought along very similar lines.

'Commençons par rendre son âme à l'Europe', Mitterrand urged (in an interview published in *Le Monde*, June 1981), while at the same time exhorting the European Council to develop the EEC's social legislation, what he called *l'espace social européen*. In a Community ravaged by high and increasing unemployment, Mitterrand's Euro-Socialist idealism was lyrical, entirely appropriate, but unlikely to be realized. What co-ordinated action was accomplished by the EEC in 1981–2 remained partial, defensive or circumstantial: common mobilization against either Japanese exports or against the monetary policies and *[le] véritable protectionnisme déguisé* (the phrase is Mitterrand's) deployed by the USA, or the adoption in support of Britain of economic sanctions against Argentina during the Falklands war. The EMS (see p. 135) functioned with sufficient normality to survive critical currency adjustments (June 1982). But otherwise European affairs were dominated, as during the later years of Giscard's presidency, by the continuous, politically linked disputes centring on British contributions to the Community's budget and the reform of the Common Agricultural Policy (CAP): after many months of deadlocked negotiation institutional crisis was averted (in May 1982) by a compromise that postponed essential reforms, determined agricultural prices for 1982, but resolved nothing. As for political relations, Mitterrand maintained the high level of positive co-operation with West Germany established by Giscard and Schmidt but complemented this with wider, more diversified bilateral relations with Britain, Italy and Denmark. This more broadly balanced approach may assist France in responding to the more conservative economic emphases expected of Chancellor Kohl.

With regard to the Middle East a similar pursuit of diplomatic equilibrium has been unremitting, infinitely delicate and, in multiple ways, costly. Known to be a long-standing friend of Israel, Mitterrand worked for what he saw as a more even-handed approach to the Palestinian conflict (guaranteed recognition of all sides, including a Palestinian State; a negotiated global settlement within the Camp David framework); the effort gave rise to considerable Arab apprehension as for the first time since 1967 France voiced active concern for Israel's interests. Humanitarian, non-partisan diplomacy was courageous but perceived as provocative as inter-Arab terrorism and anti-Zionist violence escalated in Paris. Arab criticism reached heights unknown throughout the 1970s when, in spite of Israel's annexation of the Golan Heights (December 1981), Mitterrand paid an unprecedented presidential visit to Jerusalem (March 1982). From mid-1982 however Franco-Israeli relations deteriorated in their turn following French condemnation of the Israeli invasion of Lebanon (June 1982). In consultation with the USA, in close concert with Egypt, Paris' diplomatic involvement persisted at a high pitch, culminating in the repeated participation of French troops in UN intervention forces in Beirut. As Arab and especially PLO appreciation of French positions has largely been restored (Cheysson met Arafat in October 1982), and as French arms and nuclear sales to the Arab world continue, the effective difference between the policies of Giscard and Mitterrand in this critical area appears slight.

The distance between intention and performance was inevitably widest in policies relating to the Third World. The Socialist government multiplied assertions of the pressing need for what Cheysson called *un 'new deal' planétaire* and what, more sonorously, Mitterrand referred to as *un co-développement généralisé* or *une restructuration d'ensemble* of economic relations between developed and developing worlds. North-South relations had to be co-ordinated globally, enveloping monetary, energy, industrial and commercial strategies with more orthodox development aid. To be structured progressively on the triple basis of exemplary relations with Algeria, Mexico and India, French solidarity with the Third World was repeatedly affirmed. A substantial contract for the supply to France of natural gas on terms generous to Algeria (February 1982) was presented by Paris as an example for other industrialized nations to follow. Was it a legitimate example? Or was it, as conservative critics alarmed at France's record trade deficit in late 1982 alleged, simply bad business? And what of the fact, disturbing even to some PS parliamentarians, that Mitterrand's redefinition of Third World policies did not impede substantial sales, *à la* Giscard, of Mirage 2000s to India, or (in December 1981) of admittedly defensive arms to Nicaragua?

Global reorganization was not in any case to be pursued to the exclusion of France's established bilateral ties with many African, especially francophone, states. Without exception, treaty obligations with such countries have been respected and in some cases (Zaire, for example) French financial commitment has been increased. In the light of Giscard's problems in Chad and Central Africa, interventionism has been minimized, *la non-ingérence* observed and *le développement autocentré* promoted. The latest Franco-African summit (Kinshasa, October 1982) clearly demonstrated that under Mitterrand relations with Africa have to date been restored to notably high levels of mutual understanding. It will be interesting to see if they remain there in the face of both increasing Third World indebtedness and of a stagnant metropolitan economy.

Bibliography

Books

Duhamel, A., *La République de Monsieur Mitterrand*. Paris, Grasset, 1982. Chapter V, 'La Tradition gallicane' contains an early perceptive assessment of Mitterrand's foreign policy to mid-1982; see especially pp. 179–80 and pp. 187–201.

Frears, J.R., *France in the Giscard Presidency*. London, George Allen and Unwin, 1981. Chapters 5 and 6 on foreign policy and defence under Giscard.

Giscard d'Estaing, V., *Démocratie française. Préface inédite*. Paris, Livre de Poche, 1978. Chapter XII covers briefly the principal areas of Giscard's foreign policy.

Mitterrand, F., *Ici et maintenant*. Paris, Livre de Poche, 1981. Chapters VI and VII contain a lively *tour d'horizon* of major international issues.

Pickles, D., *The Government and Politics of France*, Vol. II:

Politics. London, Methuen, 1973. Part II offers a full and stimulating account of foreign policy under De Gaulle and Pompidou. A helpful list of related French and English titles is included (pp. 481–3).

—, *Problems of Contemporary French Politics*. London, Methuen, 1982. Chapter 5: 'The decline of Gaullist foreign policy'; Chapters 6 and 7 discuss Giscardian European and defence problems.

Serfaty, S. (ed.), *The Foreign Policies of the French Left*. Boulder, Colorado, Westview Press, 1979. An informative, if frequently carping, account of PS and PCF foreign policy positions in the 1970s.

Articles

Cairns, J.C., 'France, Europe and the "design of the world" 1974–7.' *International Journal*, Toronto, vol. XXXII, no. 2 (Spring 1977), pp. 253–71.

Clark, A., 'Style and substance: Foreign Policy and the 1981 Presidential Election in France.' *Quinquereme*, vol. 5, no. 1 (January 1982), pp. 97–107.

Jospin, L., 'Politique extérieure française: le point de vue des socialistes.' *Politique internationale*, no. 10 (Hiver 1980–1), pp. 203–11.

Moisi, D., 'Mitterrand's Foreign Policy: the limits of continuity.' *Foreign Affairs*, vol. 60, no. 2 (Winter 1981/2), pp. 347–57.

Six

Education

Margaret S. Archer

Introduction

An understanding of any element in the French system of
education implies a knowledge of its history, precisely because
a system existed in France a century before its development in
England. The endurance of a structure designed to fit the needs
of pre-industrial society in the early nineteenth century leads
to problems of adjustment to modern politics, economy and
society. Even an understanding of the Events of May 1968
requires that they should be seen not only as an attack on
modern educational institutions but also on the traditional
structure of the educational system as a whole.

The historical background

The dual tradition in French education

From the French Revolution onwards, two main traditions of
educational thought and practice can be traced, whose conflict
occupied the whole of the nineteenth century and has not been
settled in the twentieth. On the one hand, the revolutionary
emphasis on individual rights to instruction is most clearly
expressed in the blueprints for educational reform put forward
in the Assemblies of the First Republic. On the other,
Napoleon's policy subordinated the amount and content of
education received by individuals to the needs of the State
efficiency.

Condorcet's blueprint, the most influential on future educationists, summarizes the basic tenets of Republican thought on education. Instruction should be given because the individual has a right to it: it should therefore be universal and for both sexes, and ought to be common to all at primary level. By contrast, Napoleon's purpose in organizing a new educational system was pragmatic. Unlike the series of revolutionary blueprints which remained largely theoretical, his reforms were immediately implemented. Napoleon's two overriding aims of bringing about efficiency in the State and stability in society could not be served by treating unequals equally. Abandoning an educational philosophy based on individual rights for one which he framed in relation to State needs, he relegated primary education to the lowest priority in his policy. As the inculcation of useful skills was to be the supreme end of instruction, and as the State required only small numbers of trained individuals, any extension of training to the masses would be economically wasteful and socially dangerous. The minimal amount of knowledge the people required could be imparted in fee-paying or charitable schools, run by the Church. Therefore the State need not create primary establishments, but could content intself with controlling the loyalty of its teachers, who were mainly members of Catholic orders. Napoleon did not want the masses to be instructed beyond a minimum level of literacy, sufficient for the needs of a mainly agricultural economy, and did not object to their being religious, since the Church encouraged social conformity by preaching the acceptance of a preordained station in life.

Unlike primary schools, secondary and higher establishments were vital to the State, since they were to provide the skilled administrators, professionals and officers who were to scrve it. As a corollary, State control over the education they gave and the degrees they granted would cnsure that the best available talent would be channelled into useful occupations. In this way Napoleon justified the State monopoly over education embodied in the Imperial University of 1808 – the name given to the centralized system of State education. This prevented any other secondary school from functioning without direct authorization by the university authorities and submitted all State establishments to the control of a rigidly hierarchical administration, whose head was directly responsible to the Emperor. Not only did this centralization remain a permanent characteristic of French education, but many component institutions of the Imperial University have survived until now. Thus the *lycées* (State secondary schools), the *baccalauréat* (degree awarded for secondary studies and permitting university entry) and the *Ecole Normale* (training establishment for teachers who become civil servants upon admission to it) are still features of the contemporary system. Not only have such specific institutions endured, but the overall educational philosophy of the Imperial University is not yet extinct. Its fundamental principle, that if the State has no need of education, the people have no right to instruction, led to the development of a bifurcated system. On the one hand, highly specialized institutions at the secondary and higher level provided skilled servants of the State; on the other limited instruction in primary schools sufficed to provide loyal citizens. The absence of a ladder between the two levels limited educational mobility and reflected the major social division between the bourgeoisie and the people.

The development of primary education under the July Monarchy

While Napoleon designed the educational system mainly to supply civil and military administrators, in connection with his policy of reconstruction in France and expansion abroad, subsequent regimes, without changing the basic structure of the Imperial University, modified some of its component parts. These reforms were largely prompted by the increasing pace of industrialization and the ensuing need for the propagation of some technical skills among the people. The July Monarchy (1830–48) was a predominantly bourgeois government, committed to industrial expansion and therefore disinclined to leave primary education to the Church, as under the Empire and the Restoration. The conservative bourgeois fear of elementary education as a source of social unrest – which had prevailed since the final phase of the Revolution – gradually gave way before the entrepreneurial awareness that industry required trained operatives. Hence the diffusion of primary schooling appeared to be a precondition of economic development and a prerequisite of the July Monarchy's motto: *Enrichissez-vous*. However, the educational structure inherited from Napoleon was ill adapted both in its form and its content to the inculcation of the skills required. The main inadequacy was the gap between an exceedingly elementary primary schooling and an exceedingly classical secondary one. The nature of secondary and higher education made it irrelevant to industry, while that of primary schooling made it insufficient. Thus the creation of *primaires supérieures* schools as an extension of primary schooling by the law of 1833 introduced the degree of expansion in popular education which the evolution of the economy demanded and a stable society could accommodate. Considerations of economic utility rather than individual rights to instruction prompted this reform. These higher grade schools created in 1833, and to which the best pupils passed after completing primary studies, were predominantly vocational. They trained workers for commerce and industry, without attempting to lead into secondary establishments. Thus the basic bifurcation was unchanged. The educational system had altered to meet economic needs, but had remained socially conservative. The sons of manual workers could gain more instruction than previously but without competing with the children of the bourgeoisie, who still monopolized secondary and higher education.

The survival of the Napoleonic structure under the Third Republic

After the fall of the July Monarchy in 1848, the Second Republic did not reform the educational system, but reorganized the division of responsibilities between secular and clerical teachers within the State system. This issue had remained contentious since the Empire, as the Church sought to retain its control over primary instruction and claimed a greater share of secondary. The *Loi Falloux* of 1850 satisfied these demands by reducing the educational qualifications required from clerics and by giving the clergy seats on the educational councils of the *Université*. Such concessions were prompted by the fear of popular unrest, exemplified by the excesses of June 1848, and by the reliance of the bourgeoisie on religious instruction to restrain radicalism.

While the Second Empire (1852–70) was a period of religious reassertion in education, the Third Republic gradually secularized the State system and the separation of Church and State in 1905 was the culminating point in this process. As a result, the Church retained only 14 per cent of existing primary schools (in 1906–7) and all its establishments, primary and secondary alike, had to be fee-paying. Apart from the religious issue, the main concern of educational policy under the Third Republic was for numerical growth and institutional adaptation within the Napoleonic framework.

Primary education

Throughout the century there had been evidence of a growing desire for instruction, witnessed by the spectacular development of adult education. The increase in school attendance predated the institution of compulsory and free primary education under the legislation introduced by Jules Ferry as Minister of Public Instruction in 1880. In a country that was still predominantly agrarian, this provision was particularly important for the rural areas, which had lagged behind the towns with regard to schooling. While it was gradually made universal, primary education remained detached from secondary but became more complex to meet the dual demands of increasing industrialization and growing parental aspirations. Thus it collected a series of additional courses, largely vocational in content, each regarded as terminal and leading to gainful employment rather than formal study. Simultaneously the higher-grade schools broadened their curricula to include more modern subjects, in sharp contrast with the classicism of secondary establishments. While these remained terminal for most pupils, they came to supply some candidates for primary teacher training institutions. It is indicative of the isolation of primary instruction that its teachers should have been recruited from those who had no secondary education themselves. While additional courses and higher-grade schools offered a modern and popular alternative to the classicism of the bourgeois *lycées*, the development of technical schools and centres of apprenticeship provided training facilities for future foremen, skilled workers and craftsmen. By 1919 it had become compulsory for primary school leavers to receive some form of vocational training until the age of eighteen. This growing differentiation within primary education mirrored the differentiation of the working class resulting from a more complex division of labour in industrial society. It did not, and was not intended to promote mobility from class to class, it merely diversified employment prospects for the working class.

Secondary education

Secondary curricula were intended to offer a preparation for higher education and the professions, and were therefore predominantly classical in content. Demands for the incorporation of modern subjects, the sciences and European languages were in direct contradiction to the traditional structure of the *baccalauréat*. They met with considerable resistance from the supporters of a purely classical definition of culture. The addition of modern subjects was construed as a move away from the cultural role of education towards vocationalism. In this debate culture was seen as totally opposed to specialization: it was in fact defined residually as 'that which remains when all else has been forgotten'. This traditional approach was symbolized by the concentration on classical languages in the *baccalauréat* which was not modernized until 1902. From that date onwards, and as a result of parental pressures for a more practical curriculum, an alternative curriculum was introduced alongside the classical. Pupils could either opt for the classical or for the modern section, each of them leading up to a different *baccalauréat*. However, classicism retained its prestige and the best pupils were systematically channelled into the classical stream. Thus the direct connection established under Napoleon between classical studies and administrative or professional careers remained unbroken. The new modern stream reflected the growing demands of industry and commerce, which had grown in economic importance rather than in social prestige.

Higher education

Higher education within the Imperial University was designed to staff the two major professions of the time – the medical and the legal. The appropriate training was dispensed by Faculties of Medicine and of Law, which were self-contained establishments. On the other hand, the Faculties of Letters and of Sciences were mainly degree-granting bodies, which organized examinations, but did not have any permanent students. The main occupation of the professors was the organization and adjudication of the *baccalauréat*. Since future lawyers and physicians were trainees rather than students, the concept of student was unknown in France until 1877 and the few lectures given were addressed to the general public. The reform of 1877 was intended to turn the faculties into teaching bodies by increasing their staff and by creating State studentships. As a result, higher education experienced an enormous expansion, doubling its intake between 1875 (9963 students) and 1891 (19,281) and doubling yet again between 1891 and 1908 (38,890). However, this numerical increase tended to be concentrated in Paris (52 per cent of students in 1888). To offset this excessive centralization, which favoured Paris residents and was detrimental to provincial interests, a policy of founding regional universities was put forward in the 1880s. This aimed at the creation of true universities, teaching a wide range of subjects and grouping many students, rather than mere collections of isolated faculties. In other words, there was a protest against the Napoleonic structure with its rigid centralization and is narrow definition of higher education. The policy proposed was to extend the range of subjects in order to include the new sciences and to incorporate the neglected specialisms, such as archaeology or modern history. All disciplines were to be taught under the same roof. These pleas for reform failed, as the law of 1896 merely conferred the title of 'university' upon groups of faculties existing in the same town, but did not amalgamate them into unitary bodies. Even if there were only two faculties in any one town, they were officially turned into a university, though neither their intake nor their courses changed. As a result, fifteen universities came into being, but their component faculties remained unaltered under this new name. Thus the law of 1896, generally considered as founding universities in France, actually destroyed the hopes of breaking away from the Napoleonic tradition.

The twentieth century

Plans for reform

Twentieth-century France inherited the Napoleonic educational system, virtually unchanged and characterized by the strict separation of primary and secondary schooling. This dichotomy firmly distinguished the bourgeoisie from the working class and the peasantry. As universal primary education threatened this distinction, the bourgeoisie strove to protect their privileged access to the *lycée* by sending their children to junior forms within the *lycée (classes élémentaires)*, which were fee-paying when primary education had become free. The efficacy of this practice as a guarantee of admission to secondary education is illustrated by the numerical growth in the number of *lycée* junior pupils: from 16,000 boys in 1881 to 55,000 in 1940. Additional obstacles debarred working-class children from entry into secondary education – the length of the course that led up to the *baccalauréat* after seven years' study, the fees payable during this period which were not completely covered by the grants available, the small number of these scholarships and the preference given to children of minor civil servants in their distribution (in 1911, 51 per cent of grants were awarded to children of civil servants and only 20 per cent to children of peasants, artisans and workers). The increase in popular demand for education was not met by an expansion of existing facilities at secondary level nor by a widening of recruitment. Therefore, it was the higher grade schools that absorbed the mass of pupils from primary school. This is evidenced by the fact that their intake in 1914 exceeded that of secondary establishments.

While in the nineteenth century it could be argued that the division into primary and secondary reflected the social structure of a predominantly agricultural country, the growth of the middle classes made this argument invalid in the twentieth. Nor could it be maintained that the adjustments whereby the primary system had developed its upper forms and the secondary its lower forms had made education more democratic. They had merely resulted in heightening class distinctions by inculcating two different cultures – excessive classicism among secondary pupils and extreme vocationalism among primary pupils. It is on these grounds that a reform movement advocating the integration of primary and secondary into an *école unique* was formed at the end of the First World War. Throughout the period between the two wars the debate about this reform was interrupted and largely unsuccessful. Indeed, while secondary establishments became free in 1928, they retained their traditional curricula and their social bias.

The main blueprint for the *école unique* was produced by Jean Zay as Minister of Education in 1937. With its stress on equalizing educational opportunities and its acceptance of a universal right to secondary education, it is reminiscent of the revolutionary philosophy and stands in sharp distinction to the Napoleonic tradition. Zay advocated the creation of a middle school (*tronc commun*), which all pupils would attend between receiving primary instruction (common to all) and entering secondary schooling. The former courses of the *lycées* and of the higher grade schools would be integrated into a new secondary, divided into three branches of study: classical, modern and technical. The middle school would be concerned with guiding pupils to the appropriate stream of secondary studies according to their ability and interests. This proposal met with strong resistance, particularly from the unions of *lycée* teachers, and was only introduced in some establishments on an experimental basis. The war in 1939 and the collapse of the Third Republic prevented further debate on educational reform. After the interlude of the Vichy regime (which was strongly conservative in educational matters) the Fourth Republic was again faced with the issues that the Third had failed to solve. In 1947 the Langevin-Wallon plan, differing only in details from Zay's blueprint, was successfully resisted by the educationists' lobby. A similar fate was suffered by the Billères plan in 1957. Thus at the beginning of the Fifth

Republic the dichotomy between primary and secondary remained almost intact.

The problem of democratization had not been solved: the main reason for this is instructive as it also accounts for failure to deal with the equally pressing issues of modernization and secularization during the same period. The answer lies in the fragmented nature of the political parties, and underlying this the cleavages dividing French society. In the first half of the twentieth century the political arithmetic of the multi-party system added up to Centre government – the alternation of power between Centre-Right and Centre-Left coalitions. Because of this, political policy was reduced to the minimum programme which the governing coalition could agree to endorse, and legislation was restricted to the even more limited measures for which parliamentary support could be marshalled. This situation, commonly described as political *immobilisme*, largely explains the long drawn out war of projects over the *école unique*, which remained unresolved at the end of the Fourth Republic. In addition, however, the failure of the Left to hold together as a political force and to steer through the legislation sought by those it represented must also be held partly responsible.

The second aspect of the twentieth-century inheritance was the inability of educational institutions to satisfy demands for modern professional training, especially for the lower levels of industry, agriculture and commerce. 'Former le producteur, l'enseignement français y répugne. Son rationalisme tourne à l'intellectualisme.' This judgement of Prost's was particularly true in the field of technical and applied instruction at all levels. Certainly the Astier law of 1919 began to tackle the problem of producing a skilled workforce by founding part-time schools and making it obligatory for municipalities to run them, employers to release their apprentices, and working youths under eighteen to attend. Its provisions initially implied decentralization, for such schools were to be controlled by the Ministry of Commerce, organized by local commissions, and financed by a tax on employers. However, in the following years they were reintegrated with the Ministry of Education and its successive directors steadily developed their general educational content at the expense of vocational specialization. As irrelevance increased so did evasion by apprentices and employers, such that by the outbreak of war apprenticeship training was still grossly deficient in quantitative and qualitative terms.

This tendency for specialized and practical training to be displaced by general education was even more marked at higher levels of technical instruction. There the creation of a series of national technical qualifications, each conferring rights to further education, resulted in uniformity rather than the diversity of skills required to match the occupational market. In particular the establishment of a *baccalauréat technique* in 1946 exerted a powerful downward influence, standardizing curricula in the upper reaches of the primary schools, the appropriate sections of secondary establishments, and the *écoles nationales professionnelles*. In one way it might seem that this recognition signalled a breakthrough in modernization (for it meant a complete hierarchy of technical studies), but in the absence of decisive legislation establishing self-standing institutions free to develop their own approach, technical education was caught up in the traditional system and loss of specialization, diversity and practical relevance were the prices paid.

Thirdly, the anti-clerical policy in education, pursued at the beginning of the century, by no means spelt a general consensus on the secular nature of public instruction. Independent Catholic schools continued to attract a substantial number of pupils, although they were facing economic difficulties in their competition with the public sector. After the First World War this led protagonists of the confessional schools to launch a political campaign for governmental funding in proportion to their pupil intake. This particular formula was never successful, due to strong Republican opposition, but after the introduction of free public secondary instruction the economic plight of the confessional schools progressively worsened and with it grew a determination to wrest support from the State in one form or another. Obviously this depended on a government favourably disposed to the Catholic educational cause, and it was not until the early fifties that the clerical issue could be politically reanimated. When, despite the vociferousness of its opponents, a law was passed in 1951 permitting State allocations towards teachers' salaries and buildings in the private sector, an MRP Deputy described this as the 'breach through which the flood will pass'. In other words the Catholic Parliamentary Association signalled its intention of achieving a much more far-reaching settlement than the politics of immobilism had allowed.

The Fifth Republic

While the powers of educational control remain concentrated at the centre, this is the source of change, whether such transformations are initiated by political negotiation or induced by political disruption. Both processes were important under the Fifth Republic and their causes and consequences are closely intertwined. The first major reforms dealing with the problems of desecularization, democratization and modernization were directed by the government in a spirit of educational pragmatism. The situations it faced were inherited from the immobilism of the Fourth Republic and the dissatisfaction which had accumulated around these three issues. The Debré, Berthoin and Fouchet measures can all be looked upon in the same light, as piecemeal changes and pragmatic concessions intended to take the edge off discontent – giving away a little in order to conserve a great deal. As such these reforms tinkered *à la marge* rather than indicating a willingness to engage in large-scale structural change or devolution of educational control. Public education remained, in the words of the then Education Minister, Christian Fouchet, 'the biggest enterprise in the world apart from the Red Army' and was just about as responsive to the expression of social interests and local demands. In turn this rigidity was partly responsible for the outbursts in May 1968.

Clericalism

The Debré law of 1959, giving State aid to private and mainly confessional schools, was justified by specific reference to the 'indispensable unity' of national education. This concession to Catholic supporters of government, which involved overriding the opinions of the vast majority of teachers' associations and trade unions, offered private schools one of four solutions to their financial difficulties – total integration with public education – a contract of association – a simpler contract – or the maintenance of the *status quo*. The first and last formulae were only used in a minority of cases, and by 1967–8 over 85 per cent of private primary and secondary schools were under one kind of contractual arrangement or the other. Both mean that the State aids such schools and pays teachers providing that, whilst conserving their 'own character', each school teaches 'with complete respect for liberty of conscience' and conforms to certain requirements about numbers of pupils, qualifications of teachers and standards of the physical environment. With the full contract all expenses are undertaken by the State at the cost of a serious loss of autonomy, for the school also becomes subject to the rules and programmes governing public education. The simple contract which provided for less aid, but less State control, was intended, however, only to be a temporary formula. Integration, loss of autonomy and standardization are all implicit in the *Loi Debré*. Its implementation leads one to wonder whether national education has not lost one of its few sources of diversity for it is difficult to see how such schools could preserve much of their 'own character' when forced to conform closely to public educational practices. De Gaulle had made the passing of this bill a matter of confidence (a sign that the new style of government was asserting itself in educational politics), and he secured his majority. What this Act did not do, however, was to solve the clerical question in education. For the Church had lost in freedom what it had gained in funding, while defenders of *l'école laïque* were outraged at this manipulation of constitutional and governmental powers and organized massive demonstrations in favour of a single secular system of instruction. Significantly perhaps, these began in earnest in 1967, since a review of the Debré law was scheduled to start two years later.

Democratization

The Berthoin reform of 1959 came as an anticlimax after forty years of struggle to establish an *école unique*, and was intended to defuse and diffuse the discontent which had build up over the repeated failures of this movement. It was imposed imperatively by decree whilst de Gaulle still possessed the special powers granted to him before the new National Assembly had met. This compromise measure thus stemmed directly from the presidency without there being opportunity for parliamentary intervention or modification.

A cycle of observation starting at the age of eleven and lasting for two years was introduced for all pupils. At the end of their elementary studies pupils could continue at primary school, attend a *collège d'enseignement général* (CEG was the new name for the old *cours complémentaires*), or enter a *lycée*. Officially this 'placement' (affected either by teachers' recommendations, parental preference, or simply by pupils staying where they were) was not viewed as decisive, for after two years of observation pupils would be orientated to the appropriate secondary course. In other words the observation cycle took place in different kinds of establishments, much to the satisfaction of the *professeurs* who had always opposed the idea of autonomous middle school for all. Moreover, the content of this cycle was not the same for all, for it was made up of the normal programmes followed in the sixth and fifth class in these different kinds of institutions. The notion of a lengthy *tronc commun* followed by all pupils and used to establish the pattern of ability of individuals, was reduced to a single term during which syllabuses were 'harmonized' in different kinds of schools.

At the end of the cycle, the *conseil d'orientation* in each school advised parents on appropriate further studies. *Classes passerelles* situated in the fourth class provided conversion courses for those who had taken the wrong turning during the orientation phase. However since assessments were made in establishments varying from the *lycée* to the primary school, and moreover were made on the basis of their respective curricula, it is not surprising that this resulted in very little individual mobility – only 1 per cent of pupils transferred from the latter to the former.

In respecting the vested interests of different groups of teachers, the compromise reform had left existing structures intact, but in doing so it had merely perpetuated these interests and the activities associated with their defence. Devices like the harmonization of curricula and the *classes passerelles* had certainly linked different parts of the system, but without providing the vast majority of pupils with more equality of educational opportunity. The dissatisfaction manifested by the primary and technical teachers, trade unions and political Left indicated that this decree was not the final solution to grievances which had rankled for half a century. Continued pressure from these quarters led the Minister to admit that the object of orientation was indeed defeated when it took place in different types of schools. Following this the *collèges d'enseignement secondaire* (CES) were founded in 1963. Theoretically they were to cater for the whole age group from eleven to fourteen, thus functioning as common or comprehensive middle schools. Some pupils would proceed from the CES to secondary establishments, others to full-time vocational training and yet others to apprenticeship schemes.

However, they were to be formed by converting the first cycle of *lycée* studies into independent units and by transforming existing CEGs, but this was opposed by *professeurs* and municipalities alike. Had the reform engaged in audacious structural change and created a multilateral institution of a self-standing type, it would have overridden vested interests: as it was it placed itself at their mercy. On the one hand conversion of schools was resisted (there were only 220 schools of this type in 1964 and 1500 in 1968 with many still refusing to transform themselves in the 1970s). On the other hand the CES was made up of a classical and a modern section from secondary, a *moderne court* section from the CET, and the old *classe de fin d'études* from the primary school, yet professional resistance prevented fusion from taking place between them. The hope was that flexibility would replace separateness, to the benefit of all pupils, but this was not discernible outside a few pilot schools that had overridden the traditional curricula – inherited from the courses making up the CES. In sum the conversion modifying the Berthoin solution drew off little of the discontent stimulated by inequality of educational opportunity.

Modernization

The Fouchet reforms at secondary and higher level were a package of changes whose contents were intended to alleviate some very different kinds of discontent – that of students with the 50 per cent failure rate at the end of the first year (likened by a subsequent Minister of Education to organizing a shipwreck to find who could swim), of large employers with an encyclopaedic culture irrelevant to occupational needs, of staff at both levels with rising numbers and falling standards, and of the Left in general with its marked social discrimination. The same mechanism was adopted at secondary and higher levels and involved the differentiation of cycles of studies within them, giving a greater opportunity for vocational specialization. Simultaneously this was intended to satisfy students (by giving greater choice, better orientation and thus a lower failure rate), to produce school leavers and graduates better suited to occupational outlets, and to have a democratic appeal because it established shorter courses for those whose cultural or financial background had previously excluded them altogether. At university level the complementary reforms were mainly intended to obviate the disadvantages inherent in lack of pre-entry selection, for all holders of the *baccalauréat* had an automatic right of admission to higher education, without further test. Faculties of Letters and Science were reorganized by creating three cycles, the first one to provide the basic knowledge required to bring entrants up to university standard. This lasted two years and students chose a particular branch of study within each faculty, which led to a diploma. Specialization became more intense in the second cycle, where after one year (that is, three years of undergraduate study in all) the *licence* could be gained, or after two years (four in all), students could obtain the masters degree. The third cycle represented the beginning of post-graduate study.

In accordance with the philosophy of 'short' alternatives, a two year course for the training of *cadres* (at supervisory and lower managerial level) was given at new institutions, *instituts universitaires de technologie*, created alongside the university faculties. Staff were to be recruited partly from

university teachers and partly from among specialists working
in nationalized industries or private enterprises. The subjects
taught were to be selected for their vocational value, assessed
in the light of current economic needs, and teaching methods
were to concentrate on practical projects in fields such as civil
engineering, electronics, information processing and statistics.

These reforms were applied identically in all institutions,
including the new universities created to cope with overcrowd-
ing. Even in broad technocratic terms they were less than
successful, to judge from the divergence between the proportions intended to follow science and technology courses under
the national plan and the much lower percentage of students
enrolling in them. Not only did this spell manpower defici-
encies *vis-à-vis* the economy, but also the continued growth
of a body of pupils and students without clear vocational
expectations or opportunities. In addition, the chaotic application of the laws (more than 2000 decrees were involved)
placed many students in an anomalous position because of
these constant changes and heightened the awareness of many
staff to continuous ministerial interference. Finally the Left
was not impressed by the democratic intentions of a reform
which created an inferior opportunity structure for the non-
privileged by consistently directing them towards the shorter
alternatives, at all levels of instruction. Clearly many of the
demands the reforms sought to assuage were mutually contra-
dictory, but it is precisely because of this that any attempt to
impose a uniform solution common to all schools and universities was bound to satisfy no one. Only a strategy which
showed a willingness to sacrifice some control and allow some
institutional autonomy, so that truly differentiated establishments could provide specialist services, could hope to satisfy
conflicting demands simultaneously.

Groups inside and outside the system publicly registered
their dissatisfaction with the educational policies of the Fifth
Republic. The Caen colloquium of university teachers meeting
in 1966 rejected the Napoleonic concept of a single national
structure, with identical regional establishments, as more
suitable for the post office or police than for education. Instead
they sought the creation of diversified universities, autonomous in policy and administration, and for which the ministry

would merely ensure adequate financing, equipment and staffing. Such universities would develop their own courses, curricula and examinations. The same demand for decentralization and the same condemnation of uniformity was issued in connection with secondary education at the Amiens colloquium, only two months before the May Events. But confronted with the highly controlled system there was little teachers could do at any level to introduce changes internally and thus to alter the nature of instruction from within. Given this position of powerlessness, the reactions of the teaching profession took two different forms.

Cut off from playing a constructive role in educational administration, or being able to respond directly to pupil requests or community requirements, much of the profession turned in upon itself and pursued an academic traditionalism which was not politically contentious. The cumulative effect of this reaction was to increase the gap between the nature of education and the facts of active life. In particular many teachers at secondary and higher level worked at reproducing themselves in their pupils and at reinforcing a *subject*-based organization of knowledge. For students the effect was to separate their present studies from any future relevance: for employers it was to deprive them of school leavers or graduates whose knowledge was organized on a *professional* basis. In his brilliant analysis, Pierre Bourdieu sums up the irrational situation which resulted as one where all were treated 'as apprentice professors and not as professional apprentices'.

At the same time, however, a different section of teachers turned to political action as a means of introducing change and pursued this end in conjunction with their professional associations, the trade unions and the left-wing parties. In 1967 the Communist Party published an issue of *l'Ecole et la Nation*, condemning Gaullist reforms as mere shunting operations, the *instituteurs'* syndicate passed a motion at its September congress condemning government policy, and in November students went on strike at Nanterre over application of the Fouchet reforms. This signalled the growth of frustration shared by certain parties, students and sections of the profession. However, it did not indicate the emergence of united action. Although teachers themselves had some unity within their professional federations, many teachers in turn were also members of the broader unions, the CGT and the CFDT, which were not themselves on good terms. Furthermore many university teachers and students looked to the parties and factions of the extreme Left which were viewed with the utmost suspicion by both the CGT and the Communist Party. Given that none of these groups, organizations or parties was in a strong enough political position peacefully to negotiate educational changes with the Gaullist majority government, the steady accumulation of grievances finally exploded into direct action – the May Events. However, their internal divisions prevented them from forming other than temporary alliances, cemented by the euphoria of revolt, but never holding together for long enough to consolidate real educational gains.

The May Events of 1968 and their aftermath

A vast amount has been written about the course of the Events and the explanations advanced have been almost as numerous. These range from various kinds of conspiracy theory, through the official chain-reaction account (endorsed by government and Communist Party alike) which interpreted the revolt as a fortuitous series of episodes tenuously linked by accident and opportunism, to explanations couched in terms of a new form of class conflict. There is not the space to assess such theories here, but the most tenable general explanation is that the events were the explosion of a number of grievances which had accumulated over the decade, as political closure replaced political immobility. More specifically, as an educational revolt, the Events appear to have represented a massive condemnation of the mania for centralization and a movement for educational autonomy and localized diversity, contrary to the revolutionary, monarchical and Republican traditions alike. It now remains to be seen how far the reforms introduced in 1968 and after reflected a willingness to concede to these demands in order to solve the crisis.

What was significant about the 1968 reform was that it set a new pattern which was consistently repeated throughout the remaining Gaullist and Giscardian periods. In the first Gaullist decade the policy had been to take the edge off discontent by scattering a few crumbs to the most persistent clamourers: the second decade opened with the realization that much greater concessions were essential to stem the rising tide of grievances. The new formula basically consisted in conceding various types of educational democratization in order to conserve the instrumentality of education to the policy. As such it represented a revised version of the Napoleonic credo, namely, 'let the people's rights to instruction not infringe upon State educational needs'. This was embodied in the *Loi d'orientation de l'enseignement supérieur* and in subsequent measures dealing with lower levels. The new principle was also to be accompanied by a distinctive method of policy implementation; generous reformism in the initial legislation followed by administrative reneging on the more radical clauses.

Higher education

The *Loi d'orientation de l'enseignement superiéur* was a typical piece of panic legislation, adopted in the National Assembly by 441 votes to none, the Communists and six Gaullists abstaining. The major political parties had restricted themselves to textual criticism and minor amendments, the whole tenor of the debate being summed up by one Deputy who commended Edgar Faure's text for having the merit of existing. The parties of the Left no less than those of the Right had an interest in defusing the educational problem. In the face of virtual parliamentary unanimity on the bill, the teachers' associations and student groups were all hopelessly divided. Thus no concerted extra-parliamentary opposition impeded either the passing or the implementation of the Act.

It was adopted in November 1968 and appeared to break away from the Napoleonic *Université* in each of the three main principles it endorsed: multi-disciplinary study, participation and autonomy. The break, however, was more moderate than it appeared since pluri-disciplinarity concealed an official concern for increased vocationalism, whilst the extent of participation and autonomy which were granted did not seriously undermine central control.

Officially *autonomy* was substantially increased. The basic unit on which the whole system of higher education was to be founded was the university and not the *Université*. Each university was to become an autonomous establishment from the financial point of view and to be free to draw up its own statutes. In the past the major limitation on academic freedom derived from the existence of national degrees and diplomas which meant that the corresponding courses were based on ministerial regulations. The new universities were now free to issue their own certificates, but even the most extreme opponents of centralization have been unwilling to relinquish the State–guaranteed qualifications which future employers still seek. Moreover the scope for experimenting with new curricula remained restricted since all universities were constrained to recognize each other's programme. Experiments with specialist subjects and approaches were largely confined to the second and third cycles and to certain isolated institutions. Furthermore the experimental excesses taking place in one or two establishments, which exploited their formal rights to the full, were counter-productive in convincing many that the only defence of academic standards lay in clinging to traditionalism. In addition a later provision that funding should be allocated according to the types and quality of courses offered was a major central infringement of institutional autonomy and the capacity for pedagogic innovation.

As far as *participation* was concerned the parity between staff and students, promised after the May Events, was in fact reduced to a maximum of one-third for students because of the distinction made between university teachers in terms of seniority. Furthermore the limitations imposed on participation were broad and excluded such areas as curricula and course design, the allocation of credits, the testing of aptitude and knowledge, the recruitment and promotion of staff and all matters of selection. Thus this legal hedging contrasted sharply with the initial statements about equal shares in university management. In consequence the French Union of Students advised UNEF members against voting in the first university elections and student voting rates have since dropped lower still. Limited participation was not perceived as genuine power-sharing and the students accordingly resented their assigned role of *électeurs mineurs*.

The first responsibility of the council elected in the 630 teaching and research units, set up to replace the former faculties, was to meet with those of other units with which the creation of a university was contemplated. Through this cumbersome procedure, which appeared to bow to the spirit of May – the initiation of reforms from the grass-roots in contrast to the centralized tradition of making decisions at the top and transmitting them downwards – *multi-disciplinarity* was to emerge. As a radical principle of reorganization, a break with the antiquated faculty structure which no longer matched the diversified occupational structure, its implicit vocational drive was diluted and distorted from the start by academic traditionalism. Article 6 of the law mentioned the desirability of an interpenetration between Arts-Letters and Science-Technology as well as within them, whilst recognizing the possibility of 'universities with a dominant vocation', that is, grouping related to specialisms. This was already tantamount to admitting that pluri-disciplinary study was a utopian ideal given academic entrenchment in traditionally defined subject areas.

To begin with a number of faculties survived in disguise by constituting themselves into the new units for teaching and research. In larger towns, greater student numbers forced a split into several units per faculty, but few original regroupings of subject matter within each unit were actually adopted. Almost everywhere, after less conventional proposals were put forward and then rejected by a majority, it was the solution most akin to traditional habits which was re-endorsed, the sub-division by subjects. For example, Faculties of Science turned themselves into units of physics, chemistry, maths and natural science. In other words a vertical division along the lines of the major courses taught in the past was the dominant pattern to emerge, rather than any radical reorganization of different knowledge systems in relation to one another.

When the units then had to engage in recombination, most played safe by avoiding co-operation with those which were unfamiliar, competetive or politically uncongenial. Thus 'compromising' entanglements were shunned and in the process few experimental combinations emerged. Most pure scientists found the social sciences too politicized for comfort, as did lawyers, and the former association between letters and social science within the old Faculties of Letters tended to endure in the new universities. The Faculties of Science and Medicine, well endowed with research facilities, did not like to merge with poorer specialisms for fear of having to share resources. Add to this the fact that partnerships were often based on shared political attitudes rather than intellectual complementarity (for example, the 'marriage of reason' between medicine and law) and we can see the types of motives which gave shape to multi-disciplinarity in practice.

The resulting mishmash of some seventy universities was a far cry from both the academic flexibility overtly demanded by the students during the May Events and the vocational orientation covertly sought by the government. The failure of the May Events to introduce radical educational change through direct action caused the membership of many participant organizations to shrink. This was particularly true of the Students' Union (UNEF), which collapsed into a number of factions, and meant that just as the legal influence of students in university administration was recognized, their disorganization made them completely ineffectual. Equally their factionalism and extremism cut the students' links with other educational interest groups, including the trade unions, and thus the possibility of aggregating educational grievances and pressurizing government was lost. To this extent the aftermath of the Events defused extra-parliamentary opposition. On the other hand, although the reform gave the Government an interval of relative peace it brought it no closer to its goal of a modernized higher education, harnessed to the mixed economy.

In sum the reform had generated institutional variegation rather than functional diversification. At the same time it had introduced changes in the decision-making processes within the universities without entailing a fundamental redistribution of authority between central government and higher education. In the next decade the official aim was to increase the functionality of education through the continued use of these central powers. Policy in the 1970s represented an increasingly conservative interpretation of the reform. The aims were to reduce the threat of autonomy associated with differentiation, by controlling politically sensitive aspects of university development and to make servicing the economy the prime aim of academic specialization.

Given the saturation of the public sector labour market (plus its preference for the products of the *grandes écoles* rather than the universities) and the endurance of non-selective entry to university (the traditional rights of the *bacheliers* had been protected during the reform), it was clear to the government that more graduates would have to be absorbed by the private sector. Yet it was equally obvious to the central authority that private enterprise was unenthusiastic about graduate employment: while the private sector employed three-quarters of the active population in 1970, it recruited less than a quarter of that year's graduates, preferring those with non-university diplomas. If opposition to selection for university entry prevailed then the projection was that private industry would have to absorb two-thirds of graduates. Attempts were thus made to articulate university outputs with occupational outlets.

The vehicle for the professionalization of the universities was the violently contested reform of 1976 which sought to transform the *licence* and *maîtrise* degrees into self-contained, one-year vocational programmes. Universities were instructed to evaluate their existing courses, eliminating those without occupational outlets and redeploying their resources to create new vocationally relevant courses. Proposed programmes would then be reviewed by 'technical study groups', with representatives from the appropriate vocational area, to estimate market demand for them before final authorization was given by the new Secretariat for Higher Education. This authorization process represented increased power for the central authority and a further clawing-back of autonomy from the universities. Official approval meant that a university could offer a course as a national degree for five years, after which renewed authorization was needed; unapproved degrees, whilst permissible, would lack national recognition.

The response was the largest protest since 1968 and most universities were closed for several months. On the one hand the students objected to their studies being limited to vocational and terminal courses as well as to 'handing over the university to the service of capitalism'. On the other hand the faculty abhorred this new infringement of academic freedom in which curricula assessment was in terms of marketability, and their unions tenaciously defended existing courses. Thus academic traditionalism and student radicalism joined forces to repulse this renewed central incursion and hostilities intensified between the Secretariat and the universities.

Although these reforms became law in 1977, the concessions wrested from the (now) Minister for Universities by internal opposition effectively nullified the professionalization of the universities. In particular, the centrally organized unions of teachers and students, which counter-balance ministerial control, precluded the direct manipulation of individual universities by the central authority. These oppositional forces extracted the crucial concession that automatic authorization would be granted to such existing programmes as gave fundamental training in a discipline. In turn this killed vocational reorganization for it left no redeployable funds for the development of new practical courses. Equally importantly it compelled the Minister to re-endorse the principle of disinterested cultural study for the majority of students, which was precisely what the government had sought to make a minority affair.

Thus central attempts to rationalize the diversification conceded in 1968 have been wholly frustrated through internal counterpressures against professionalization – by the traditional vested interests of academics and the radical political opposition of students. But this stalemate has benefited neither side. Rationalization from the centre having failed, some believe that the government then started to abandon the universities – witness a 20 per cent financial reduction in real terms since 1973; the reliance for its own recruitment on the *grandes écoles*; and changes like selection for medical degrees and the reform of teacher training when the polity did seek specific university outputs. Talk of abandonment is too strong – at the end of the Giscardian period the government was still supporting a vast enterprise which in its view was instrumental to neither the public nor the private sector. Yet the universities themselves had not benefited from their opposition: the devaluation of degrees continues through over-production in relation to job opportunities, the divorce between studies and active life is perpetuated, and the social advancement of university students is enfeebled as the élite *grandes écoles* have reinforced their superior standing.

Primary and secondary education

In broad terms the same pattern of legislative reform followed by administrative retreat also characterized lower levels of education. The trade-off between concessions towards democratization, to pacify the Left, and vocationally-orientated diversification, to satisfy the Right, was even more striking. The course of reform can be divided into three main phases – first a series of Gaullist changes in which technocratic concerns outweighed democratic concessions; second the official recognition, contained in the Haby reform, that these priorities had to be reversed in the face of parental, pedagogic and political pressures; and finally the Giscardian implementation of these new provisions during which vocational relevance regained priority over equality of opportunity.

(i) In the aftermath of the May Events de Gaulle had also contemplated a *Loi d'orientation de l'enseignement secondaire* to introduce selective university entry among holders of the *baccalauréat*. To the Right, the termination of the historic open-door policy would have reduced the numbers in higher education, increased the standards of those graduating in the new specialisms, and improved the employability of those for whom the *baccalauréat* was terminal. At the time organized public opinion was so hostile to the un-democratic implication of selection that this policy was dropped in favour of reforming the examination itself – on vocational lines.

Consequently, in 1969, the last years of the *lycée* were transformed into specialized sections leading to different kinds of *baccalauréats*, defined with reference to the modernizing economy. Thus sixteen technical examinations (for example in electronics, biochemistry, administration, management, or computer programming) were differentiated from twelve general ones and accorded parity with the latter. But parity involved the same automatic right of entry to university for its holders, so although the new technical options were attracting over a quarter of all candidates by 1976, this became an additional avenue to further education rather than a preparation for active life.

By 1973 the failure of this reform to attain its technocratic aims was accepted and Joseph Fontanet, then Minister of Education, attempted a further trade-off, this time within secondary education itself. In basic terms his plan entailed grading the *baccalauréat* into a 'good' pass (giving university entry) and a 'straight' pass (giving admission to vocational training centres): to propitiate left-wing opinion the Minister proposed stepping-up democratization at the *start* of secondary studies. Here the three parallel tracks, which had largely confirmed pupils' social origins, would be replaced by ability grouping, supplementary teaching for the disadvantaged, and mixed-ability work in some subjects to reinforce the democratic principle. However what the government had seen as a concession to left-wing and pedagogic egalitarianism was received as precisely the opposite – instead, ability-grouping would merely accentuate differences in social background. The intensity of criticism meant that these proposals were never implemented, but the fact that a reform of the lower levels had officially been mooted then fuelled demand for their complete transformation on egalitarian lines. Thus not only had the policy of intensifying vocationalism in the *lycée* failed, it had backfired by stimulating pressures for a genuine democratic reform of the secondary level in its entirety – to which the government had to bow.

(ii) In this context, the Act of 1975, initiated by the new Minister René Haby (a former *recteur*) did not represent an official conversion to educational equality but rather the political realization that further democratization was the price of national unity – essential for the development of the technocratic society.

Haby's own proposals sought to cut through the tangle of past compromises which, without significantly improving the equality of educational opportunity, had merely cluttered the interface between the primary and secondary levels. His major reform was to install a common middle school (*collège unique*) which, as an independent institution for all pupils, would place the 'same opportunities in every satchel'. Nor, initially were the proposals to be limited to streamlining the secondary level, but also included reforms of nursery, primary, technical and 'long' *lycée* instruction.

Passage into the *collège unique* would be monitored by teachers, parents, doctors and psychologists and based on an assessment of the mental age of each child. The middle school itself would have a common curriculum for its first two years, plus compensatory tuition designed to bring all up to roughly the same standard, even if this involved abridging the syllabus. Then in the last two years options would be selected in relation to individual aptitudes. Although some could leave early to receive special vocational training, most would gain the leaving certificate after the four years, or then proceed to an apprenticeship scheme or a *lycée*, guidance again being given by an advisory panel with parents having the right of appeal against its decision.

(iii) On the one hand the *collège unique* was not far removed from what the egalitarian *compagnons* had sought fifty years earlier, for the new plan embodied a *tronc commun*, *observation* and *orientation*. The new Act however, was not an unmitigated victory for the reformist tradition. For, on the other hand, these proposals which aimed at a full-scale trans-formation of the system suffered from the eternal bane of centralization – truncation in order to fit in with existing provisions or priorities, and standardization such that one universal 'model school' was centrally imposed throughout the nation. Truncation of scope affected both 'ends' of the proposals. The nursery provisions and the earlier start (at five years not six) remained unimplemented, undermining the notion of getting pupils off on a more even footing; so did reform of the *lycées* (now giving only the 'long' general or technical course) and of the *baccalauréat*. In practice the Haby reform was topped and tailed during implementation. The *collège unique* was inserted between the upper and lower levels and the fact that the *lycées* remained virtually unchanged meant that the spirit of the secondary school reform petered out carefully short of the universities. Once again, instead of the reform of the whole system, a reform had been fitted into the existing system.

The effects of the centralized introduction of the *collège unique* (which involved 11 decrees, 19 *arrêtés* and 20 circulars in the first two years) were immediately apparent in its uniformity. Indeed the very concession of a whole 10 per cent of the timetable, to be used at the teachers' discretion, highlighted this enduring feature of the French educational system. From the start the justification for imposing a standardized plan was, as ever, the goal of national unity, a theme which could always harmonize with egalitarianism if emphasis was placed on 'the same provisions for all citizens'. Gradually, however, the tune changed and more stress began to be laid on the Giscardian notion of citizenship for an advanced industrial society – witness the introduction of 'manual and technical training' as a new compulsory subject.

Moreover, the orchestration of change from the centre meant that the new Minister appointed in 1978, Christian Beullac, had the means to manoeuvre the reform into closer alignment with the economy whilst professing that he was simply continuing with its implementation. Consequently the innovation of *éducation concertée* in 1979 placed pupils taking the shorter secondary courses in industrial firms for probationary periods. This redirection not only tightened the links with industry but also served to conceal the failure of the existing reform to redistribute educational opportunities. By that time it was already known that after two years of post-primary instruction 30 per cent of pupils did not proceed along the common course but received pre-occupational tuition or were channelled into apprenticeship schemes. As such they nullified the notion of a common school, let alone equality of outcome. What *éducation concertée* did was to give a positive face to this failure in democratization by presenting the scheme as an opportunity for all rather than a device which served to confirm the restricted opportunities of the socially disadvantaged. The fact that educational change had been centrally engineered, rather than change spelling decentralized powers of control, meant once again that a new governing élite could make it reverberate to its current political philosophy.

Conclusion

The advent of Socialism

Throughout the twentieth century those seeking greater equality in education (the unions, primary teachers, students and political parties of the Left) recognized that its attainment depended upon a change of government, away from the Right or the Centre-Right. During their long sojourns in the political wilderness the tenuous left-wing coalitions shared a common educational cause and elaborated detailed programmes of reform. However, their brief periods of office (in the 1920s and 1930s) were taken-up with economic disputes which prevented the delivery of educational promises. Throughout the *longue durée* of Gaullism, these groups still pinned their educational hopes on an electoral victory for the Left. Given the centralized nature of the educational system and the failure of direct action in May 1968, there was no other means through which they could introduce significant changes in education. When the Socialists assumed office in 1981 the new government became the focus of half a century's frustrated aspirations for educational reform.

Mitterrand immediately stated that his aim was for 'national education as a great secular and unified public service', but one which should be developed by persuasion not constraint and involve 'ni spoliation ni monopole'. This method has been adhered to and the Minister for Education, Alain Savary, devoted the first year to reflection – to listening rather than to legislating. Commissions were set up to investigate different levels of instruction, types of institution and personnel. After receiving delegations, each commission presented a report on the basis of which the Minister was to draft proposals for parliamentary consideration. By now most reports are complete, ministerial reactions are slowly emerging, but legislative change still lies in the future. However, since methods of policy-making affect the nature of policies themselves, this procedure of consultation and conciliation does not seem to herald thorough-going or visionary reform. Nevertheless, only one thing is certain, that neither dramatic nor radical transformation of the educational system has been – or is on the point of being – introduced by the new government. Once again education is not a top political priority.

To assess the probable direction of change involves reading between the lines of the Minister's responses in two different ways – examining specific reactions to reports on given problems and then trying to detect common underlying themes, an exercise which is extremely tentative. In specific areas the following policies appear to be crystallizing:

i) *Private schools* (now mainly Catholic and enrolling 16 per cent of all pupils) will not be abolished nor will State aid to them be withdrawn. The first year of Socialist government did not celebrate the centenary of the Ferry reform by consolidating a universal *école laïque*. Instead the official response stressed tolerance and a respect for pluralism. The likelihood is that the contract of association will be universalized (probably with increased State control over outputs and growing municipal discretion over local relations between the two sectors), rather than a full contract of integration being introduced, assimilating private to public instruction.

ii) In the public sector itself the commissions have concentrated on the upper reaches and a common theme emerges in relation to the *lycées* and higher education. The main aim is to destroy the closed status of the *lycées*, through demolishing the wall between 'training' and 'study' and through creating new channels (*passerelles*) to 'long' secondary courses. Thus, for example, in the 'professional' *lycées* (equalling half the total) credits for periods of placement in various enterprises will be combined with academic modules. This notion of accumulated credits is also intended to remove the 'diploma guillotine', for even the incomplete diploma will give its holder *'unités capitalisables'* on the job market whilst he or she will later be able to add the credits needed for the award of the full diploma.

iii) Legislative reform is most advanced for the universities and the same theme reappears – democratization is to procede hand in hand with more vocationalism. The principle of democratization will entail accepting increased student numbers, retaining unselective entry and probably awarding more grants. The vocational principle will involve periods of practical placement, a professional rather than an academic definition of instruction, and more courses geared to careers. The basic plan appears to comprise a foundation year, devoted to orientation, followed by a second year which can be a self-contained and certificated form of professional training, or may then lead on to long forms of training, which again would be complete.

iv) The *grandes écoles* do not seem in danger of extinction. At most these specialist, competitive and élitist institutions (and their preparatory classes) will become more closely integrated with the universities, probably through the development of *passerelles* between them. Here the aim seems to be to *unifier sans uniformiser*, to integrate them without destroying their diversity, and to democratize their intake without damaging the employability of their outputs.

v) The *teaching profession* and its past alienation from the central authority is of prime concern to the Socialists. They are trying to resurrect a working partnership between the government and the profession and to weld all teachers into an integrated body, less divided by sectional interests. Unification of the profession (with its six major categories, differentiated by qualifications, pay, functions and workload) necessarily means uniting the existing body of teachers, for new entrants were less than 3 per cent of the whole in 1981. Hence Mitterrand was quick to promise continuous training for all and it appears that this may eventually enable the *instituteur* to advance to a *lycée* post. Again many favour the formula of acquiring 'capitalizable units', of a more advanced academic nature, in the course of a teaching career as this would make promotion integral to the profession.

Perhaps, then, it is the Socialists' determination to pursue democratization and vocationalism in tandem which will constitute the major contrast with the Gaullist and Giscardian regimes, both of which consistently subordinated educational equality to educational instrumentality. Beyond this, however, there are few pointers to audacious reforms – the new joint goals seem about to be accomplished by *petits pas*, after consultation, concession and accommodation. The structure appears unlikely to undergo radical transformation: no familiar part of it is yet marked for extinction, no novel institutional innovation has yet been mooted.

180   *France today*

What the new government sets out to achieve it hopes actually to accomplish by making existing institutions work better, by building bridges between them, by placing flexible joints in what was once rigidly articulated. In this process it remains unclear whether the Socialists will resist the eternal temptation of maintaining the centralized structure of education in order to make it serve their own goals. Historically this has always been politically irresistible, but equally it has always proved socially defeating: education as an instrument which is supremely responsive to the polity is simultaneously a lumbering over-standardized machine, insensitive to regional, sectional or internal interests. If Socialism is to break with the Napoleonic structure it can only be by thorough decentralization: without this, new policies introduced in the traditional uniform manner will generate the time-honoured effect – a swelling reservoir of educational grievances threatening to break its political banks.

Bibliography

The books recommended below refer to the two parts of this chapter.

The historical background

Anderson, R.D., *Education in France 1848-1870*. Oxford, Clarendon Press, 1975. A detailed historical account with an extensive bibliography.

Prost, A., *L'Enseignement en France: 1800-1967*. Paris, Colin, 1968. Perhaps the best account existing to date of the historical changes in the French educational system; contains extracts from major reform bills and influential authors.

Vaughan, M. and Archer, M., *Social Conflict and Educational Change in England and France. 1789-1848*. Cambridge University Press, 1971. A comparative sociological approach to educational development in the two countries.

The twentieth century

Archer, M.S. (ed.), *Students, University and Society*. London, Heinemann, 1972. Chapter 6 presents an analysis of the May Events.

Archer, M.S. *Social Origins of Educational Systems*. London, Sage, 1979. See in particular pp. 306-81 and pp. 639-69.

Bourdieu, P. and Passeron, J-C., *Les Héritiers, les étudiants et la culture*. Paris, Minuit, 1964. An extremely good summary of the influences of pupils' social origins on school and university entry, followed by an analysis of the student condition in the 1960s.

Fournier, J., *Politique de l'education*. Paris, Seuil, 1971. An excellent review of contemporary educational problems and their relationship to the political structure.

Fraser, W.R., *Reform and Restraint in French Education*. London, Routledge & Kegan Paul, 1971. An examination of the difficulties of introducing educational change in a highly centralized system.

Talbott, J.E., *The Politics of Educational Reform in France 1918-40*. Princeton University Press, 1969. The best account available in English of the *école unique* movement before the Second World War.

Seven

The Church

J.E. Flower

Introduction

The erosion within the structure and organization of the Catholic Church in France which has been substantial during the last thirty years shows little sign of diminishing. The recruitment of seminarists continues to fall by approximately 200 per year; the number of ordinations at about 100 per year (and likely to remain at this level until the mid-1990s) is now only slightly above what it was in 1800; only one priest in every ten will be less than 40 by the mid-1980s; more parishes become priestless as retirement and death create vacancies, more than 1000 rural churches have fallen into disuse and are threatened with demolition, and regular attendance at Sunday Mass has fallen, according to figures published by *La Vie* in August 1979, to less that 12 per cent. Yet evidence of another form presents a different picture. In spite of widespread disaffection, according to a survey carried out by *Le Pèlerin* in October 1981, 79 per cent of French nationals are Catholic; Lourdes continues to welcome hundreds of thousands each year; confessionals are busy; baptism, confirmation, marriage and the last rites are accepted without question even by those whose religious practice otherwise is minimal; the Catholic press remains healthy and vigorous. The review *Prier* has also claimed that private worship is increasing.

Such conflicting evidence and information suggests a fundamental instability which has in fact been echoed in the debates and activities within the Protestant Church as well. Even since the Second Vatican Council the Catholic Church has been obliged to examine itself with increasing regularity and thoroughness and in France as elsewhere (especially in Holland) the results have frequently been contentious.

Pope Paul VI (an 'artisan consciencieux' as *Témoignage chrétien* called him) who had continued to implement much of the spirit of the council had in particular been responsible for initiating liturgical changes, and for encouraging both decentralization of the Catholic Church itself and ecumenicalism. Inevitably such measures met with some opposition, but they also encouraged important developments and were welcomed in the main by other religious communities in France: the Protestants of whom there are nearly 1 million, Jews (*c*. 700,000 of whom 15 per cent practise regularly), members of the Orthodox Church (*c*. 600,000) and the Moslems (*c*. 2.5 million of whom about 700,000 are of French nationality).

By their choice of papal name, his successors, John-Paul I (26 August–28 September 1978) and John-Paul II, have been considered by many to be willing to continue to work within a similar tradition. By 1979, however, John-Paul II had intimated that he considered the time right for a widescale reappraisal of the situation and role of the French Catholic Church. After nearly a century during which the Church has moved, if sometimes rather unsteadily, towards a greater degree of understanding of and co-operation with the secular and political world, the Pope has made it clear that some re-emphasis on fundamental spiritual and pastoral values are to be encouraged. In October 1978 in his sermon given on the return of Parliament, Cardinal Marty's words were indeed prophetic: 'L'Eglise est aujourd'hui moins politique et administrative, elle est plus pastorale et prophétique'.

Catholic Action: the early years

Despite its many diverse forms modern Catholic action in France has its roots in the efforts of a number of prominent lay Catholics like Albert de Mun, René de la Tour du Pin, Léon Harmel and above all Marc Sangnier who, during the last years of the nineteenth century, attempted to give practical expression to Pope Leo XIII's policy of *ralliement*. This policy, continued after the First World War by Pius XI who referred to

Leo XIII as his 'spiritual father', was essentially an attempt to encourage French Catholics to accept the Republican government and to make the Catholic Church an accessible and meaningful institution for the working class. Once traditional barriers and attitudes had been broken down spiritual unity and national solidarity would develop to mutual advantage. The task was a difficult one however. Whatever political and social changes may have occurred since the late nineteenth century, the view that the Church should represent authority and discipline died hard. Maurras, whose right-wing extra-parliamentary movement, the *Action Française*, campaigned for a restoration of the monarchy and propounded a political philosophy based on the principles of heredity and social hierarchy, had not only found a perfect prototype in the structure of the Catholic Church but also a ready ally during the immediate pre-war years in Leo's successor Pius X. Remembered today for his strict conservatism (his policy centralizing the Church firmly on the Vatican became known as 'integrism'), Pius attacked all attempts at compromise with democratic Republican ideas or systems. With hindsight it is tempting to see his policies as an obstacle to a course of events which had already become apparent, but at the time Pius was in a difficult position. The growing anti-clericalism of the Third Republic had come to a head in 1904-5 when Emile Combes had broken off diplomatic relations with the Vatican. Perhaps Pius X was repaying the minister's intransigence in kind, but his attitude did sound a warning note for all subsequent attempts to draw Catholicism and matters of political and social importance too close together.

In the early 1920s and in a political climate in which the Left was becoming increasingly influential, and in a spiritual one generally referred to as a state of 'dechristianization', Pius X's rigid policies were replaced by Pius XI's attempt to introduce a second *ralliement*. With the disastrous reduction in the number of priests – a direct consequence of war casualties – Pius saw that there was now more than ever a need for lay participation in ecclesiastical matters. In 1929, for example, he remarked: 'Le clergé actuel ne suffit malheureusement plus aux besoins de notre temps. ... Aussi est-il nécessaire que tous se fassent apôtres; que le laïcat ne se prenne pas dans une

indifférence boudeuse, mais prenne sa part dans la lutte sacrée
. . . .' It was clear, however, that for the young in particular the
institution of study circles of the type that had been
encouraged during that last twenty-five years or so of the nineteenth century was too intellectual a method: instruction, it
was thought, should be replaced by example. Youth groups
within different social environments were established, all of
them affiliated to the *Association catholique de la jeunesse
française* (ACJF) – itself founded long before in 1886 – but
retaining their own distinctive autonomy. Of these the
Jeunesse ouvrière chrétienne (JOC) was the first (1926), soon
followed by a number of others: *Jeunesse agricole chrétienne*
(1929), *Jeunesse étudiante chrétienne* (1930), *Jeunesse
maritime chrétienne* (1932), *Jeunesse indépendante chrétienne*
(1936). The aims and consequently the developments of each
of these groups were different but the control exercised by the
central ecclesiastical body in France, the *Assemblée des
cardinaux et des archevêques* (ACA), which had been established in 1919 was, in these early years, near absolute. Yet
while even the JOC was able for the most part to comply with
Pius's wishes and remain apart from party politics, it was
inevitable that with such a deep concern for the working class,
one of the most striking features of the Church during this
period should be the relationship between Catholics and
Communists. Essential ideological differences made any deep
rapprochement seem impossible, of course, and in spite of a
number of statements in the *Osservatore Romano* (the *Pravda*
of the Vatican as it has been described) encouraging tolerance,
many Catholics remained openly hostile. As General Castel-
nau, leader of the conservative *Fédération nationale des catholiques* maintained, Communists were atheists, subversive
elements in society, and quite beyond salvation – an attitude
echoed in the 1970s by the traditionalist Catholic group
around Lefebvre. The matter was further complicated by the
growing threat of Fascism. The Italian invasion of Ethiopia and
the Spanish Civil War both provoked extremist reactions. Over
the latter in particular a large number of French Catholics at
first accepted the simplistic formula of Church versus
heathens, and talked in terms of a crusade. Gradually, however,
more and more of them sympathized with the republican posi-

tion and deplored Rome's reluctance to condemn the extreme Spanish Right. Such approval for the side to which Communists also gave their support added a further dimension to a situation that had already arisen internally in France in matters of industrial dispute. The 1936 elections revealed that the Communists, whose numbers had increased tenfold during the last few years, were by now a real political force. On 17 April their leader Maurice Thorez made his famous appeal for collaboration: 'Nous te tendons la main, catholique, ouvrier, employé, artisan, paysan, nous qui sommes des laïques, parce que tu es notre frère, et que tu es comme nous accablé par les mêmes soucis.' When in the following year Léon Blum echoed Thorez and suggested that collaboration was not only possible but desirable, *Sept*, the Catholic weekly, printed his words. In September the paper was ordered by Rome to cease publication; such an open declaration of sympathy was not to be tolerated, and for all his progressive measures Pius XI, like his predecessors, was adamant that religion should be above and quite distinct from the affairs of the political world.

Catholics and the Occupation

In his *Histoire du Catholicisme en France* André Latreille suggests that the Second World War stifled the promise of the 1930s, and in terms of a continuous development of the various groups that had been formed during these years this is largely true. But after a period of uncertainty the experience of war and the Occupation led to a number of developments that were to have far greater significance than anything previously undertaken, and of these the worker-priest experiment is the best example.

Under the catalytic influence of the Occupation the French people's sense of religion was expressed as it had been after 1870–1 in highly emotive terms. Divine punishment was the inevitable and just result for the sins of the Third Republic – a theme taken up by Camus in *La Peste*. As General Weygand remarked: 'La France a mérité sa défaite, elle a été battue parce que ses gouvernements depuis un siècle ont chassé Dieu de l'école.' However aware the Church may have seen of the Occupation, it was hardly in a position of authority, and some of its high-ranking members, more politically astute than others perhaps, saw that they should make the best of the situation. Cardinal Gerlier, Bishop of Lyons, advised Catholics to group themselves around Pétain who was greeted in 1940 by Gerlier himself as a kind of providential hero: 'La France avait beosoin d'un chef qui la conduise vers son éternel destin. Dieu a permis que vous fussiez là.'

None the less, there were at the same time other leading ecclesiastics who were aware of the dangers inherent in such idolatry. Feltin, Archbishop of Paris, remarked in 1941 that respect and deification should not be confused: 'le respect dû à l'autorité ne demande pas que nous déïfions celui qui la personnifie.' Yet in general Gerlier's views were predominant and in 1941 the French episcopate published a declaration of loyalty to the Pétain regime, even though it cautiously suggested at the same time that actual political commitment should be avoided. During the following months more statements on these lines from important members of the French Church were pumped out by the *Services d'information de Vichy* with, if necessary, censorship of the more cautionary passages. The effect of such propaganda was quickly apparent: a Pétain cult developed accompanied by invocations, poems and prayers including a parody of the Lord's Prayer. Moreover, the Vichy slogan of *Travail, famille, patrie* also appealed to those many Catholics who had already considered the growing readiness to agree to a liberal interpretation of their faith and the flirtation with Communism as real threats to the stability and traditions of Catholicism.

Yet this, as Jacques Duquesne has remarked in his book *Les Catholiques français sous l'occupation*, is a rather one-sided and even unfair picture. There were from the very beginning of the Occupation signs of resistance among Catholics, voiced in particular by *Le Temps présent*, a left-wing Catholic paper, which had been founded as a successor to *Sept* by, among others, Jacques Maritain and François Mauriac. But large-scale participation by Catholics in the Resistance movement was comparatively slow in developing. The dissolution of the trade unions, the CFTC and the CGT in 1940 (an action which, ironically perhaps, drew their leaders closer together), the growing drain on French manpower for the *Service du travail obligatoire* (STO), and the large-scale deportation of Jews in 1942, however, were sufficient reasons for inducing action. On the second of these issues Rome remained embarrassingly silent and it was left to Cardinal Liénart to take the initiative. He argued that Catholics as a whole and regular clerics in particular should accept this as a challenge and should feel responsible for those in Germany whom they were to join, whatever their political or religious beliefs. At the same time in France itself the appeal of the *Assemblée des cardinaux et des archevêques*, to respect the legitimacy of the Vichy regime, was swept aside by a wave of indignation hardened by an awareness of the increasing viciousness of reprisals against civilians and by the arrests of some higher members of the clergy. It was such realizations as these that began to draw Catholics and left-wing (frequently communist) Resistance fighters together: here was the opportunity that had been sought already on several occasions in the past.

In the early 1940s a number of positive steps were taken, which were to lead to important post-war developments in the sphere of Catholic action. In 1941 the *Mission de France* was founded by Cardinal Suhard in an attempt to train priests to form part of an inter-diocesan body that would reach out into the dechristianized areas of France. Two years later a book written by two Paris chaplains, the abbés Daniel and Godin, *France, pays de mission*, argued that the continuing association of Catholicism and the bourgeoisie not only rendered the former unknown to the workers but, more importantly, *unknowable*. This view, together with the situation in Germany, had much to do with the creation in the same year (1943) of the *Mission de Paris* from which the worker-priest experiment essentially sprang.

Post-war developments

After the war Pius XII emphasized once more the eternal and absolute qualities of the Church, but at the same time made it clear that its immediate task of missionary work was vital. While participation of lay Catholics in this was to be encouraged, some of the Pope's statements indicated that control by senior ecclesiastics was imperative if a second *ralliement* was to be avoided. In spite of such encouragement it should not be imagined that there was a great resurgence of religious fervour. After the war the pattern of dechristianization that had characterized the 1920s was still as apparent, and the recovery in the numbers of the clergy that had been achieved by the late 1930s had been lost. But many of the lay Catholics who were active were so in a new way. They were less inclined to consider politics as a danger to their spiritual state and also their Resistance record meant that they were more readily accepted. The first ministry of the provisional government contained five former members of the general committee of the ACJF and the MRP in its early years at least enjoyed the support of a number of bishops.

Catholic action groups

In the decade following the war these developed in number and in outlook much more rapidly than their predecessors some twenty years before had done. Some were short-lived: the *Ligue ouvrière catholique* (LOC) for example, founded during the war as a body to be responsible for providing aid for prisoners and refugees, was disowned in 1945 by the ACA as it became increasingly political, and changed its name a year later to the *Mouvement de libération du peuple* (MLP). Others remained, even though they were to modify their attitudes quite significantly in subsequent years. The *Action catholique ouvrière*, for example, formed in 1950 and concerned, as its name suggests, with the working-class areas of France, remained for some while apart from political commitment. But this did not last for long. By 1980 more than 10 per cent of its members including seven of its national committee were members of the Communist Party.

Perhaps the most influential of all, however, was the *Mission de France*. Founded also in 1941 by the ACA as an inter-diocesan association, it provided a special training for the priests it sent to work in teams in dechristianized areas. In this it differed significantly from the worker-priests who worked individually and who were criticized by the *Mission de France* for doing so. At first the *Mission* directed its attentions to rural areas, but gradually realized that it was in the towns that its activities were most needed. Soon, however, its priests were criticized by the bishops with whom they were meant to work in close collaboration. In 1952 and 1953 they complained (like the worker-priests) that the Vatican had very little idea of what was happening in the dechristianized areas of France. Also in 1953 rumours of Marxist literature being read by the seminarists prompted an investigation, and in August the *Mission* was closed to await a new statute to be promulgated by Rome. In the following year the new conditions of the *Mission's* activities were published, and it was now noticeable that only those bishops who actually requested the assistance of priests from the *Mission* had them; an episcopal commission was also set up to be responsible for them and to give them their directives. Although such centralization and control may have disappointed some members of the *Mission*, an attempt had been made to create an organic unit linking missionary priests, Catholic Action groups and the general clergy. Today there are over 300 priests from the *Mission* spread throughout France of whom more than two-thirds are in full employment. At its annual congress in September 1980 the *Mission* reaffirmed its basic aim which, in Suhard's original words, is to 'rendre au Christ les foules qui l'ont perdu'. Teamwork is considered essential and an emphasis is placed on a liberal (but not free) interpretation of Christian teaching as it is contained in the Gospels.

Worker-priests

When the Vatican finally decided to discontinue the first phase of the worker-priest experiment in 1954, Cardinal Feltin, Archbishop of Paris, summed up the views of many who were sympathetic to the movement with the following words: 'Le monde ouvrier, éloigné de l'Eglise, a son histoire, ses traditions, ses valeurs morales, ses richesses spirituelles et une certaine unité qui fait qu'il n'accepte pas l'étranger à son milieu qui vient lui donner des leçons. Pour exercer sur lui une influence, il faut être naturalisé, reconnu comme membre de ce monde.'

Attempts to take Catholicism to the working-class world had, as we have seen, been various, but none had sought to penetrate it in such a total way as the worker-priest experiment. Individual priests had already made some efforts before the war: the Franciscan Bousquet or the Dominican Loew, who went respectively to Ivry and Marseilles, were well in advance of the general movement created during the years of the Occupation. In many ways those priests who went to Germany found themselves in an artificial situation, and their complete independence was not something from which worker-priests in France were subsequently to benefit. In *France, pays de mission*, Daniel and Godin outlined some of the major problems to be faced: the working-class conception of the Church as a capitalist stronghold must be overcome, the priest should assimilate himself completely with his new environment and only when accepted reveal his true identity, and also there should be some kind of preparatory training. While these points were recognized they tended to be over-ambitious. Assimilation quickly led in many cases to complete identification, with political and emotional ties becoming particularly strong. As one worker-priest remarked: 'Le fait formidable, c'est que lorsqu'on devient ouvrier, le monde bascule du côté ouvrier.' Although a number of them disagreed with Gilbert Cesbron's portrayal of the worker-priest's dilemma in his novel *Les Saints vont en enfer*, the fact remains that they were very much alone, regarded often with suspicion by more traditionally minded Catholics and by their bishops, who had little or no conception of working-class conditions. Such a situation could lead only to friction and discontent, and in 1951 uneasiness in Rome led to a suspension in recruitment. In 1952 two worker-priests were arrested in a Communist-inspired demonstration against General Ridgway when he arrived as Allied Commander in Europe, and in the following year the experiment was stopped altogether and the priests withdrawn. The majority of them obeyed Rome's decision without hesitation, and in January 1954 a number were linked with the teams trained by the *Mission de France* and known as 'prêtres de la mission ouvrière'. For some worker-priests, however, the Vatican's decision was little more than a betrayal, while, more embarrassingly still, the three French cardinals at that time (Feltin, Suhard and Gerlier) all approved of the experiment and yet were bound to enforce the ban.

Outside the Church, militant lay Catholics, particularly those in the JOC and the ACO, were quick to criticize: 'L'Eglise nous a trompés deux fois, une première fois en ne s'occupant pas de nous malgré ses promesses, une seconde fois en s'occupant de nous par les prêtres-ouvriers pour nous les retirer quand ils n'ont plus fait ce qu'elle voulait.'

Such criticism as this, together with considerable sympathy and pressure within the Church itself, was sufficient to ensure that the ban could only be short–lived, and in 1959 Cardinal Feltin made a specific request to Pope John XXIII for it to be lifted. John refused but during the Second Vatican Council (called by John himself) the question was reopened with a new enthusiasm. There were, now, a number of indications why the whole concept of the worker-priests should be more favourably received. Political contamination was now for some reason less feared; Paul VI, John's papal successor, was more determined in the view that workers would not come to the priests if priests did not first go to the workers; and in addition the Curia in Rome was beginning to realize that bishops might well understand local problems better than someone several hundred kilometres away. As Henri Fesquet writing in *Le Monde* remarked, what did an Italian cardinal who had never been to France know about the mind of a Renault factory worker near Paris? Such a view is to some extent clearly an oversimplified one, but it does single out the crucial issue of the whole experiment and one that was largely met by the new conditions imposed on the worker-priests, or 'prêtres au travail' as they were now to be called.

In 1965 the second phase of the worker-priest experiment was revived for a trial period of three years. In addition to the change in name which some argued was too fine a distinction to be generally recognized, there were five important modifications. No priest would be allowed to assume union or other responsibilities during his years of office, though he could become a member of a trade union; there should be a more thorough training before the position was actually taken; the priest should remember that he is and must remain 'un homme d'église'; he should not be isolated but remain in contact with other ecclesiastical bodies in his parish – an idea already practised by the *Mission de France* teams; and as a body the worker-priests should come under the jurisdiction of an episcopal committee headed by the Archbishop of Paris. The two major differences, therefore, were the attempts to limit the priests' political activities and also to create some kind of organic missionary unit, of which the worker-priest would be a single (albeit the most important) element.

For the most part these reforms were greeted with enthusiasm, though there was some criticism from the ever-present traditional and conservative right-wing Catholics who remained in opposition to the whole action of missionary work expressed in these terms; from the few worker-priests who had chosen to disobey their superiors in 1953–4; and from those priests who had continued in 1954 as 'prêtres de la mission ouvrière', some of whom now considered that they and their efforts were being overlooked. In spite of such criticism, however, Paul VI saw fit in November 1968 to prolong this second phase of the worker-priest experiment (during which forty-eight priests had been used) for another three years. During this period further reforms were announced: numbers were no longer to be limited and priests could exercise union responsibilities – a directive which appeared to have been left sufficiently vague to enable Rome to intervene if it was felt that political commitment was becoming excessive. The immediate results were impressive; over 400 worker-priests were active throughout France by the end of 1971, a number which has swelled to more than a thousand. But increase in numbers has not been accompanied by any noticeable increase in effectiveness. Certainly the elevation in May 1975 of Jean Rémond, a priest within the *Mission de France* since 1950, to the rank of bishop was an acknowledgement of the movement's status, but it may also have been a sign that it was less of a revolutionary and critical force than it had been before. Certainly Rémond continues to be ready with criticism of the Church's attitude to society ('Elle vit dans un monde à elle, un monde qui n'est pas réel'), but other groups and movements have developed since the Second Vatican Council whose members are much more outspoken and active than the worker-priests. Furthermore, the fact that such a high percentage of them are now members of unions and overtly political groups does suggest, together with the relatively low attendances at the annual worker-priest assemblies, that even in its most recently conceived form the experiment is considered by many of those who take part in it to be relatively ineffective. Indeed, given developments during the last fifteen years in particular, the whole worker-priest movement must now be considered to have little more than historical interest.

Some structural and organizational changes

During this same period from the early 1940s to the present day a number of far-reaching and influential changes have been made in such disparate matters as parish reorganization and the liturgy in an attempt to refashion the image of the Church in the eyes of the modern world. In 1967 a new catechism written in a language which, it was hoped, would be more suitable for children was brought into use and in 1981 an illustrated 'encyclopedia of faith', *Pierres vivantes*, was published under the auspices of the Episcopal Assembly and again specifically intended for children. Religious education in schools has also been a matter of concern – since the late 1970s 25 per cent of all French schools have had no specialist teacher – as has the provision of special courses for adult lay members of the Church. Although change has frequently been opposed by the traditionalists, groups like *Catachèse 80* and school courses put out by the national committee for Catholic education have become established and have been influential in the organi-zation of annual gatherings of young Catholics at Taizé, the formation of youth groups like *Frat 78* which encourages all movement towards ecumenicalism, or in the development of non-confessional cultural centres like the one at La Sainte Baume in Provence.

Other important developments include the territorial rearrangement of a number of parishes (most recently in the Paris area), the gradual decentralization of certain admini-strative and consultative duties, and an examination of the conditions under which many priests are required to live and work (though the decision to launch a pension fund was only taken in 1972). Significant too in recent years has been the awareness shown by the *Assemblée plénière de l'épiscopat français* of the potential value of broadcasting. Televised masses attract an enormous audience, a fact which has not escaped the attention of the most recent presidents of the Assembly, Etchegaray and his successor (since 1981) Jean Vilnet. Together with missionary work, communication and the media have featured as major items for discussion on the agenda of the last four annual assemblies.

The aftermath of the Second Vatican Council

Towards a religious revolution?

In many ways such changes as these are relatively superficial, however. Much more crucial has been the growing unrest among the clergy – progressive and traditionalist alike. For the former there has been, particularly since the mid-1960s, what the late Jean Daniélou described as 'une crise des vocations sacerdotales'. In 1964, for example, those priests responsible for country parishes undertook a survey of their position. Like the worker-priests before them, they felt that their attempts to integrate themselves with their parishioners were doomed to failure from the beginning: inadequate training, insufficient opportunity for integration, and a sense of isolation within the ecclesiastical framework, were all listed as major contributory factors. As one priest was recorded as having remarked on his relationship with his bishop: 'L'évêque est un personnage qui passe . . . qui ne sait rien de vous, comme vous ne savez rien de lui.' Objections of this kind are regularly examined by the bishops at their annual assemblies but response has not been positive and radical enough for many priests. As a result a wave of revolutionary groups and movements has appeared during the last fifteen years often leading, in particular, to direct confrontation with the Church hierarchy.

In November 1968 a letter signed by over a hundred priests and sympathizers belonging to a movement known as *Echanges et dialogue* appeared. Their demands and proposals, like those of many progressive Catholics before them, though now more strongly expressed, were for priests to become independent of the structure and the constitution of the Church. They wished to alter, radically, the image and the position of the priest in society and maintained that changes made in the past had ignored this fundamental problem. The priest, they argued, should act independently of his order; he should have the right to express himself freely, to participate in political affairs, to marry and to be allowed a voice in the nomination and deployment of new priests.

By January 1969 over 400 priests had joined the movement. In the same month a further statement was issued in which the whole question of authority within the Church was challenged. What they sought, they maintained, was to introduce 'de nouvelles formes de relations entre évêques, prêtres, et laïcs, indispensables à l'annonce du Christ au monde d'aujourd'hui'. In the spring of 1969 the movement was partly responsible for interrupting a service held by Jean Daniélou, showering the congregation with pamphlets released from the roof questioning Daniélou's right to be a bishop: for whom and by whom had he been elected?

Nor surprisingly *Echanges et dialogue* was received by many bishops with considerable hostility. Some attempts were made to meet the issues raised and in March 1969 the Episcopal Assembly issued in particular a statement arguing the case for celibacy. The movement continued to grow but in December 1974 was formally replaced by *Camarades chrétiens critiques*, a movement which is openly more political and seeks to overthrow the Church hierarchy:

> Nous refusons une Eglise qui a choisi le savoir, l'avoir et l'ordre établi. Nous refusons un Credo, une théologie et une morale préfabriqués. Nous refusons une image de Dieu qui renforce la notion du pouvoir. L'important est d'appeler les chrétiens à prendre leur destin en main, à devenir eux-mêmes théologiens, à gérer eux-mêmes leur vie sexuelle. (June 1975).

More recently still in 1979 another movement, *Le Collectif pour une église du peuple*, has developed supported by priests from the north and east of the country in particular who are critical of the role they are obliged to fill: 'Dans le monde où nous vivons, nous ne pouvons pas être prisonniers d'un modèle de prêtre qui a sa valeur, mais qui ne correspond plus aujourd'hui aux exigences de l'annonce de l'Evangile.'

Such movements as these coming from within the body of

the Church itself clearly present special problems. The unrest and dissatisfaction which they express has also been reflected in the growth of a large number of smaller, often essentially lay groups whose criticism has been no less strong. In this period of 'pluralisme inconfortable', as the Episcopal Assembly defined it in 1975, we find, for example, *La Vie nouvelle*, *Témoignage chrétien*, *Chrétiens marxistes révolutionnaires*, the *Communion de Boquen* under its leader Bernard Besret or the *Communauté chrétienne de Béthania* whose members share a simple but non-programmed faith. Some like the last are quite apolitical, others only moderately so, preferring to work instead towards the establishment of ecumenicalism; others, particularly lay groups, can be uncompromisingly militant. In July 1974, for example, Huguette Delanne, leader of the JOCF, remarked: 'Nous agissons d'abord parce que nous sommes de la classe ouvrière et non parce que nous sommes chrétiens.' And in June 1977 the movement *Chrétiens pour le socialisme* which, recognized by neither the ACO nor the JOC, maintained that for Christians and non-Christians alike there could be a 'cohérence entre les engagements pour le socialisme et les exigences de l'Evangile'. Within what many consider to be a general climate of liberalization, it is not surprising that the way to some form of compromise between the pastoral and the political has been growing clearer. Indeed in June 1976 Marchais, in words which recalled Thorez' famous 'main tendue' forty years earlier, appealed to Catholics to join Communists in a struggle against all forms of oppression. And since the late 1970s theologians have increasingly emerged as propounders of progressive ideas, drawing the Church more deeply into debates concerning, for example, divorce, abortion, homosexuality and the position of immigrants.

In the face of such rapid, not to say turbulent developments the episcopacy's position has been difficult. Ready acquiescence is unlikely of course and however progressive individual bishops might have wished to be, official statements have, not surprisingly, been cautious. In October 1972 in a speech entitled 'Pour une pratique chrétienne de la politique' Cardinal Marty, while still underlining the need for debate and discussion also stressed the view that the Church should not allow itself to become a victim of political struggles; its pastoral mission should remain pre-eminent: 'le comportement des évêques et des prêtres en matière politique doit toujours être cohérent avec la mission de l'Eglise et leur mission spécifique dans l'Eglise.' In 1977, admittedly with the Lefebvre affair much in evidence, he observed that 'on ne peut pas être à la fois bon communiste et bon chrétien' and in October 1978: 'L'Eglise est aujourd'hui moins politique et administrative, elle est plus pastorale.' Etchegaray, Archbishop of Marseilles, and, since June 1979, a cardinal, also warned priests against excessive political involvement at the Episcopal Assembly in 1977, and in May 1978 on the fiftieth anniversary of the JOC pointed to what he called a no-man's-land between the world of the working class and the Church – an attitude for which he was quickly rebuked by *Témoignage Chrétien*. Elchinger, Bishop of Strasbourg, in a message to his diocese in March 1980 accused a number of Catholic Action groups of 'ambiguïtés doctrinales' and of 'une confusion dans le rôle des laïcs et des prêtres', and he warned against misinterpretations of the Gospels which made Christ into a political figure.

Such caution as this is not only the result of natural conservatism, however. Since his first Easter message in 1979 Pope John-Paul has consistently reminded the French clerics that, after a period of dialogue and some liberalism, certain traditional positions should be recovered and even strengthened. From this message three main points emerged: first that in the spirit of the Second Vatican Council seminaries are to be reviewed and reinvigorated; second that whatever their activities priests should remember that they are 'porteurs de la grâce de Christ' and that expectations of them are by definition greater than those of a lay member of the Church ('on attend de vous, prêtres, une sollicitude et un engagement bien supérieurs et différents d'un laïc'); third, that celibacy is essential. These are positions from which he has shown little sign of shifting despite his undisguised sympathy for the underprivileged and the working class. There have been hints too that within the institution of the French Church some careful planning has been taking place. The arrival in 1979 in Paris of the new papal nuncio Angelo Felici, who had played an important role in the problems surrounding the Dutch Church, has been seen as a conservative and even disciplinary appointment. Perhaps more significant is the appointment of Jean Lustiger as Marty's successor. Of Polish origin (his parents were Polish Jews) Lustiger has already been seen as having a role to play in the increasing concern for ecumenicalism. In general he is considered to be a moderate who prefers to base his decisions on experience rather than impersonal reports ('je préfère le terrain aux dossiers'). He has made some organizational changes in the Paris region, but has yet to take a firm position towards either his progressive colleagues or the traditionalists.

The traditionalist reaction

Left-wing progressive Catholics have not been alone in voicing their opinions and in some cases in challenging the Vatican head-on. Since the early 1970s various traditionalist groups which all to some degree or other chose to ignore the Second Vatican Council have expressed concern at what they see to be a severe erosion of the Church's authority and true role. The abbé Georges (*Centre réforme catholique*) in 1972 accused both the Second Vatican Council and Paul VI of revolutionary activity; the *Alliance Saint-Michel* whose members profess themselves to be 'excédés par la situation révolutionnaire' have interrupted Paris masses chanting Latin; and late in 1980 the *Union pour la fidélité* called on French bishops to reject 'cette nouvelle église' and to assist all those 'qui se meurent dans les ténèbres de la secte conciliaire'.

No one however has undertaken such a sustained and vigorous defence of traditional Catholicism as the former Archbishop of Dakar and Bishop of Tulle, Marcel Lefebvre, who late in 1978 claimed to have established thirty centres throughout the world, especially in the USA and Europe. A man who admits to having been vitally influenced by Maurras and for whom Communism is 'la plus monstrueuse erreur jamais sortie de l'esprit de Satan'. Lefebvre has, by his activities, clashed directly with the Pope, the Archbishop of Paris and the French episcopacy in general. In 1974 his book *Un Evêque parle* expressed his feelings unambiguously. Having challenged social and political trends within the Catholic Church since the early 1960s (he had been part of a minority opposition group at the Second Vatican Council), in March 1972 he founded a seminary at Ecône in Switzerland for his movement *Fraternité sacerdotale de Saint-Pie-X* and for the training of priests along traditionalist lines. His refusal to accept the Pope's ruling led in 1976 to his being forbidden to ordain priests and on 12 July he was officially suspended from his priestly function – *a divinis* – a position in which he remains today even though he has seen fit to continue to celebrate Mass and administer the sacraments. He has also maintained that papal directives may be misguided or wrongly inspired. Thus in New York in November 1977, for example, he recognized that he and his followers were ready to follow Paul VI but only when the Pope showed himself to belong to the true Catholic Church: 'Nous sommes prêts à suivre les instructions du pape. Mais lorsqu'il ne suit pas les instructions des deux cent soixante-deux papes qui l'ont précédé, nous ne pouvons pas suivre les siennes.' From the moment of his suspension, in fact, his masses have been enthusiastically attended and the faithful have regularly heard the same message in his sermons – a warning against what he sees as neo-modernist and neo-Protestant developments in the Catholic Church, against the threat of Communism in particular and against all attempts to undermine authority and discipline in secular and religious society alike. In September 1979, for example, at the celebration of an open air mass attended by about 15,000 people in Versailles he claimed in his sermon: 'La messe est essentiellement anticommuniste. Le communisme c'est: tout pour le parti, tout pour la révolution; la messe c'est: tout pour Dieu. Elle s'oppose au programme du parti, qui est un programme satanique.' Lefebvre has continued to defy the Vatican too over confirmation (in many cases the *re*confirmation of children into what he considers the true Catholic faith) and the ordination of priests of whom there are now about forty each year.

The most direct clash with the established Church in France, however, has occurred in Paris. Late in February 1977 the Pope announced he would not grant Lefebvre an audience until he had satisfactorily responded to his requests of the previous year. On 27 February, as an instant response, traditionalist Catholics, organized by one of Lefebvre's principal supporters, the abbé Ducaud-Bourget, occupied the church of Saint-Nicolas du Chardonnet in the fifth *arrondissement*. In spite of various 'threats' by Marty – notably of recourse to the civil authorities – the occupation has continued and neither Marty nor his successor Jean Lustiger have been able to do anything about it. In May 1979 the parishioners of Saint-Nicolas wrote to the President of the Republic demanding action: not only is it a matter of civil liberty, they have argued, but also of religious tolerance and political activity. Certainly this last point has been increasingly noticeable. The church of Saint-Nicolas is in the heart of Chirac country and in addition to a large proportion of elderly people at Mass are found younger members of extreme right-wing groups, often anti-Semitic and racist in attitude, and others who look somewhat nostalgically back to the period of collaboration during the Occupation and are sympathetic to the OAS. Marty, who tried to maintain a nice distinction between 'tradition' and 'fixisme' or 'passéisme', was in a difficult position even as archbishop, but he allowed the parish to call in the civil authorities and offered the traditionalists another church, the rather aptly named Marie-Méditrice near the Porte des Lilas.

The problem remains unresolved, however, and the parishioners' plea to the civic authorities – and indeed to the National Assembly – unanswered. Lustiger has acknowledged the problem but has so far taken no action. In September 1982 Lefebvre handed over the responsibility for the Ecône seminary to the abbé Franz Schmidberger, still only thirty-six years of age and presumably destined to replace Lefebvre as head of the movement as a whole. For the moment, however, Lefebvre at seventy-three shows no sign of giving up his overall control though when he does the Saint-Nicolas problem could, ironically, become even more entrenched once he assumes some kind of historical authority. He personally appears to remain convinced that he and the Vatican will ultimately resolve their differences. Meanwhile support for his movement increases, particularly at a time when new Socialist policies are meeting with increasing opposition. A remark reported from one of his supporters has interesting and typical social and political overtones: 'Pétain, de Gaulle et Monseigneur Lefebvre sont curieusement tous trois originaires du nord de la

France. Je les crois tous les trois également utiles. Ce sont souvent les minoritaires qui ont raison et font avancer les choses.' This confrontation is not limited strictly to the Church. Like many of the debates which are being conducted in progressive Catholic circles it relates to and reflects crises and tensions present in society at large.

Conclusion

Whereas by the mid-1970s it would, not unreasonably, have seemed to any outside observer that in general the progressive forces within the Catholic Church in France (and indeed in many ways in the world at large) were beginning to make their presence felt, early in the 1980s the situation is much more difficult to assess. Progressive trends continue – witness for example the new catechism or the ever increasing number of married priests. At the same time traditionalists, grouped in the main around Lefebvre, look not only for a restoration of the Tridentine Mass, but in a more general way for the reaffirmation of values like discipline, order and hierarchy which they consider to be important socially and politically as well as religiously. Nor have the Pope's position and attitude always appeared consistent. When he visited France in May-June 1980 the first Pope to do so since Pius VII in 1804) he made a particularly marked impression on the young and the working class. He was warmly welcomed by the PCF, expressed approval for the worker-priests, was cautious and even authoritarian in discussions concerning doctrinal and pastoral issues, and was as disapproving of progressive as he was of integrist tendencies. (His criticism of the latter emerges more clearly from his second encyclical letter *Dives in misericordia* issued in November 1980.) He has been criticized by the Catholic Left and Right alike, but it does appear as though he is attempting to reaffirm the traditional pastoral values of Catholic teaching and is expecting to receive rather more support from the French episcopacy than has been forthcoming in recent years.

In terms of its own development, therefore, the French Catholic Church is at an interesting stage in its development. It is also becoming more aware of and involved with debates being conducted by the other Churches. The Protestant Church, for example, reacted strongly to the Pope's views about the qualitative superiority of the priest. At its annual synods the role of the Church in society and in political activity has been regularly debated, and an increasingly liberal attitude has been adopted towards, for example, sexual matters. Doctrinal narrowness has been disapproved. As Max-Alain Chevalier remarked in his final speech as president of the synod in May 1980: 'L'unité plurielle est un défi, un bel et bon défi. Aimer Dieu n'est pas avoir peur des divergences.' The Catholic Church has also contributed to a collective response by the Churches to the problems faced by immigrant communities, to the call for greater ecumenicalism and for some awareness of the role which the Church (any Church) has to play within the expanded European Community.

Bibliography

For a general survey of the period covered by this chapter consult:

Latreille, A. and Rémond, R. (eds), *Histoire du Catholicisme en France*, Vol III, pp. 487–684. Paris, Spes, 1962.

Mayeur, J–M. (ed.), *L'Histoire religieuse de la France, XIXe, XXe siècles. Problèmes et méthodes*. Paris, Beauchesne, 1975. Adopts a thematic rather than a chronological approach. Deals with overseas as well as internal issues.

For a more substantial treatment the following books will prove useful:

Dansette, A., *Destin du Catholicisme français*. Paris, Flammarion, 1957. Detailed survey of the period 1926–56.

Duquesne, J., *Les Catholiques français sous l'occupation*. Paris, Grasset, 1966. A fascinating, well-documented account.

Rémond, R., *L'Anticléricalisme en France de 1815 à nos jours*. Paris, Fayard, 1976. An introduction in which anticlericalism is discussed from a variety of angles – sociological, cultural, and so on – and is followed by a long historical account of the phenomenon in France. Particularly good on the period from the Second Vatican Council to the present.

Other books or articles on particular topics or problems include:

Casalis, Georges, *Les Idées justes ne tombent pas du ciel.* Paris, Cerf, 1972. A handbook of progressive Protestant ideas.

Etchegaray, R. and Marty, F. (eds), *France que fais-tu de ton baptême?* Paris, Centurion, 1980. A collection of the speeches and comments made by John-Paul II during his visit to France.

Fesquet, H. (ed.), *Une Brassée de confessions de foi.* Paris, Seuil, 1979. A collection of interview-articles originally published in *Le Monde* which deal with the problem of talking to a non-believer about religious faith.

Hourdin, G. and Marchais, G., *Communistes et Chrétiens, Communistes ou Chrétiens.* Paris, Desclée, 1978. An interesting discussion of a key issue by sympathetic representatives of opposing sides.

Solé, R., *Les Chrétiens en France.* Paris, PUF, 1972. In the main a collection of texts relating to all the central problems which confront both the Protestant and Catholic Churches. An interesting discussion in the last chapter on sexuality, love, celibacy, and so on.

A collection of documents concerning the worker-priests is *The Worker Priests: A Collective Documentation*, translated by J. Petrie. London, Routledge & Kegan Paul, 1956. Valuable surveys of the influence and position of the Church in France have been carried out by *Le Nouvel Observateur* (no. 106, November 1966, and nos. 242 and 243, July 1969) and by *Esprit*, October 1967, 'Nouveau monde et Parole de Dieu', and November 1971, 'Réinventer l'Eglise', which deal with both general and specific issues. The role and status of the priest in particular is examined. Documents relating to the pontificate of Paul VI are contained in *Paul VI et les évêques de France*, Dossier présenté par J. Vandrisse. Paris, Editions SOS, 1978.

Eight

The press

W.D. Redfern

Introduction

As with the world's press, the crisis of the French press has become endemic. Falling sales, decrease in advertising revenue, huge increases in the cost of paper, highly paid yet often superfluous staffs, are some of the material causes. Yet there is no shortage of groups or individuals anxious to buy up or to initiate newspapers.

France comes twenty-ninth in the world tables for the number of newspapers sold per 1000 people; and consumption is about half that of Britain. The obvious inference that French citizens are less thoroughly informed on public events than Anglo-Saxons is tempting but, despite such statistics, unproven. The French also read fewer books and go less often to the theatre or cinema; radio and television have developed there less rapidly. Proportionately fewer papers are read today in France than before 1939. The Paris dailies are essentially a press for the Paris area. Before the war they sold twice as many copies as the provincial press, but now sell only half as many. This exchange of position started in 1945, when the metropolitan press was too poorly equipped to develop provincial editions. Nowadays the regional dailies can obtain news as quickly as those in the capital, and are physically and temperamentally nearer to their readers. They continue to expand their circulation but, rather surprisingly, more in the countryside than in the towns. This situation stems from the multiplicity of editions, each specializing in local, even parochial, news. At the same time, they have experienced the same concentration of resources as the Paris press. There is an increasing tendency for regional papers to form *couplages* (partial mergers), especially in the fields of advertising, printing and distribution. The aim is to avoid mutually unprofitable competition, particularly on the boundaries of regions where some overlap occurs. Hence the reciprocal non-aggression pacts. One result is that *Ouest-France* (700,000 circulation) has become the largest daily in France. On the other hand, *Le Progrès de Lyon* and *Le Dauphin libéré* have recently split up. In general the strength and independence of the provincial press have impeded so far the creation of huge newspaper chains, like those of Great Britain, the United States, Japan or Germany.

Of late, however, there have been long and loud protests from journalists and some politicians, when Robert Hersant, a financial manipulator of talent, by adding control of *France-Soir*, *L'Aurore* and *Le Parisien libéré* to that of *Le Figaro*, extended his empire. These acts defied the 1944 edict aimed at thwarting press monopolies. Despite some resistance by the journalists he employs and frequently sacks, Hersant is well on the way to deserving the title of 'the French Axel Springer': already one in five Frenchmen reads one of his publications. It does not seem likely that the present Socialist government will be any prompter than previous administrations to act on the question of monopolies, especially as it is more preoccupied with the audio-visual media. The Socialist Party gave little support to its daily, *Combat Socialiste*, which survived for only a few months in 1981.

There are fewer French papers, national or regional, than before the war, and those that survive are, in the main, examples of *la presse industrielle*. Like all industries, it has its victims. *Paris-Jour*, with a circulation of a quarter of a million, had to close down in 1972, after large-scale sackings had led to strikes and fruitless government intervention. It is heartening, however, that the most reliable French newspaper, *Le Monde*, has made the best progress in circulation and been the only daily to make a regular profit. The press in France nevertheless remains big business, and figures about twentieth in the list of French economic giants. It employs nearly 100,000 people and ensures the livelihood of twice that number. The State helps it by indiscriminate aid of various kinds, which amounts to a form of indirect subsidy. Newspapers are wholly exempted from taxes on turnover and various local taxes. They can start tax-free funds to fit themselves out with new equipment or can obtain loans from the State. They enjoy preferential postal, telegraph and telephone rates. Overseas sales are subsidized, in keeping with the official policy of spreading French 'culture' the world over.

In France, unlike Germany, the United States or Britain, there are no appreciable differences in price between 'quality' and 'popular' papers. Until 1967, the selling price of French dailies was fixed by the government. The increase in price that year caused a big drop in sales from which most papers have not yet recovered. A chasm separates the cost price and the selling price, and it can be bridged only by actively encouraging advertisers to buy space. Three-quarters of the income of *Le Figaro* comes from advertisements. The pursuit of advertisers is even more fierce than that of readers. Between the two wars, a feudal consortium of five leading Paris dailies, together with the chief agency, conspired to keep the price of advertising space high and thus to shut out any rivals. This stranglehold was eventually broken, but today advertising continues to favour the more flourishing papers and to accelerate the downfall of the less successful ones. It is sometimes argued that a paper which is well off for advertisers eager to use its columns is freer from any pressure they might try to apply than is an economically weak paper. In addition, it is not really necessary for advertisers to pressurize newspapers, for the interests of both sides are identical: to sell as much as possible. Perhaps collusion is a more apt term.

The post-war press and the Algerian crisis

Just as the political militants engaged in Resistance work were already manoeuvring for supremacy after the Liberation, so newspapermen were determined after the war to make a clean sweep. A great purge of the collaborationist press was carried out. The avengers confiscated and shared out its equipment, premises and capital; the former clandestine press benefited. There were high hopes (still alive in some journalistic quarters) of setting up a completely reformed, 'decapitalized' press – that is, one freed from the control of financial interests. Polemics erupted as to whether the essential auxiliaries of the press (the paper industries, distributing organizations and news agencies) should be nationalized, or whether this step would put the press at the mercy of arbitrary government. In fact, because of such hesitation, a considerable part of the old order was able to re-establish itself. The much needed statute of the press was blocked in the National Assembly. In the confusion of post-war France, a large sector of the press pushed out varying forms of propaganda, often anti-Communist. Much of it was gutter-journalism. When the editor of *Le Monde* advocated neutralism as the only solution to the Indo-Chinese dilemma, he was derided as a eunuch.

As well as the civil war waged at various points in history between newspapers themselves, the French government has occasionally laid its heavy hand on the press. There is a long tradition in France of governmental confiscation or censorship of 'dangerous' publications, dating back to the suppression of anti-government pamphlets in the seventeenth and eighteenth centuries. In fact, the care taken by authoritarian regimes to muzzle the press indicates its importance, especially in those countries where, as in France, the expression of ideas is valued highly (Karl Marx's comment has a sting in the tail: 'La France est le seul pays de l'idée, c'est-à-dire de l'idée qu'elle se fait d'elle-même'). During the Algerian crisis, the government had many reasons for wishing to limit dissent in the communications media. One reason was the hostility of the army officers to what they considered a 'treason press', which they had already blamed for helping to lose them the Indo-Chinese war, by its critical and therefore 'demoralizing' reports. In addition, the government wanted at first to represent the Algerian rebellion as the handiwork of mere terrorists, and later tried to make out that the end had come when it was nowhere in sight, and that peace could be obtained without negotiating with Algerian nationalists. A strong opposition press would obviously hinder such aims. During the Algerian war therefore, papers and periodicals were seized by the police on over 250 occasions in France. The irony was that few convictions followed these seizures, as open trials would have given too much publicity to the government's dubious right of confiscation. To show its 'impartiality', the government sometimes suppressed both right- and left-wing papers.

Its various actions did not in fact arrest the spread of information, at least to the educated reading public. A heavy responsibility lay on the French press, because of the State control over television and radio. In addition, the sole French news agency, the *Agence française de presse*, often withheld cables containing items detrimental to the government or other vested interests. In many such ways, public opinion in the 1950s slowly lost contact with events, despite the efforts by several organs to keep readers informed. *Le Monde, L'Express, France-Observateur, Le Canard enchaîné, L'Humanité* and the Catholic monthly *Esprit*, all made sustained protests, or simply printed factual statements that spoke for themselves, especially on the question of torture. The big-selling dailies told very little. Like the torturers themselves who used jargon to shroud their doings, these papers tended to camouflage the whole issue in euphemisms.

The popular press

Randolph Churchill once said that the popular press provided a meal, in which murder was the hors-d'œuvre, a juicy sex-story the dessert, and a Royal Family scandal the main course (*Le Parisien libéré* hinted broadly that on his honeymoon Captain Phillips had, as a result of regal demands on him, 'gorn lame'). The first 'yellow' journal in the world was French. *La Gazette burlesque* (Paris, 1650–65) abounded in reports of scandals, crime and society gossip. *France-Soir* continues and extends this tradition. It has a circulation of around 400,000 (which has slumped from nearly a million a few years ago), and covers most of the day and night with successive editions. It took up where the pre-war *Paris-Soir* (nicknamed *Pourri-Soir*, because of its unscrupulousness) left off. In eight years during the 1930s, *Paris-Soir* jumped from sales of 60,000 to 2 million by reason of its masses of photos (thus reducing eye strain and brain fag), an enormous staff of reporters everywhere (thus ensuring widest coverage and frequent scoops), and a calculated exploitation of sensationalism. The stress, now as then, falls on 'human interest' stories, strip cartoons and picture serials; on American-style gossip columns and belligerent opinionating (on non-political topics). *France-Soir* also uses the typically French trick of occasionally employing an academician to act as special envoy or commentator on big events. It is doubtful whether it has ever wielded much political influence (popular papers have been called 'leaders who bring up the rear') but, in its pandering to the lower instincts of its readers, it probably has a stultifying effect on their minds. The French popular press, like that of other countries, tends to melodramatize news by presenting politicians as actors in some exotic drama rather than as functionaries, to trivialize it by anecdotage, to warp it by innuendoes and suppositions. All this is so that the reader may have the illusion of living, by proxy, more intensely. Such an escapist press offers collective psychotherapy. René Pucheu has said: 'Le journal est beaucoup moins un moyen d'information qu'un moyen d'incantation, il est à la société technicienne ce que le sorcier est à la religion primitive.'

Although *Le Figaro* and *Le Matin de Paris* have tried weekend supplements, a Sunday press on the Anglo-Saxon model does not yet exist in France. On the other hand, photojournalism, now virtually defunct in Britain, is represented by *Paris-Match*, with a weekly circulation of 750,000 and sometimes considered to be the best picture magazine in Europe. With its commandos of reporters and photographers always on standby to rush to any big event ('*Match* men move in on a story like locusts. After they're through, there's nothing left for anyone else to reap.'), *Paris-Match* maintains an 'apolitical' but essentially anti-Communist line. Aiming to attract the greatest number possible, it tries to offend none of them, and consequently works hard at smoothing the rough angles of any item. But photos, its staple produce, can bias reporting more insidiously than words do: the camera can and does lie.

Some leading papers

Le Figaro

Le Figaro is a rough equivalent to the *Daily Telegraph*, and is the traditional organ of the conservative and moderate bourgeoisie. It had the advantage of reappearing as early as August 1944, with the same title as before the war and with much the same staff. Moreover it is the oldest Paris daily, but, despite its circulation of around 300,000 is heavily dependent for revenue on advertisements for the Paris property market. Its professed policy is eclecticism, and it is proud of its long tradition of using established writers and academicians as contributors. *Le Figaro* was the paper that, in his cork-lined room, Proust relied on to keep in touch with the outside world, especially the affairs of high society. Readers of this paper are unlikely to be extremist, avant-garde or very intellectual. Since its takeover by Hersant in 1975, there have been many struggles between the owner and the editorial staff, some of whom have resigned in order to affirm what was never a very strong independence. Recently it has shown signs of moving more frankly to the Right: its offshoot, *Figaro-Magazine*, is already there, and indeed provides a platform for the New Right. *L' Aurore*, long the journal for small businessmen, and now also under Hersant's control, has gradually become an almost identical paper to *Le Figaro*.

L'Humanité

At the other end of the social spectrum, *L'Humanité* has existed for eighty years and has been the official organ of the French Communist Party for three-quarters of that period. In the 1920s, soon after it became specifically Communist, *L'Humanité* was subjected to harsh treatment by the government. Several seizures of whole issues were made and contributors imprisoned, for inciting the proletariat to strike for better wages and working conditions, and for denouncing French imperialist exploitation in the colonies. At various times in its career, it has supported the Viet-Cong, the Algerian *FLN (Front de libération national)* and the rebels in Cuba. But it wore Stalin-coloured spectacles when reporting on the Hungarian uprising in 1956. It suffers attacks from Socialists, moderates, extreme right-wingers and, increasingly, is outflanked on the Left by more radical elements. As well as calls to direct action, it also plays more often nowadays the waiting game of political alliances. It has half the number of pages of its rivals and has always had to scratch along financially by means of appeal funds and unpaid assistance from readers. The present readership is oldish and the circulation drops steadily. Once a year it has its day of glory, when it organizes a fête attracting hundreds of thousands. There, among the fun fair and the candy floss, Marxist dogma can be more easily disguised than in the daily paper. For all its numerous faults, however, by its continued existence and its occasional campaigns, *L'Humanité* does remind the world that a large number of often militant Communists live in France, and that the French proletariat is probably more politically conscious than its British counterpart.

La Croix

The only truly national daily is the Catholic evening paper *La Croix*, as, unlike the other Paris dailies, it sells its 120,000 copies mainly in the provinces. Starting in 1883 and up to 1914, it published two versions of the daily (one for the élite and one for the popular audience), in keeping with the Catholic convention of hierarchy. After the Second World War, it was regarded with some suspicion, despite de Gaulle's *Nihil obstat* and the support of the Christian democrat MRP, because it was rather late in 'scuttling itself' (June 1944). It fulfils a semi-official role as the vehicle of Church opinion. Far from being obsessed, however, with religious matters, *La Croix* devotes more space to foreign news than, for example, *Le Figaro*. Its crucifix symbol was dropped in 1956 with an ensuing increase in sales of several thousand but, in the main, the Catholic press in France remains very much a closed-circuit organization, conceived principally for the faithful – though there are millions of such faithful. Its financial independence surpasses that of the commercial press, largely because its distribution system excludes costly middlemen. The pattern is: postal subscriptions (90 per cent of the sales of *La Croix*), unpaid home delivery, or stands set up after Mass. On the other hand, *La Croix* wins little advertising revenue, for its readership, oldish and relatively well-educated, is socially too undifferentiated. Its losses are made up by other enterprises, such as printing, in its group. Ecclesiastical advisers sit on the boards of all Catholic publications, but usually exercise their control only after the journal has been published. There is little need for overt interference by the church hierarchy when self-censorship already prevails. Since 1968, a whole page in *La Croix* called 'Dialogue' has been devoted to readers' letters, which over the years seem to have improved in thoughtfulness and to avoid the wasteful jokiness often found in the correspondence columns of the British 'quality' press.

Le Monde

Le Monde is the major serious paper. In shape, it resembles the *Daily Mirror*, but there the likeness ends. Instead of yelling headlines, the reader sees a rather forbidding mass of small print, broken only by the occasional map or graph. The paper's policy is *faire dense*; and the density of its lay-out is counteracted by the intelligence of its content.

Its title reflects its readership, which is worldwide: one tenth of its 425,000 readers are non-French. It is the paper of the urban élite: the magistrature, administrative grades, diplomats, the whole *Université* (that is, *lycée* teachers, students and academics), and top men in industry and commerce. Nevertheless, *Le Monde* is often praised by militant trade unionists for the honesty of its reporting. It has the youngest readership of any major French daily, which might explain what many see as its recent movement towards the Left.

It was born four months after the Liberation of Paris, and so was rather late on the scene. Most of the team that got it going belonged to the pre-war *Le Temps*. Its initial line was support for de Gaulle and a plea for overdue reforms to benefit the workers and young people of France. Clearly, *Le Monde* set out to be less conservative than *Le Temps*, but it placed the same emphasis on the arts and on international affairs. From the beginning, the guiding idea was to launch a paper free from all kinds of influence, such as big business and political parties. It was immediately attacked by left-wing journals, who thought that it would continue where *Le Temps* had left off, as a semi-official source of government news. But very quickly *Le Monde* differentiated itself from its predecessor. Apart from combating external opponents, the staff at times disagreed among themselves, and *La Monde* did not try to conceal its internal difficulties. With similar frankness, it decided to publish its accounts regularly, a practice unheard of in the French press, in order to prove that no financial lobbies were influencing its policies. In 1951, some former editorial staff attempted to return in order to change the paper's neutralist line on foreign affairs. The reigning editor, Beuve-Méry, offered his resignation, but received so much support from his staff and from readers that he agreed to remain. This was an important stage in the development of the French press, as it established a precedent whereby editorial staff were enabled to demand more participation in running the newspapers they work on. Above all, it was a notable victory against the widespread hatred of independence and fair play. It is said that the Communists are less afraid of their biased antithesis *Le Figaro* than of the more objective *Le Monde*. Beuve-Méry believed unashamedly in certain intellectual and moral values, and was always hostile to the lies, scandalmongering and muckraking of so much of the world's press. At the risk of boring his readers, he gave a full-spread treatment to all important documents.

Le Monde has naturally made mistakes. Over Suez, it urged that Nasser should be jumped on heavily. On the Algerian question, its policy shifted from one of supporting the spineless Guy Mollet to that of pleading for negotiation with the rebel nationalists. On the other hand, its apparent indecision on some issues is caused by its attempts to represent conflicting opinions: it acts as a forum for discussions. Of all French journals, the non-kow-towing Catholic monthly *Esprit* is perhaps closest in outlook to *Le Monde*, whose staff sometimes publish articles there. Both stand for moderation, independence, liberalism of a realistic kind, 'révolution par la loi'.

Le Monde has no photos, horoscopes or gaudy advertisements. Precise and vivid reporting is the house rule. It has agreements with *The Guardian*, *La Stampa* and *Die Welt* to interchange articles. It diversifies continuously, with regular supplements on the arts, literature, leisure, science, education and economic affairs. It was run until quite recently by a benevolent despot, in close co-operation with a disciplined team. Beuve-Méry was called 'the misanthrope of the French press', a 'cactus', a 'Cassandra-figure'. He was hardly any wealthier than his assistants and had a profound scorn for money. He was not anaemic in his moderation and commanded a caustic and, if need be, crude style. His instructions to his staff were twofold: 'Pas de bourrage de crâne, pas de léchage de cul'. *Le Monde* is more reliable than *The Guardian*, less shifty than *The Times*, and far less conservative than the *Daily Telegraph*. Its comprehensive and well-informed coverage of foreign news makes all British papers look very insular indeed. Beuve-Méry obviously relished difficulties, 'like selling a boring, expensive newspaper', as he once said. His pseudonym, Sirius, was reminiscent of the French term denoting remoteness of viewpoint, 'le point de vue de Sirius', and it is true that *Le Monde* often takes itself too humourlessly and regards common reality from too Olympian a vantage. The recent attack on it by an ex-staff reporter who charged it with secret subversiveness provoked a pompously self-righteous rejoinder signed by all the members of the team and Beuve-Méry himself. For all its efforts at objectivity, *Le Monde* has never claimed to support the conservative side of the great divide in France, and its recent insertion of political cartoons reveals a readiness to offer on occasion very slanted opinions on current events. Even this most trustworthy of papers needs to be read mistrustfully, but its courage, shown recently in criticizing the French judiciary's many faults, is indisputable. Most recently, the lengthy and divisive process of finding a successor to the previous editor has exacerbated the growing financial difficulties of *Le Monde*.

The only other sizable daily not beholden to the Right is *Le Matin*, founded in 1977, and closely linked to *Le Nouvel Observateur*. It has a circulation of 180,000.

Some weeklies

L'Express and *Le Point*

As no serious Sunday press yet exists in France, there is a greater market than in Britain for weeklies, which have more time for reflection and a more sifted and glamorous presentation. *L'Express*, with a circulation of half a million, is an interesting case of a journal starting out with a pronounced conscience which is gradually shed or made more sophisticated in tune with changes of the times. It first appeared in 1953, as a weekly supplement of the financial daily *Les Echos* (and despite the growth of its financial press France has still no match for *The Economist* or *The Financial Times*). In 1955–6 it tried to transform itself into a daily and failed. In 1964 it changed to the news magazine formula and an editorial that year proclaimed that the era of crusades was over. In the last few years, *L'Express* has revealed a taste for its own peace of mind, and the stimulation of its readers' well-fed bodies. Like its founding editor, Jean-Jacques Servan-Schreiber, it has generally striven to appear young, vigorous, non-conformist but 'with it', explanatory rather than partisan, and slick. It does very well for advertisers. Its public is composed mainly of *cadres*: the 'technocrat' sector, youngish, well equipped with creature comforts and avid for more. It has been said that *L'Express* aims at 'Americanizing' the Left in France. Certainly its present appearance, a near carbon copy of *Time*, suggests that this may be partly true. It extensively 're-writes' in the house style, and its articles present a pretty uniform idiom. In 1977 it was taken over by the financier, Sir James Goldsmith, and now proclaims itself centrist. It is experimenting with regional editions.

Le Point, with sales of 300,000, was founded in 1972 by several refugees from *L'Express*. It is largely non-oppositional and in effect a replica of *L'Express* in lay-out (intellectual/commercial incest, like hypochondria, is a French national sport). But with its practised policy of simplification, *Le Point* makes a point: too much indeed of the language of the French press is self-consciously inaccessible to the general public. *Le Point* successfully escaped when its parent company, Hachette, was taken over by the armaments manufacturer, Matra.

Le Nouvel Observateur

A much more individualistic production than *L'Express* is *Le*

Nouvel Observateur, earlier called *L'Observateur*, then *France-Observateur*. It was founded with the intention of playing in the French press the role once taken by the *New Statesman* in Britain. It has always been firmly anti-colonialist and anti-Gaullist, and has frequently supported the PSU. *Nouvel Observateur* had opted to go against the current, once favoured (e.g. Mendès-France), when it finds them compromising their stated beliefs. Like *L'Express* it lost a good many readers after the end of the exciting Algerian crisis. Yet in 1964 an editorial stated that, in the face of the Americanization of Europe and the alleged depolitization of the public, *Le Nouvel Observateur* had opted to go against the current, convinced that a sufficiently large body of readers wanted to be informed and guided by a left-wing journal dedicated to the democratic revival of France. This faith has proved justified, for this weekly steadily increases in circulation. After the Events of May 1968, it rediscovered its old belligerence and today tends, sometimes to the point of silliness, to look for signs of revolutionary change in every walk of life: education, employment and literature, but also films, motoring and fashion. It boasts a team of idiosyncratic writers and a more than average number of tough, intelligent women columnists. Although some firms withdraw copy because of the frequent intransigence of its political stances, it carries a good deal of quality advertising, for its readers include many well-off liberals. Its readership is young (twenty to forty-five in the main) and composed principally of *cadres moyens et supérieurs*, students, teachers, the liberal professions and trade union executives. Its rather pompously stated ambition (to remain 'un journal d'opinion, pur et dur') is being largely fulfilled. When it changed its format in 1972, to look more like *L'Express*, it sent a questionnaire to many political, academic and cultural luminaries, asking them what kind of paper they wanted it to be. Most replied: carry on as before, but avoid the trap of radical chic, *suivisme*. Its current circulation is 370,000.

Le Canard enchaîné

Le Canard enchaîné is the leading French satirical journal. It began as a trench news sheet in 1916, dedicated to resisting the government's *bourrage de crâne* of the common soldier and citizen. It sought to unmask all official pronouncements, by lampooning the gaps between policy and practice. Its title stemmed from the old word *canard*, meaning first any printed matter offered for public (especially popular) consumption, and second, false news. The only papers that the masses, if literate enough to read them, could afford throughout most of the nineteenth century were *canards*, as the high cost of proper newspapers reserved them for an élite. *Le Canard enchaîné* exploits this tradition towards a more honourable goal: 'the demystification of the man in the street'. Its professed policy is to provide 'a clownish but critical parody of the daily press'. To this end, its lay-out apes that of a normal daily and, though it appears weekly, its team's powers of improvisation ensure that its commentary on the news is always up to the minute. It aims to have the same relationship to the daily press as puppet-shows have to the theatre.

Its articles are specifically 'made in France'. It reflects what many Frenchmen like to think of as typical Frenchness: *débrouillardise*, *bon sens*, occasional *engueulades*. Neither *Punch* nor the *New Yorker* is a close equivalent. *Private Eye* is nearer, in its often schoolboyish thumbing of the nose at authority, though the *Canard*'s writers are mostly middle-aged, and their dissidence is less flashily contemporary. The *Canard* receives a heavy mail from readers: letters of support, rockets, snippets for that section of the paper devoted to the howlers and other idiocies of public pronouncements. This close contact of readers and journalists lends the *Canard* the air of a club. It is a club, too, in another sense: its comic tactics range from winking innuendoes to thumping puns ('Ne disiez-vous pas, Monsieur de Gaulle, que les Français étaient des veaux? Ils ont veauté pour vous'). With its circulation of 600,000 (three-quarters of that in the provinces) it clearly has, by French standards, a wide audience. It is most popular with school and university teachers, students and the less affluent members of the professional classes. Its editorial staff work as a co-operative, taking a share of the profits. Each has freedom of expression, but the chief editor retains the right to excommunicate. One of its leading columnists was once sacked for accepting the *Légion d'honneur*.

Its policy of accepting no advertising, either open or concealed, makes it unique in the French press. The result, however, is a rather grubby and old-fashioned appearance, which is perhaps part of its image as a rebellious old war horse. Its standpoint is that of the *frondeur*, the defender of individual and minority rights. Its strong polemical tradition prevents its taking sides easily, and it tends to oppose those in power, whether Right, Left or Centre. This is especially valuable at present, when the Socialist government reveals itself to be every bit as self-righteously touchy about its press image as the preceding one had been.

Its satire is not exclusively political. It features a good deal of purely verbal humour and some analysis of cultural trends (it is very rude towards the whole concept of modishness). The tone is frequently that of an embittered but still virulent idealism. It is not an anti-social paper. The ideal is 'constructive anarchism'.

Often the rumours it reports are exclusive and well-informed (generally leaked by disgruntled insiders). De Gaulle was a godsend. Easily caricatured, his regal style inspired one *Canard* writer to describe his entourage regularly in terms of the court of Louis XIV, and Gaullist politics were in this way presented as a court entertainment in a France that had reverted to monarchy.

In many ways, *Le Canard enchaîné* is outdated and sentimental (one of its heroes is Victor Hugo), but it undoubtedly reflects a native distrust of politicians and a strong desire on the part of most people to be left in peace by the 'powers that be'. The *Canard* has never been seized. One Prime Minister, urged to suppress a particularly outspoken issue, retorted that he had no desire to become a national laughing stock. This peculiar kind of immunity goes with its status as an institution. Licensed fools, however, lose some of their bite and governments can point to the *Canard*'s untroubled existence as proof of their own liberalism, though this myth was recently punctured when the *Canard*'s offices were found to be bugged. Another weakness: regular readers note the strain behind the *Canard*'s attempts to be funny about everything; news items are often milked dry. In this age of hidden persuaders, all the same, *Le Canard enchaîné*, like its cousins, the geese on the Capitol in Rome, sounds an appealing alarm at every encroachment on freedom. In 1972 it was central to the publicizing of the scandals which disclosed corruption in high Gaullist circles. More recently its leaks about the gifts of diamonds to Giscard may well have cost him some credibility. Financially, it has the last laugh: the *Canard* is the least lame duck of the French press.

The regional press

Though the metropolitan press is not noted for recognizing its own distortions and omissions, in 1972 *Le Nouvel Observateur* published an article calling the regional press 'la presse du silence'. In response, provincial owners and editors protested, too much. Content analyses have in fact shown that regional papers studiously avoid raising important local issues in many cases. 'Pour l'infiniment petit', said the director of the Bordeaux-based *Sud-Ouest*, 'nous sommes irremplaçables.' When provincial papers fail to appear, statistics show that social, economic and cultural life in the catchment area suffers badly, and that attendance at funerals drops markedly. 'La nécrologie constitue la base de la vie d'un journal de province', as a *Sud-Ouest* editor said with a straight face. The regional paper is undoubtedly an agent of interconnection between scattered localities and individuals.

Pressures from all quarters, the commonly expressed but inadequately justified fear of upsetting advertisers, the notorious closeness of provincial community life, these are all reasons why the regional press treads carefully. In its defence it should be stressed that the Paris press lets the provinces down by talking more readily of national or foreign issues than of purely regional ones. Besides, the large provincial papers, because of their often monopolistic position, are perhaps wise in trying to remain politically neutral. There are, however, exceptions to the general rule. *L'Est républicain*, for instance, gave extensive support in 1970 to the candidature at Nancy of Jean-Jacques Servan-Schreiber. And for all its glaring short-comings of moral cowardice, political conservatism, its care not to ruffle the hair of local bigwigs, the regional press at least talks of what interests its readers. It is helped in this service by its elaborate network of local correspondents, a luxury that the

Paris dailies simply cannot afford. Indeed, the provincials win both ways, for a good number of top Parisian journalists contribute articles to the regional press. However, with the introduction of modern techniques, the Paris dailies can now add local pages to their standard editions and transmit these rapidly to the provinces, thus rivalling the regional press on its own ground. Nevertheless the situation at present is that Paris papers seem to function mainly in the hothouse atmosphere of the capital, largely divorced from the provincial life led by the majority of Frenchmen.

The parallel press

1968 saw the resurrected phenomenon of the *journal mural* (a means of conveying information, slogans, insults, credos and morale-boosts among the rebels), which to many optimistic observers and participants was the writing on the wall for the old France. The often beautiful posters produced by the students of the Beaux-Arts demanded 'information libre!' Liberty of expression was indeed one of the main freedoms sought and temporarily practised by the insurgents. From 1968 and until the late 1970s, this new press (called variously 'parallel', 'wildcat', 'impressionist', 'underground', 'alternative' or *gauchiste*) has had a remarkable and turbulent career. The sudden emergence of such papers and often equally sudden extinction (they have been called 'exploding ephemera') were their facts of life, the extinction caused both by governmental measures of harassment and by internecine strife amongst the *groupuscules*. At their peak, sales of some reached 100,000.

Their innovation was principally to give a voice to the previously stifled protest of workers, servicemen, convicts, students, pupils and ethnic or sexual minorities. Readers were encouraged to participate directly via letters, the gathering and transmitting of news, the constitution of dossiers. Revolutionary press agencies were formed in order to co-ordinate this mass of material. What were at first mainly militants' news sheets, badly printed and arid in content, were often transformed into attractive, exciting and professional products.

Of all of them, *Libération*, founded in 1973, is enjoying the

longest life. Early in 1981, a split developed between those of
its staff who favoured keeping it as it was – no hierarchy, rotation of jobs, identical wages for all, no advertising – and those
who wanted a more competitively modern paper run on truly
professional lines. The latter won, and sales climbed to 70,000.
No doubt, as before, it will try to steer clear of all constituted
organizations ('militants de la vie et non d'un parti', as many
new journalists see themselves).

In France, by law, any publication, even small or contentious, is guaranteed access to distribution and display, unlike
the situation in the Smith/Menzies chains in the United Kingdom. This might help to explain why many wildcat papers
survived as long as they did. Some became blunter through
repetition. Scatology was rampant. It sometimes seemed that,
if the widespread manure could be reprocessed, by some
natural organic method of course, and passed on to the
ecological press, the gardens of communes might flourish.
Another development of this press was strip cartoons in which
even the heroes were grotesque (though this might stem from
slapdash draughtsmanship). All suffered from the debilitating
fact of life that, to vie with the established press, they needed
to emulate its organization: distribution systems, advertising,
the hard sell. In fact, a type of short-circuit occurred, by which
underground journalists write mainly for the initiated.
'Aspirant à réaliser la révolution par le plaisir, elle a souvent du
mal à exister pour autre chose que son propre plaisir', as *Le
Monde* once said. In addition to these newspapers, proper or
improper, roneotyped sheets continue to serve a necessary
function in barracks, factories, schools and universities for
those disillusioned by traditional organs, parties or *syndicats*.

The anarchist press answers the needs of those sickened by
endless doctrinal dispute, and it has strong links with the
Women's and Gay Liberation movements. The aim of one
such publication is typical of many: 'considérer chaque
individu comme artiste afin d'éliminer l'artiste'. The
motivation is often as much cultural or 'counter-cultural' as
political. Yet, just as no truly national daily exists in France, so
no comprehensive paper unites all the variegated elements of
the counter-culture, which are, in comparison with Anglo-
Saxon youth, still relatively unemancipated.

The whole phenomenon of the parallel press has clearly alarmed the authorities, which have sometimes resorted, in what seems like panic, to seizures and trials. Sartre (the 'lightning-conductor' of the new press), by accepting the function of director of, and therefore legal responsibility for, several *gauchiste* papers, tried repeatedly to prove that justice in France as regards the press has 'deux poids, deux mesures'. After he provoked the authorities to haul him in, the official response was a perfect example of Marcuse's concept of repressive tolerance: 'On n'arrête pas Voltaire.' All in all, however, this alternative press acts as a constant thorn in the fleshy side of the Establishment. But it was Sartre himself who said soberingly, in 1970: 'Les journaux bourgeois disent plus la vérité que la presse révolutionnaire.'

Depolitization

Like all young media, television is often credited with almost magical powers of influence. None the less, as it and the radio are controlled by the State in France, the temptation to use both as conditioning agents has frequently proved irrestistible. De Gaulle's big appearances on the little screen were in keeping with his general attitude towards the Fifth Republic: he could make direct appeals, bypassing such encumbrances as Parliament. There is, then, all the more need for a vigorous independent press to counterbalance such pressures. It seems likely that the 'audio-visual press' has mainly shock value, and that people wishing to inform themselves properly on current affairs need to turn for commentary and extended explanation to the written word. In short, radio and television do not necessarily kill off the press, but rather stimulate the appetite for a serious press.

The introduction of advertising on French television hit newspapers, but perhaps not so severely as the decline in 'small ads', due to the general economic situation. Furthermore, the monopoly system favours the big papers, and Paris dailies kill each other off more often than they succumb to competition from television. Television is dangerous, not so much in that it steals advertising and thus weakens the press economically, but more in that, being a monolithic and largely unquestioned institution, it stifles thought.

It is difficult to deny that all forms of public communication in France, and this is where Gaullism most demoralized the nation, bear witness to the phenomenon of depolitization: public apathy in the face of often crucial political matters. Since 1945, the Communist *Ce Soir*, the Socialist *Le Peuple*, the liberal *Combat* and the Gaullist *La Nation* have died; there are no extreme right-wing dailies at all, though the sales of the satirical weekly *Minute* doubled in the Paris area after May 1981 and now run at 200,000. It is openly racist and features personalized attacks on Socialists and Communists.

It can be argued, of course, that as the style of politics itself changes, so does public interest, but it is hard to distinguish what new forms of political awareness may have appeared. Many people are clearly bored with the increasingly formalized nature of politics in France, and transfer their energies to more private concerns (hence the rapid growth of the specialist press, the 'mini-media', dealing in hobbies). The *apolitisme*, especially of the regional press, leads naturally to conservative stances. And yet 'there is a monarchist way of reporting on road accidents'. Every journal has a slant, and none more so than those that claim to be 'pure' newspapers. In these the manipulation of readers' attitudes is at its most surreptitious. Their style of reporting is often neither neutral enough to be 'information', nor intellectualized enough to be 'opinion'. It is governed by and it promotes *attitudes* (unconscious prejudices, fallacies, stereotypes). It has been claimed that educated Russians are better at decoding *Pravda* than western thinking people are at reading between the lines of our own 'free' press. In addition to editorial bias, there is the matter of that loaded information, on which papers rely so heavily, supplied by press attachés and public relations officers – the whole question of the filtering and packaging of facts.

Proust spoke of 'cet acte abominable et voluptueux qui s'appelle: lire le journal'. Perhaps inevitably, the relationship of many readers with the paper of their choice is narcissistic. They gaze at their own face, hear their own voice, their own fears and desires, suitably embellished and projected back to them. There can be few people who read with the express intention, or even the readiness, to be jolted. Most of us can shut off what we do not wish to hear (conversely, attention, once polarized, can be acute). Few readers have time or patience to collate differing versions of the same news in different papers. As a result, opinions are often refuges, non-opinions. Today the temptation is not to *read* a paper but to 'spectate' it. The pages often resemble supermarkets, the new 'iconosphere'. The eclecticism of the present-day press, offering a bit to everyone, works against the notion of responsibility. The number and variousness of readers are too great for any one line to be presented. While the weeklies can afford to be rather more committed, because they serve fairly faithful and homogeneous groups, the daily press as a whole is diversifying its contents; papers and magazines are getting closer together in style and material. Some of the more serious organs like *Le Monde* resist the contemporary craze for built-in obsolescence, by stressing the documentary function of the press (for example, the publication of annual indexes of articles to facilitate reference back), but this is exceptional.

Sociétés de rédacteurs

Some of the most obvious shortcomings of the French press date back a long way. Over the past twenty years, the most hopeful signs of reform have come from within the journalistic profession itself, in which three warring factions predominate: the owners, the editorial staffs, and the technical operatives. The complexity of agreements and the marked individualism of the parties concerned have impeded the growth of honourable efficiency. The powerful union of printers has imposed high wages and under-employment of staff, by using archaic standards for calculating work loads. Although modern machines have been introduced, profitability has shown little increase, because the same number of men as before work them. In the 1969 troubles at *Le Figaro*, the technicians did not side with the editorial staff in its resistance to the owner's bid for complete control.

For three years recently, open war raged on *Le Parisien Libéré*, a big-selling popular daily, between the owner Amaury and the monopolizing printing-workers' union (the *Fédération du livre*-CGT). There were broken agreements, sieges of premises, assaults on blackleg personnel, hijacking of pirate editions. The owner and his chief executive, Claude Bellanger, both made great play of their Resistance records, although in this particular confrontation it was hard for outsiders to tell which side was the *maquis* and which the repressive occupying force. The owner presented his struggle as a democratic crusade against would-be totalitarian Communism and its attempts to control editorial matter and dictate the size of the workforce. The only clear results in three years of battling were the owner's decision to spend large sums in order to construct alternative printing-works and new distribution systems, and the drop in circulation by one half. Elsewhere, in July 1976, Paris paper owners, including Amaury, and printers' unions settled their long dispute over technical modernization (photo-composition and computer typesetting).

A good many journalists refuse to envisage the press as simply a commercial proposition, and are haunted by theories about the corrupting power of money and by romantic visions of a press akin to knight-errantry. For them, papers should offer their readers 'daily refresher courses', an *éducation permanente*. To idealistic journalists, it is as scandalous that industrialists should control papers as it would be to most people if they controlled law courts or universities. And this statement by a powerful press lord, taxed with having sold out to big business interests, unwittingly illustrates what they are reacting against: 'Je ne me suis jamais vendu qu'à mes lecteurs.' The spokesmen for reform realize that the opponents of any proposed *co-gestion* in producing papers will raise the old alarmist bogyman of 'des soviets partout!' Few reformers are as radical as this. Some would settle for American-style foundations, which would run papers as limited-profit companies. The *sociétés de rédacteurs* that have been set up on *Le Monde* (in which the editorial staff hold shares), *Le Figaro* and *Ouest-France*, see themselves as active watchdodgs, ensuring that news is not treated purely as a commercial product and that editiorial staff have a real say in all decision-making – but only at *Le Monde* do they have any true influence.

The common belief of such *sociétés* is that the press faces the same problems as society at large: in particular, the need to democratize the remaining autocratic structures. They recognize that part of their programme must include a better training for journalists themselves; and university degree courses have been established at Paris, Lille, Strasbourg and Bordeaux. Refresher courses, especially in economics, about which many journalists are as under-informed as the general public, have also been laid on. In this whole area of reform, the French pressmen have outstripped their British colleagues, who only recently have begun actively to question the present functioning of the mass media and to propose needed changes.

One recent proposal made in *Esprit* is that *sociétés de lecteurs*, akin to consumer-protection groups, are at least as necessary as those of journalists. There is clearly a need for 'informational militants': self-appointed journalists who cross-check reports from news agencies or who raise hushed up and forgotten issues. The biggest need is for plurality of viewpoints, though even pluralism should have its limits. Why, for instance, weep over the material difficulties of badly conceived and ill-run rags?

Conclusion

Edmund Burke spoke of the press as the Fourth Estate, alongside the judiciary, executive and legislative powers. What kind of a force is the French press? It has been suggested that, like that of the Latin nations in general, it is more of a 'tribune' press, which goes to the people instead of coming from it, or at least conversing with it. Hence the large amount of pontificating, the paternalism, and the lack of attention given to readers' letters (which could act as a feedback and the start of a dialogue). One explanation, among many others, for the depolitization of the French press is the inhibiting historical example of *Le Petit Journal*. At the time of the Dreyfus Affair, it had the widest circulation of all French papers. It campaigned for Dreyfus; it lost half its readers. Consequently, there is a widespread reluctance to meddle or to shock, at least openly, for all papers try to direct opinion indirectly by veiled allusions, undocumented sources, omissions or by effects of juxtaposition. Comment disguised as news is a constant ploy.

Perhaps the two features of the French press that most strike a foreign reader are, first, the *médisance*, the personal bitchiness, the bristly sense of 'honour' common to French journalists of all persuasions; this derives in part from the importance granted to ideas, to ideologies. Second, there is the impression that French journalists, even mediocre ones, are soaked in history, politics and literature. Occasionally, this cultural formation proves too facile, turns to *déformation professionnelle*, and produces (like French lawyers, and like many of the readers who do write to their papers) a kind of cheap sub-literature, replete with rhetorical effects. Just as there is a long tradition of sedentary anthropology in France, so there is one of armchair journalism, which relies too much on printed sources or imagination and too little on going to look for oneself. Perhaps a better result is that, in *L'Humanité*, addressed among others to manual workers, can be found long words and cultural allusion beyond the imaginings of the British popular press. Even *France-Soir* publishes occasional serious articles. A lack of matter-of-factness can be a handicap but also a blessing.

Prophets see both the press and printed books as moribund industries. It might well be that papers will fairly soon become (as they started out) a privilege for the well-off minority, because costs in future will be more closely matched by much increased selling prices. *Paris-Jour*, in that it had most blue-collar workers in its readership, was the most 'popular' paper in Paris before it died in 1972. After it closed, it seems that its readers did not switch to any other paper. It is sometimes said that Paris has room for only two morning and two evening papers. The sad part of the success of *Le Monde*, over which it would be snobbish to rejoice too much, is that readers at the bottom end of the earning scale might eventually be deprived of what is in many cases their sole source of reading matter. It is yet another indication of the separate orbits in France of the intelligentsia and the masses. René Pucheu offers a salutary reminder that 'la bêtise n'est pas un privilège des non-privilégiés'.

Bibliography

Agnès, Y. and Croissandeau, J.M., *Lire le journal*. Paris, Lobiès, 1979. Excellent on using the press as a teaching aid.

Albert, P., *La Presse*. Paris, PUF, 1968. A general study, short but accurate.

Archambault, F. and Lemoine, J.F., *Quatre Milliards de journaux*. Paris, Moreau, 1977.

Bellanger, C. (ed.), *Histoire générale de la presse française*, 5 vols. Paris, PUF, 1969-77.

Bercoff, A., *L'Autre France: l'underpresse*. Paris, Stock, 1975.

Cayrol, R., *La Presse écrite et audiovisualle*. Paris, PUF, 1973.

Derieux, E. and Texier, J.C., *La Presse quotidienne française*. Paris, Colin, 1974.

Freiberg, J.W., *The French Press: Class, State and Ideology*. New York, Praeger, 1981.

Jeanneney, J.-N. and Julliard, J., *Le Monde de Beuve-Méry*. Paris, Seuil, 1979.

Pucheu, R., *Le Journal, les mythes et les hommes*. Paris, Editions Ouvrières, 1962.

Schwoebel, J., *La Presse, le pouvoir et l'argent*. Paris, Seuil, 1968. Good on the *sociétés de rédacteurs*.

Varin D'Ainville, M., *La Presse en France*. Paris, PUF, 1965.

Voyenne, B., *L'Information aujourd'hui*. Paris, Colin, 1979. A completely rewritten version of *La Presse dans la société contemporaine* (1962) and the best general study.

The 'Kiosque' series published by Colin contain several fascinating studies of the press in action, for example, *La Gauche hebdomadaire*, *La Presse clandestine*, *Le Monde et ses lecteurs*, *Le Cas Paris-Soir*.

The monthly *Presse-Actualité* is a goldmine of up-to-date information. *La Documentation française* published in May 1978, no. 4469, an excellent review of the whole question of the French press.

Nine

The broadcasting media

Neil Harris

Introduction

A study of the media in any country tends to arrive at conclu-
sions that are heavy with implication, most obviously concerning the attitude of a government towards its news and
information services. The fact that television has developed so
rapidly in the past thirty years or so, resulting in an increasing
reliance on it as the supplier of news, has made this question
into a crucial factor in assessing the state of democracy anywhere. In Britain, we like to think that the relative freedom of
the media to broadcast material critical of the State is a
symptom of a healthy society; loss of free speech, the argument goes, is a serious threat to more fundamental liberties.
The BBC has indeed established an international reputation as
a voice of freedom. It did so particularly during the Second
World War, and if it was impossible to say as much of the
French broadcasting system until recently, it is back to the
same time that we must look to find the cause. The considerable governmental influence to be seen in the workings of the
media, where a head of broadcasting can say confidently 'a
journalist should be French first, objective second', has
allowed many commentators to observe, via the different
concessions and crackdowns made by the government, the
various pressures on it from within and without.

The arrival of a new regime, as well as the imminent communications revolution, has tossed a stone into the stagnant
pool of the broadcasting monopoly, although it will take years

before the full impact of Socialist reforms becomes apparent; indeed, the definitive text of many of these reforms has yet to appear. It is true to say, however, that those who anticipated instant translation to a world of free, vigorous broadcasting have been in large measure disappointed. Despite the tremendous upheavals following May 1981, quite a lot of the old-style way of thinking has been preserved. Undoubtedly the Gaullist tradition of autocratic rule dies hard, in broadcasting as elsewhere; and this can only hinder an industry that is already behind in an extremely competitive market.

Background

The effectiveness of radio as a vehicle for political propaganda was discovered before, but particularly during the Second World War. De Gaulle in exile recognized the vital part it could play in rallying loyal Frenchmen to his cause, and once the war was over he lost no time in nationalizing the radio networks, thereby driving home the Gaullist message and expunging the collaborationist image created by the private radio stations in the pre-war years. As television spread in the late 1950s, de Gaulle proved himself as much a master of this new and even more powerful means of mass communication. His appearances on television, particularly as President, were virtuoso displays in the art of controlling an audience and he even reserved some of his major policy decisions for his televised press conferences. As long as he was able to exercise total control over the political content of radio and television, he had no fear of a serious rival.

Not surprisingly, this absolute veto came in for much criticism. Gaullist assertions that such control was necessary to counterbalance opposition in some of the press did not cut much ice, since the rapid spread of television, and falling newspaper sales, had quickly made both radio and television more powerful and lasting means of putting over a message. In order as much as anything to placate their critics, the Gaullists created in 1964 the *Office de la radiodiffusion et télévision française* (ORTF). ORTF was ostensibly an autonomous body which assumed responsibility for programming; but many of the posts in the organization remained government appointments – was this then such a large step towards a broadcasting service free from State control?

Discontent with this lack of freedom, together with the problems of a cumbersome bureaucracy and unsatisfactory working conditions, reached its head, like so much else, in 1968. The ensuing 'liberalization' of the ORTF from 1969-72, the work of the Prime Minister Jacques Chaban-Delmas, was fiercely criticized by many in the government; and the Office retained its unitary structure until 1974 when the incoming President Giscard d'Estaing, having based his electoral campaign on more flexible policies than those of his predecessors, rapidly (some say now much too rapidly) pushed through legislation breaking up the ORTF into seven independent companies, or *sociétés*. It was hoped that competition between these would prove beneficial for broadcasting at large, but the companies soon ran into financial difficulties. Furthermore the government, by making those at the head of the companies its own nominees, showed itself reluctant to grant real independence to these *filles de l'ORTF*. The very strong Gaullist presence in the administration no doubt contributed largely to this measure.

May 1981 and afterwards

Like President Giscard in 1974, the Socialists saw the reform of broadcasting as one of their first tasks on coming to power. But this, the fifth reform of the service in twenty-five years, was to be the most radical. The new administration undertook to ensure that the public service (as they called it, significantly discarding the term 'monopoly') was protected from government intervention. In order to 'cut this umbilical cord', an *Haute Autorité* was created, a council of nine members, their mandate (doubtless intentionally) longer than that of the presidential term. The Authority has taken upon itself the task of appointing the directors of the *sociétés*, drawing up the 'cahier des charges' which define the exact scope of broadcasting for each company, plus several other tasks which hitherto were handled exclusively by the government. Its personnel come from professions other than politics; the judiciary is represented, for example and the Assembly and Senate as well as the President have put up names for this council. The intention clearly has been to set up an independent body whose staff, while perhaps lacking éclat, is solidly professional and capable of instilling confidence in the troubled world of broadcasting.

All this, however, has taken a year to become law, and at first the arrival of the new regime caused much consternation. There was a flurry of activity amongst those at the top, with the government subsequently being accused, justifiably, of rough treatment in its handling of those it considered particularly at fault. Within the rank and file there was an expectation that rapid reforms would follow; but much of this optimism was to disappear over the next twelve months. If journalists had felt repressed under Giscard, they now felt frustrated and leaderless. Those appointed as directors were 'hommes de dialogue' rather than men with new ideas; they appeared to have as little interest in the day-to-day running of the channels as their predecessors. There was no real sense of contact between those in charge and the programme makers. The temporary nature of the appointments also made things difficult for everyone: a director naturally feels reluctant to elaborate a long-term strategy for his company if he is not sure he will be in the job in a year's time; and the personnel feel a corresponding insecurity ('Our *patrons* are whirling dervishes' said one, 'three turns and they're gone.')

It is to be hoped therefore that the naming in September 1982 of the company presidents for a period of three years will act as a steadying influence. In fact the case of one of these nominations is particularly interesting. Pierre Desgraupes is an old hand in television, having been on the team of one of the most influential news magazines of the early 1960s, *Cinq colonnes à la une*. He survived a reputation for liberalism under the Gaullists and became one of the most respected journalists of the post-1968 era. He is now head of the second French television channel Antenne 2, but in the year since the Socialists came to office his presence has not acted as a stimulus; indeed the views expressed by his staff have an all too familiar ring about them: they find him over-cautious, wary of change, even contemptuous of incoming talent and fresh ideas. This kind of sterile age/youth conflict has appeared in the past, but may conceivably be less of an issue once a more stable situation is created.

The malaise within television has certainly communicated itself to the viewing audience. The majority of French people have long expressed themselves dissatisfied with the service and a year after the euphoria of mid-1981, there were still headlines in magazines reading: 'What is wrong with our television?' The public has no doubt on that score: they are resentful at seeing prime-time schedules given over to arid discussions of society's problems, at once garrulous and muddled, which leave them feeling half-bored, half-patronized. The Left may try to defend this sort of programme as attempting to explode the myth that the nation returns home in the evening too tired to think for itself; others suggest that instruction is not incompatible with entertainment.

Television structures

The TV companies created in the 1974 reform still exist, for the most part, in 1982. They include the three present channels TF1, Antenne 2, and FR3, together with *Télédiffusion de France* (technical problems of broadcasting and maintenance of transmitters), and the *Société française de production* (making of films, video productions and marketing). It was intended that the new companies should commission programmes from the SFP, but they soon went their own way and the SFP ran further and further into debt. Eight years on this problem seems no nearer a solution.

TF1 commands the largest audience of the three channels, deliberately fostering a more 'popular' image than its sister A2, which has more cultural aspirations. FR3 is the company which concerns itself to a certain extent with regional affairs, and up until very recently has been rather the poor relation (a journalist dismissed from TF1 in 1981 was told that he could 'always go and work for FR3', apparently the equivalent of the Russian Front). The channel has frequently been called 'pseudo-regionalist', as its outposts were ideologically responsible to Paris ('Ils n'ont de régional que leur adresse' said *Le Monde*). This is now changing, as the government implements its decentralization policy for broadcasting: the intention is to make all the regional stations independent, beginning with the three largest – Lille, Marseille and Lyon. For the moment, these local branches have to content themselves with an increase in the amount of time they may devote to programmes of specifically local interest. Even this seems to be paying dividends: one station, Midi-Pyrénées, has registered a considerable increase in its audience to coincide with an extension of its local news programmes. If until now FR3 has been the 'chaîne du cinéma' – much of its airtime has been spent showing films – its ambition is to become a true 'chaîne des régions'.

Finance and a fourth channel

The intention of the government in 1974 was that the three TV channels should be dependent on licence fees, shared out according to a formula based on audience and quality ratings, plus a fixed proportion of advertising revenue. In 1982 the resources of the licence fee (approximately 450 francs a year in 1983) and the revenue from publicity barely sufficed to keep TF1 and A2 afloat, and further cutbacks are planned. The new regime has inherited many difficulties; in the years between 1974 and 1981 the same wastage of resources that crippled the ORTF was in evidence among the companies (especially the SFP). There was a surfeit of administrators, while the number of *réalisateurs* (those responsible for the actual making of programmes) on the payroll was far in excess of those needed in work at any one time. Squandering money here and elsewhere naturally reduced the opportunities for the channels to be vigorous and creative; no risks can be taken where any further serious loss would result in financial disaster. In 1980 the SFP announced a loss of 50 million francs; it remains to be seen whether the new plans to bind it together with TF1 and A2 in a *groupement d'intérêts économiques* will help. 'Hollywood gérée par la Sécurité Sociale' is a not-so-recent description it may well be stuck with for some time yet.

While TF1 and A2 during the Giscard years derived more than half their income from advertising (despite a ruling which fixed the ceiling at 25 per cent, a figure which in theory still exists), FR3 has hitherto been free of publicity. Now there are plans to introduce a ten-minute daily spot in certain areas from January 1983. This has caused difficulties particularly with regard to the local press, and the interest of the State-owned publicity agency Havas and the lesser, privately-owned Publicis has caused conflicts with the *Régie française de publicité*, the overseeing company which specializes in television advertising. In any case, the government has made the matter of publicity subject to annual review and it will certainly adapt its policies to the circumstances of the moment.

There are plans to introduce a fourth channel sometime in 1983. This appears to be the cradle of many hopes for the middle-term financial security of the production companies. It will only be received in certain areas to begin with, but by 1986 it is hoped that it will cover 70 per cent of French territory. This will coincide, as we shall see, with a large-scale cabling operation, and the channel will undoubtedly take a very different form to the three others. At the moment it seems likely that it will be operated as a hybrid, on a part-free, part-pay basis. One worry is that a new channel will be opening without – as long as output from production companies remains stagnant – many home-produced programmes to put on it, thus opening the way to a flood of imports; as it is, the three channels buy their cartoons from Japan, most of their television films from the US, and most of their documentaries from Britain . . . . Further, it may be risky to launch a fourth channel in the regions where FR3 has been expanding and draining off the advertising revenue. Add to this the expense of adapting existing transmitters and the whole enterprise seems fraught with difficulty. Nevertheless the government is committed to it and appears confident that it will work.

News and information on the media

1956 is often cited as the year in which government interference in the media became particularly obvious. Political censorship was rigorous throughout the duration of the Algerian crisis, and by 1961 was firmly entrenched as a way of life in France. News bulletins contained items evidently designed to induce unconditional admiration for government policies; reflection on events was not encouraged. The items had to be presented in the right order: one head of news almost lost his job for putting a description of a strike before an account of a presidential visit. Critics of such an attitude were not only concerned by the political bias, but also by the fact that everything that was not propaganda was of scant interest. Even after the creation of the ORTF, the director-general had the right to make every appointment, to veto news missions (applications made by investigative teams for permission to go out on assignments), also to choose political commentators for fifteen-minute 'journals' (interviews with prominent government figures), and to preview news sequences if required.

The 1965 presidential campaign changed the situation considerably by showing for the first time on television an opposition candidate who was allowed to present his case on the same terms as his government counterpart. This made an extraordinary impression on the public, and resulted in the government failing to win a clear majority at the first ballot (de Gaulle had not bothered to appear at all, but was obliged to do so before the second ballot). Between 1965 and 1968 several current affairs programmes appeared. The hierarchical structure of the ORTF remained, however, and little protection was afforded to journalists by the terms of their contracts; the threat of dismissal hung constantly over their heads. When the two news services were combined into one early in 1968 discontent reached a new pitch, and the upheaval of May gave the journalists a chance to express themselves vigorously. The nature of their protest (involving the complete taking over of the networks for a time) brought the attention of the public to bear on the way in which the coverage of the riots by the media was being controlled by the government. Subsequently, polls showed that 85 per cent of viewers would like to see the news services made independent of the State.

Reforms however were not immediately forthcoming. It was only after the presidential elections of 1969 that the new Prime Minister, Jacques Chaban-Delmas, promised an independent news unit for each channel, each with a director having full responsibility for choosing his own team of journalists. The directors had secure tenure, and could only be dismissed in cases of exceptional professional misconduct. Some sacked journalists were reinstated, and in general there were hopeful signs that the news services were becoming more attractive.

Nevertheless the ORTF was still the 'voice of France'. Following the 1972 'clandestine publicity' scandals a new statute tightened the hold of the government; elections were approaching, and Pierre Messmer, the Prime Minister, was less tolerant than Chaban-Delmas when it came to freedom for broadcasting. The government was also angry at the news teams' treatment of the Common Market referendum earlier that year. Many contracts were not renewed. News was placed in the control of the directors of channels who were themselves responsible to the president. In spite of the strenuous denials of the head of the ORTF, Arthur Conte, that there existed control of news in the Office, a gradual decline in audiences followed. The journalists themselves were describing the pressures on them as representing a return to pre-1968 levels of censorship. Conte was known to have weekly meetings with Messmer over breakfast, presumably to be 'briefed'. Even after the 1974 reforms journalists realized that the heads of television news were directly responsible to the government.

To those who attempted to make the best of a bad job and remain within the organization, the effects of such censorship from above were all too evident. A group of journalists made known their difficulties via *Le Monde* in 1979, describing the discouragement felt by all who aspired to lively coverage of news and its objective presentation; with their jobs at stake, even the most dedicated of their number were disinclined to make any attempt at impartial reporting. The problems were such that in March 1979, following a demonstration in Paris and the imprisonment of many of those who took part, it took an enquiry by a BBC team to make known the dubious judicial processes leading up to the jailings. The team even managed to interview Alain Peyrefitte, the Privy Seal and a key figure in the affair; it is doubtful whether an investigation by the French services would have got anywhere near this far, much less have received permission to broadcast the results.

The news programmes on Antenne 2 were particularly mistrusted at this time, and on the night of the Socialist victory a large crowd assembled in the Place de la Bastille, in their fervour calling for the news editor, Jean-Pierre Elkabbach, to be strung up (*Elkabbach à la lanterne!*). He was one focus of resentment, but in the weeks following May 1981 many top newsmen left. Their replacements were in some cases journalists not seen since 1968. Communists have even made an appearance on the staff. Some of the measures taken were injudicious: a newsman of pre-1968 vintage hardly finds it easy to adapt to the techniques of the 1980s, and some of the young people hired seem quite out of their depth.

In certain ways more freedoms and scope have drawn attention to technical inadequacies. There is even an attempt to make a virtue of amateurism, one illustration of this being the current evening news magazine on FR3. It has received much criticism, not only for its strong slant to the Left, but also for the deliberately rough-edged quality of its presentation, sacrificing elegance and continuity for (it is hoped) immediacy of impact and 'authenticity' (the programme makes no use of the autocue, for example). It is also perhaps representative of a narrowly 'Socialist' view of broadcasting in the way it eschews the 'star-system' of political reporting in favour of a team: the use of a single well-known face, it is argued, allows a personality to get in the way of the news (1000 dead in Iraq against a badly knotted tie).

By an irony, it is the old liberal Desgraupes who has been the cause of the most worrying event in broadcasting of recent months. In September 1982 a news presenter on Antenne 2 was removed from his post for remarks 'in bad taste' concerning Princess Grace of Monaco, who had died earlier that day. This was seen as unprecedented, since even when the veteran Roger Gicquel announced the *Affaire des Diamants* (diamonds given to President Giscard by Emperor Bokassa) on TF1 in the autumn of 1979, he was not sacked nor even 'posted'. The matter has revived fears that the bad old days of summary dismissals have not yet disappeared. In fact the aforementioned *Haute Autorité* has made it clear that a journalist's conscience will henceforth be his guide in such matters, and that it will not intervene. However, although this in theory protects the staff from the consequences of ministerial wrath, the channel's *président* may still take action.

Other programmes

Nowhere on French television have the financial difficulties experienced by the *Sociétés* been more in evidence than in more 'highbrow' entertainment. There is little studio-based drama; and despite the plethora of *réalisateurs*, there is a shortage of good directors for television productions of all kinds. Frequently, eminent cinema directors such as Chabrol or Barbet Schroeder are called upon to take charge of the more ambitious projects. There has been a 50 per cent decline in the number of *créations* on French television since 1970, as it costs ten times as much to produce a ninety-minute play in a studio than to show a film of the same length. 'Culture' as such has, however, had a good deal of importance for programme planners: this is another legacy from Gaullist days, when productions of French classical drama served up in the time-honoured traditional way were considered an essential ingredient of television scheduling. A programme devoted to the cultural interests of the President was made in 1982, but was not screened owing to its excessively obsequious approach, which apparently embarrassed even Mitterrand himself. Nevertheless it indicates that the concept of high culture on the media still receives the sanction of those at the very top.

Unfortunately such programmes do not sell enormously world-wide. A very high proportion, nearly 70 per cent, of foreign material is used on all three channels. Foreign imports, particularly American serials, are about as popular in France as in their country of origin (oddly, Antenne 2, the channel which aspires to the most cultural image, has the largest quantity of American imports). The companies have not succeeded in exporting a great deal up till now; the Anglophone market is the most profitable in this respect, and the French are here inevitably at a loss. However France does produce *séries de prestige* such as the recent *La Chartreuse de Parme* with Marthe Keller, and yet another adaptation of *Les Misérables* is being planned, but money is too often wanting. An indication of the French lack of confidence in their ability, in the short term, to make quality products for sale abroad is the intention in 1983 to produce programmes for the bicentennial of the Revolution, all of six years away! The view of an American producer at the Cannes festival of 1982, that the French are good at making programmes on gastronomy, culture (occasionally), and Edith Piaf, though not necessarily in that order, may be somewhat inaccurate but seems widely-held abroad. The present financial anxieties do not inspire much optimism. The SFP and the programme companies are both concerned, for different reasons, with audience ratings rather than the merits of the programmes themselves (the former because it feels bound to produce the most profitable programmes, the latter because of the rivalry between them), and forthcoming financial stringencies make any recovery seem a long way off.

French radio

The situation with regard to radio is very similar as far as government interference is concerned (Roger Gicquel, head of radio news from April 1973, was said to have been appointed after a personal telephone call from Alain Peyrefitte); but the challenge represented here by commercial interests has been much more obvious. The stations of the national network are France-Inter, France-Culture, France-Musique, FIP, and Radio-France Internationale for broadcasting overseas (a 1982 innovation), all gathered under the collective name 'Radio-France'. France-Inter is the most popular of the government stations (FIP is an exclusively popular music station, intended as a *radio d'accompagnement*, and confined to the Paris area), and, doubtless because of its official nature, still commands a large audience for its news programmes. Its avowed aim is to appeal to the largest possible audience, and so it ranges over a wide field, from light entertainment to interviews with eminent figures in the political and cultural worlds. The most popular and enduring of this last type is *Radioscopie* with Jacques Chancel, a programme which in many ways is typical of the French approach to person-to-person interview; the 'chat show' format, so beloved of media personalities, is perhaps less to be seen on French than on British television, but is popular, naturally enough, on radio. The French are keen on the 'in-depth' interview, and these are often lengthy and occasionally highly revealing. No question of eight gramophone records in half-an-hour and a quick, painless résumé of one's life; if asked to choose his favourite music, for example, a guest may be faced with an interviewer who berates him for lack of taste and forces him to justify his choice. Chancel has recently deve-

loped his programme even further by stretching out an interview with a single personality over a period of a week.

France-Culture and France-Musique, as their names suggest,
cater for more highbrow tastes, and the fact that there are two
'cultural' stations indicates the importance still placed on high
art on the media in France. The stations see their relationship
as that of *petites cousines*. France-Culture presents a broadly-
based fare, using radio for *composition sonore* and
experimenting with combinations of music and drama. For
this, it has the resources of the excellent *Atelier de création
radiophonique*, an enviable asset for any radio company. For its
part, France-Musique limits itself largely to more conventional
music broadcasts, but leaves itself scope for experimentation,
and devotes a considerable amount of time to the promotion of
new music. The stations occasionally pool their resources to
good effect, sometimes in order to cover the same event
(perhaps the Aix festival, for example). However, such
enterprise is often counter-balanced elsewhere by carelessness
over simple things: on one occasion, for example, France-
Musique broadcast an extended classical piece, covering two
sides of a record, which began and ended halfway-through
because the second side had been played first. Accidents
happen anywhere, of course, but it was surprising that the
mistake went unnoticed for three-quarters of an hour.

The chief rivals to Radio-France are the commercial stations
Radio Luxembourg (RTL), Europe-1 and Radio Monte-Carlo,
all known as *périphériques* as they broadcast from just outside
French territory. For a long time these stations have poached
listeners from the State network, largely because they offer
news programmes less subject to government pressure. Radio-
France has tried experimenting with new *grilles* but to no
effect: the latest polls show that it is lagging behind quite
badly. In fact RTL is the most popular station by a long way,
although Europe-1 is most listened to for news. There is a
curious anomaly, however, with regard to the *périphériques*:
although they are all commercial in terms of their ethos, programming and dependence on advertising revenue, the French
State none the less has large shareholdings in all three, via
Havas in the case of RTL and via the *Société française de
radiodiffusion* (SOFIRAD) in the case of Europe-1 and RMC.

The government took them over gradually as the stations' need for French co-operation became evident, particularly in the matters of offices in Paris, transmitters and cables on French territory. Prime Minister Chirac is thought to have engineered the dismissal of the head of Europe-1, a declared supporter of Giscard's rival Chaban-Delmas in the 1974 election. The motive for this was evidently not commercial, as audience ratings were healthy and advertising revenue high. A further illustration is provided by the former President's last-minute broadcast on Europe-1 on the eve of the 1979 European elections: two editions of a popular magazine programme were cancelled to make way for him. No one seems to have pointed out at the time that this was the exact procedure used by de Gaulle – eleventh-hour appeals to the electorate and no time given for adversaries to reply.

The departure of some of the people in important positions in these companies after May 1981 may be seen to be a continuation of the same kind of political pressurization. However that may be, the government's post-election pledge to 'davantage les associer à sa politique générale de développement culturel' hardly contains precise proposals; and certainly the *périphériques* from most points of view seem healthy enough. Europe-1, for example, is becoming involved in the video business, and has set up a local radio in Brussels. *L'après-dix mai* may have been as traumatic for the *périphériques* as for the others, but their audience ratings give them cause to feel reasonably cheerful about the future.

Other radio stations

The issue of pirate radio has assumed great importance in France in recent years. In 1978 a law was passed which reinforced the State monopoly, and one of its most controversial rulings was that banning outright *radios libres*. Any station found still operating was subject to jamming (*brouillages*), or else the equipment was seized. This practice was found particularly iniquitous by the opposition, and they determined that the question of pirate radio would be given priority when they came to power. To this end, a commission was set up to examine the especially tricky problem of radios in the Paris region, where the airwaves in 1981 were crammed with operators. The difficulty of the commission's task was clear when it received a total of 155 *dossiers* for a maximum possible allocation of 18 wavelengths, and the applicants were forced to make the most unlikely shotgun marriages in order to give themselves sufficient clout to win through. The final choices show the range of interest catered for: from those concerned with ethnic minorities (particularly North African) to the homosexual (Radio Gaie) and Catholic communities. Elsewhere in France it seems that everyone wants to get in on the act, almost as if a radio station is a necessary adjunct of any political activity. An example was seen recently in Lozère, where a mayor, a supporter of the Republican Party, has been engaged in a battle of the airwaves with his Socialist rivals. As a local pensioner observed, 'This is straight out of *Clochemerle*'.

Under the 1982 reform private local radios are permitted to come into being, provided that the bulk of their finance comes from non-municipal and non-advertising sources. A most successful example of just such a regional station in 1982 has been Alouette FM in the Vendée, broadcasting to an area including the towns of Nantes, Angers and La Rochelle. It deliberately avoids any strong political stance and takes pains to indicate that it receives no municipal funding, relying for its patronage (*mécénat*) on local industries and associations. The people of the district have responded and on present reckoning, the station has an audience of half a million. Nevertheless its popularity has, as elsewhere, not been a guarantee of its legitimacy, as it still has to obtain a *dérogation*, or authorization to transmit; until it has this, it is, in effect, 'pirate' (applications for a permit are now made to the independent *Haute Autorité*, not direct to the government).

It should be emphasized that such radio stations, legitimate or not, are not meant to be alternatives to any national radio service (along the lines of our own Radio Caroline in the 1960s, for example), but are local networks, deeply preoccupied with the problems of the regions they serve. In many cases, any lack of technical expertise is made up for by the enthusiasm of the operators, largely based on the delighted rediscovery of the social utility of this type of radio. Such a station prides itself on the fact that it allows anyone living in the region to take part in its programmes, thereby creating grass-roots participation and allowing problems to be debated which might otherwise be dispatched on the national media 'entre la météo du lendemain et le hold-up de la veille'. There is no doubt that local radio is attracting a growing audience, including an increasing number disenchanted with the bland format of much of what the State networks and *périphériques* have to offer. Perhaps their proliferation is due also to the growing diversification of the audience, a fact which the coming cable TV will make use of; indeed, multiplicity of choice is the *raison d'être* of cable. But there is of course no real comparison to be made between the two, at least at the moment; local radio treasures its close involvement with its public, and the reciprocity of the relationship is what gives it its value.

The future: cables and satellites

The extraordinary developments in audiovisual technology have left their mark everywhere, but in no country are they giving rise to more rapid thinking than in France. Much of the progress made in the field has simply passed the French by, and her industries find themselves ill-adapted at the moment to meet the challenge. This has been another charge laid at the door of the monopoly, whose dominance has been such that any interest in events elsewhere was firmly discouraged. However it has rapidly become clear to the government that the revolution was upon them come what may, and steps had to be taken if France was not to be left even farther behind. For a country with a strong broadcasting system, with resources and expertise, the arrival of cable seems a bewildering prospect; if the resources are absent, then one may feel that the most drastic measures may not be sufficient. As it is, the government is hoping that the new technology will in turn stimulate new industry; it wants above all to avoid a situation where new channels are opening but there is a shortage of home-produced programmes to furnish them.

The cabling of French territory should coincide with a large-scale (and sorely-needed) modernization of the telephone system, itself a first step towards acknowledging the realities of present-day communication. After that, the possibilities seem endless, as elsewhere; one estimate has it that by 1990 approximately ten satellites will serve France, and cable is the only means of accommodating all these efficiently. The Post Office is currently proposing a law whereby 1.5 million homes will have the use of cable by 1987; and by 1995 half of France could receive the same service. This phase of the operation would cost about 8 billion francs. The town of Biarritz has been chosen as a touchstone of the success of the scheme; by 1983, 1500 homes there will be switched in to the cable. The choice of a frontier town may be significant: it is doubtless important to monitor the reception of foreign programmes via the facility. In the matter of satellites, the first purely French one (TDF 1) will be launched in 1986 and will have three channels: one reserved for TF1, one for A2, and the other for an unknown, possibly private customer. Other projects are under negotiation, notably with Luxemburg and Germany. Thus by 1986-7 the Parisian viewer might have the choice of some twenty channels. One undoubted advantage of satellites would be that it would eliminate the *zones d'ombres*, areas which because of their position cannot receive the signal.

Conclusion

A former head of the ORTF has stated that until the media services sort out exactly what they consider their function in society to be, their situation will not improve. In fact, there is enormous interest taken in France in the role of the television presenter: not many weeks go by without another earnest discussion of his links with and responsibilities towards his audience. He is part journalist, part pedagogue, part technician, part *animateur social*, a real *homme-orchestre*; but the trouble of course arises when he is faced with a lack of technical resources and unhelpful attitudes from those in power. If twenty years of monopoly have 'frozen' the structures of French broadcasting, a year of reform has certainly not been enough to loosen them, although it is undeniable that advances have already been made. One experienced journalist remarked in the wake of May 1981 that it would take two or three years before the 'new television' appeared: it would take that long to *maîtriser la machine*. Others find it hard to believe that the situation for those working in television will essentially change; as long as the medium retains its influence, indeed, a journalist should consider the extent of interference from above as a measure of his success at the job ('un journaliste qui ne subit pas de pression est comme une femme qu'on ne courtise plus'). Such an attitude shows the difficulty they have in thinking in terms which are other than narrowly *contestataires*, a forgivable fault perhaps, but one which may hinder the services at a time when a solid base is needed on which to work for the future. If, as many believe, network television is finished in France and does not possess structures flexible enough to meet changing demand, the old oppositions could turn out to be redundant. 'We must go slowly, try to assess these changes, encompass what is happening,' sounds an admirable and necessary course of action – one hopes there will be time to carry it out.

Bibliography

Ardagh, J., *France in the 1980s*. Harmondsworth, Pelican, 1982. Gives a good account of the history of the broadcasting media until the beginning of 1982.

Kühn, R., *Government and Broadcasting in France 1969–75*. Department of Politics, University of Warwick, Working Paper no. 8, December 1975. A detailed account tracing the relationship of State to TV and radio over six highly eventful years.

Mamère, N., *Telle est ma télé*. Editions Megrelis, February 1982. The story of the events of May 1981 by a former journalist on Antenne 2. A graphic account of the struggles within one channel during this turbulent time.

Thomas, R., *Broadcasting and Democracy in France*. London, Crosby Lockwood Staples, 1976. A detailed exploration of the subject, giving an outline of the 1974 reforms.

Also of use are:

Astoux, A., *Ondes de choc*. Paris, Plon, 1978.

Caillavet, H., *Changer la télévision, ou la réalité imaginaire*. Paris, Flammarion, 1978.

Durieux, C., *La Télécratie*. Paris, Tema, 1976.

Louis, R., *L'ORTF un combat*. Paris, Seuil, 1968.

Thibau, J., *Une Télévision pour tous les Français*. Paris, Seuil, 1970.

Montaldo, J., *Dossier ORTF tous coupables*. Paris, Albin Michel, 1974.

The television channels each publish their own handbook, plus a *cahier des charges* containing more technical data. *Le Monde* publishes a weekly column on radio and television. In London, the IBA library keeps a useful collection of press cuttings on the subject as well as books and periodicals.

Contributors

J.E. FLOWER, M.A., Ph.D., Professor of French, University of Exeter. Main interests: French literature and history of ideas, literature and politics from the late nineteenth century to the present day. Publications include *Intention and Achievement: an essay on the novels of François Mauriac* (Oxford University Press), *Georges Bernanos: 'Journal d'un curé de campagne'* (Edward Arnold), *Roger Vailland, the Man and his Masks* and *Writers and Politics in Modern France* (Hodder & Stoughton), *Literature and the Left in France since the Late Nineteenth Century* (Macmillan). Editor of the *Journal of European Studies*.

ANDRÉE SHEPHERD, L. ès L., Agrégée d'Anglais, Lecturer in English, University of Tours. Main interests: twentieth-century French and English sociology and politics. Publications include a study of the occupation of French factories in May 1968, *Imagination in Power* (Spokesman Books), a translation of Serge Mallet's book *The New Working Class* (Spokesman Books), and contributions to the *Encyclopédie de civilisation britannique* (Larousse) and *Littérature anglaise* (Bordas). Research in progress on the New Left in Britain.

ERIC CAHM, B.A., Chevalier des Palmes Académiques, Head of the School of Languages and Area Studies, Portsmouth Polytechnic. Main interests: France since May 1981, and the Dreyfus Affair. Publications include *Politics and Society in*

Contemporary France 1789–1971: a documentary history (Harrap), *Péguy et le nationalisme français* (Amitié Charles Péguy) and an edition of D. Halévy, *Péguy et les Cahiers de la Quinzaine* (Le Livre de Poche).

RICHARD McALLISTER, M.A., Lecturer in Politics, University of Edinburgh. Has also been a member of the British Diplomatic Service and a Visiting Assistant Professor, University of California, Los Angeles. Main interests: the politics and policies of the European Community; central-local relations in west European States. Author (with D. Hunter) of *Local Government – Death or Devolution?* (for the Outer Circle Policy Unit, London), and of contributions to books and to journals including *Common Market Law Review, Futures* and *The New Atlantis*.

BRIAN FITZPATRICK, M.A., Ph.D., Lecturer in European History, Ulster Polytechnic. Main interest: the French Right since the French Revolution. Recent publications include *Catholic Royalism in the Department of the Gard, 1814–1852* (Cambridge University Press).

ALAN CLARK, B.A., Ph.D., Senior Lecturer in French, University of Canterbury, Christchurch, New Zealand. Main interests: French literature, intellectual, social and political history since 1870. Publications include *La France dans l'histoire selon Bernanos* (Lettres Modernes), an edition of Valéry Giscard d'Estaing's *Démocratie française* (Methuen) and numerous articles on French foreign and Pacific policy.

MARGARET S. ARCHER, B.Sc. (Econ), Ph.D., Professor of Sociology, University of Warwick, and Chairperson of the ISA's Publications Committee. Main interests: the development and change of educational systems, European social structure, and macro-sociological theory. Publications include *Social Conflict and Educational Change in England and France: 1789–1848* (with Michalina Vaughan; Cambridge University Press), *Students, University and Society* (Heinemann), *Contemporary Europe: Class, Status and Power* (edited with S. Giner; Weidenfeld &

Nicolson), *Social Origins of Educational Systems* (Sage), *Contemporary Europe: Social Structures and Cultural Patterns* (Routledge & Kegan Paul) and *The Sociology of Educational Expansion: Take-off, Growth and Inflation* (Sage).

WALTER REDFERN, M.A., Ph.D., Professor in French Studies, University of Reading. Main interests: French literature and in particular the novel from the eighteenth century to the present day. Publications include *The Private World of Jean Giono* (Blackwell), *Paul Nizan: Committed Literature in a Conspiratorial World* (Princeton University Press) and *Queneau: 'Zazie dans le métro'* (Grant & Cutler).

NEIL HARRIS, B.A., freelance teacher and translator, formerly Tutorial Assistant in French, University of Exeter. Main interests: French literature since 1800, Stendhal and the relationship of music to literature.

Index